The European Union and Developing Countries

The European Union and Developing Countries: Trade, Aid and Growth in an Integrating World

Edited by

Yves Bourdet, Joakim Gullstrand and Karin Olofsdotter
Lund University, Sweden

Edward Elgar
Cheltenham, UK • Northampton, MA, USA

Published by
Edward Elgar Publishing Limited
Glensanda House
Montpellier Parade
Cheltenham
Glos GL50 1UA
UK

Edward Elgar Publishing, Inc.
William Pratt House
9 Dewey Court
Northampton
Massachusetts 01060
USA

A catalogue record for this book is available from the British Library

Library of Congress Cataloguing in Publication Data

The European Union and developing countries : trade, aid, and growth in an
integrating world / edited by Yves Bourdet, Joakim Gullstrand, and Karin
Olofsdotter.
    p. cm.
  Includes bibliographical references and index.
  1. European Union countries–Foreign economic relations–Developing
countries–Congresses. 2. Developing countries–Foreign economic
relations–European Union countries–Congresses. I. Bourdet, Yves. II.
Gullstrand, J. (Joakim) III. Olofsdotter, Karin, 1970-
  HF1531.Z4D4439 2007
  337.1'42091724–dc22
                            2006034557

ISBN 978 1 84542 246 2
Printed and bound in Great Britain by MPG Books Ltd, Bodmin, Cornwall

Contents

Contributors

Adenäuer, Marcel, Ph.D., Institute for Food and Resource Economics, Bonn University
Belfrage, Carl-Johan, Assistant Professor, Lund University
Bourdet, Yves, Associate Professor, Lund University
Gullstrand, Joakim, Assistant Professor, Lund University, and Senior Researcher, Swedish Institute for Food and Agricultural Economics
Hansson, Pontus, Assistant Professor, Lund University
Jansson, Torbjörn, Agricultural Economist, Agricultural Economics Research Institute (LEI), The Hague
Johansson, Helena, Ph.D., Senior Researcher, Swedish Institute for Food and Agricultural Economics, Lund
Nilsson, Lars, Ph.D., European Commission, Directorate-General for Trade
Olofsdotter, Karin, Assistant Professor, Lund University
Persson, Maria, Ph.D. Candidate, Lund University
Petersson, Lennart, Associate Professor, Lund University
Söderling, Ludvig, Ph.D., International Monetary Fund
Wilhelmsson, Fredrik, Ph.D., Lund University

1. Introduction

Yves Bourdet, Joakim Gullstrand and
Karin Olofsdotter

Issues related to the effectiveness of industrial countries' trade and aid policies on promoting growth and economic development in the Third World are topical for at least three reasons. The first is the lingering negotiations of the Doha Round within the framework of the World Trade Organization (WTO), and the difficulties in completing them. The main objective of the Doha Round is to design a world trade system that is more favourable to the long-term growth of developing countries. The second reason refers to the strong emigration pressures that exist in developing countries, in particular in Africa, and the urgent need to address, through development policy, the main factor behind the desire to emigrate, namely the poor economic performance and prospects of many countries in the Southern hemisphere. Third, there is a need for policy makers and organisations of the civil society in industrial countries to substantiate the efficient use of aid and its positive effects on the economic development and well being of recipient countries. This is all the more important today when increased tax resources are required to finance the scaling up of aid necessary to achieve the Millennium Development Goals (MDGs), which were agreed upon by political leaders from around the world.

The European Union is the main trading partner of developing countries and provider of development aid (when the aid of both Member States and the European Commission is taken together). The development policy of the European Union consists of three components. The first is the trade policy preferences granted to various groupings of developing countries in order to boost their export and growth. The second is the financial assistance granted to developing countries. The volume of development assistance has increased over time and its form has changed, with greater scope for budget and sector support and lesser scope for project aid. The third component concerns policies and measures that focus on specific sectors and have contributed to securing some forms of economic rents for beneficiary developing countries. Illustrative examples are the sugar and banana regimes that have given some developing countries economic rents that have been used, more or less efficiently, to finance their long-term development.

The European Union trade and aid policy towards developing countries is at the crossroads. Each of its three components has recently experienced, or is currently experiencing, dramatic changes. The trade preferences that have been granted the so-called ACP (African-Caribbean-Pacific) countries are planned to be phased out and will be replaced by free trade areas between the European Union and regional groupings of developing countries. These free trade areas will be equipped with rules of origin, the final nature and degree of restrictiveness of which are still to be decided. For those developing countries that do not belong to these regional groupings the current preference scheme (Generalised System of Preferences) will remain, with its less generous and predictable stance. The aid component has changed substantially with the signing of the Cotonou agreement and the establishment of six Economic Partnership Agreements between the European Union and regional groupings of developing countries among the ACP states. Emphasis in these agreements is placed on 'new development issues', hopefully with high catalytic content, like good governance, deeper policy dialogue between development partners, improved donor coordination, trade facilitation, respect for the rule of law and the like. Finally, the specific sugar and banana regimes have been reformed, with far-reaching implications and economic losses for some developing countries.

The main purpose of the various studies included in this book is to evaluate critical aspects of the European Union's trade and aid policies and to assess their impact on the economic development of the Third World. Where relevant, the studies integrate the current policy changes. Numerous implementation studies scrutinise the coverage and depth of trade preferences or the way European aid is designed and implemented in recipient countries (or groupings of countries). Such studies are of limited help when it comes to providing feedback for the improvement of the current policy stance. The last few years have witnessed a growing interest in a more systematic and regular evaluation of the European Union's trade and aid policies with a view to providing a better basis for decision-making. This kind of evaluation, based on the assessment of the real impact of policy and specific measures, can work as a form of voice and, in a situation where exit is difficult and costly (for a recipient country that rejects assistance), it is the best way to improve the effectiveness of the European Union development policy in promoting economic growth in recipient countries.

It is now generally admitted that trade can contribute more to long-term growth and economic development than aid, in particular when aid is poor in catalytic content. The structure and content of this book reflect this contention. Chapter 2 of this book, written by Joakim Gullstrand and Karin Olofsdotter, is devoted to developing countries' specialisation patterns and participation in world trade. The purpose of this study is to provide both a background for the following chapters and a picture of the link between trade and economic development. One important result in the chapter is that although developing countries experienced a sharp increase in their share of world exports in the 1990s, there does not seem to be a corresponding effect on the world structure of specialisation. Also, and in line with other studies, a growing divergence in trade and factor endowments is observed between low- and middle-income countries. Regarding the developing countries' trade with the EU, a pattern that has emerged is one in which countries in East and South Asia in particular appear to have gained market access in the EU at the expense of countries in Africa and the Middle East.

The following four chapters deal, in various ways, with EU trade arrangements with developing countries. In Chapter 3, Maria Persson and Fredrik Wilhelmsson examine the effects of EU trade preferences on developing countries' exports. The growing complexity of EU preference schemes has made it difficult to grasp the extent of their impact, and there is a common view that non-reciprocal preferences have not boosted export growth in developing countries as expected. Moreover, the value of these preferences has been eroded as multilateral trade liberalisation under the WTO has proceeded and the number of beneficiary countries increased. The authors analyse these issues by considering changes in various EU trade preferences granted to developing countries over an extended period of time. The main finding in the study is that more generous preferences have larger positive effects on recipient countries' exports. Hence, the ACP countries seem to have benefited the most, followed by the Mediterranean countries. On the other hand, no effect is found for those countries only obtaining preferences under the Generalised System of Preferences (GSP). Since many ACP countries belong to the group of countries that have experienced falling shares of exports to the EU, this also suggests that their situation could have been even worse without preferences. In addition, the study points at the potentially disadvantageous effects of EU enlargement from the developing countries' perspective, as new entrants seem to divert their imports from developing countries to other EU members.

The European Union and the United States are the most important providers of preferential market access to developing countries. The preference schemes of the EU and the US differ in both depth and coverage and, in general, EU trade preferences are considered to be more beneficial than US preferences. In Chapter 4, Lars Nilsson assesses the relative impact of these preferences. Using recent trade data, he estimates and compares the export-generating effects of the EU and US overall trade policy vis-à-vis developing countries. The results point to larger trade-creating effects of EU trade policy, especially for the least developed countries that gain additional benefits within GSP with the Everything but Arms (EBA initiative). The chapter also indicates that the differences in the developing countries' access to EU versus US markets have increased in recent years.

The Mediterranean partnership between the EU and 12 Southern and Eastern Mediterranean countries was launched by the Barcelona process in 1995, with the goal of creating a free trade area by the year 2010. Chapter 5, by Ludvig

Söderling, examines the effects of these integration efforts with the EU for six of the Mediterranean countries belonging to the Middle East and North Africa Region (MENA). The study tries to establish these countries' export potential to EU as well as non-EU countries by comparing actual and predicted trade levels. The analysis shows that there is probably considerable potential for trade with the EU, even though there are differences across the MENA countries. However, it also shows that there are significant untapped markets outside the EU, in particular the US. This of course raises the question of the possible trade-diverting effects of the Barcelona process. This does not seem to be a problem for most of the MENA countries in the study, although there is some evidence of Tunisia achieving its trade potential with the EU.

The history of trade relations between the EU and South Africa differs from that between the EU and the other Sub-Saharan countries. The imposition of trade sanctions during apartheid excluded South Africa from the successive conventions linking the EU and the ACP countries. The lifting of sanctions in the mid-1990s was first followed by the inclusion of South Africa in the group of GSP countries. On 1 January 2000, the EU and South Africa established a free trade agreement. In Chapter 6, Lennart Petersson analyses to what extent the agreement contributed to boosting trade between the EU and South Africa, and diversifying exports from South Africa towards products with higher value added. The results of his study indicate that free trade between the EU and South Africa contributed to South Africa's export increase and diversification. He also shows that the form of specialisation has changed appreciably, with the share of intra-industry trade, i.e. exchange of similar products within industries, in total EU-South Africa trade having increased markedly since the mid-1990s.

A critical aspect of the new EU policy towards developing countries is to support the creation of regional integration arrangements among developing countries so as to, in a second stage, enter into Economic Partnership Agreements with the EU. Six Economic Partnership Agreements are planned between the EU and regional groupings of ACP countries, four of them with Sub-Saharan African countries. Another reason invoked by the EU is that regional integration *per se* can work as an engine for growth largely via its impact on trade and specialisation. In Chapter 7, Yves Bourdet and Joakim Gullstrand evaluate the EU policy of promoting regional integration of developing countries. They focus on West Africa where the EU and some EU member countries have contributed most to shaping the form and comprehensiveness of regional integration. The study quantifies the impact of both the deepening of integration among UEMOA (Union Économique et Monétaire Ouest Africaine) and the enlargement of regional integration to ECOWAS (Economic Community of West African States). In addition, it is shown that regional integration in West Africa is likely to fall short of expectations and have limited effects on trade creation and subsequently on economic growth.

The European Union is in the process of reforming policy in sectors like bananas and sugar. Chapter 8, written by Marcel Adenäuer, Torbjörn Jansson and Helena Johansson, assesses the effects of the reform of the EU Common Market Organisation for sugar on developing countries. The study quantifies changes in prices, production, consumption and trade with the help of the CAPRI model. Special attention is given in the study to the distribution of benefits and losses among developing countries, both prior to and after the reform of the EU sugar policy. A main result of the study is that some developing countries, mostly sugar-producing countries of the ACP group and developing countries that import sugar, will suffer significantly from preference erosion. The analysis underlines, however, that the *status quo* is a costly and inefficient way of transferring resources to developing countries, and that the reform is likely to give rise to substantial welfare gains in the EU, which will pave the way for more sizeable and efficient transfers to developing countries hit by the reform.

Food aid accounts for a mere 3 percent of world trade in food, but as much as 80 percent of food availability in some recipient countries. The main donors are the USA, with more than half of the total donations in quantity terms, and the EU, with about a quarter. In Chapter 9, Carl-Johan Belfrage investigates the impact of food aid from the EU and USA on local agricultural production and import of agricultural products by recipient countries. He shows that food aid from the EU and USA has no discernible influence over local production, except when the analysis is confined to Sub-Saharan Africa. As far as the impact of different forms of food aid on local production is concerned, only project aid (typically involving the use of donated food in food-for-work projects designed to improve rural infrastructure) seems to impact on local production. While EU project aid has clear positive effects for several years after it is received, US project aid has more limited, but also positive, effects on local production. Comparisons between EU and US food aid clearly reveal different effects on commercial imports. Apart from the case of aid to Sub-Saharan Africa, where trade effects appear quite limited, the general pattern is that while US aid, as expected, replaces commercial imports, EU aid appears to be import-stimulating. With the phasing out of program aid from EU food aid operations, observable in the wake of the introduction of new norms for EU food aid policy in 1996, the trade effects of EU aid have become fairly neutral, while the negative impact of US aid on recipient country commercial imports has remained. The concerns over trade distortions from food aid by the main donor thus seem to carry some substance.

How development aid affects economic growth has been on the research agenda in the past decade. The impact of aid has been shown to depend upon the quality of economic policy in recipient countries. This result is, however, not robust and depends upon the period and the sample of countries examined. On a priori grounds, we expect the impact of multilateral aid, like that given by the European Commission, to be more growth-enhancing than that of bilateral aid, which we believe to be more politicised and tied to the purchase of goods and services from the donor country. In Chapter 10, Pontus Hansson assesses the impact of EU multilateral aid on the growth of developing countries. The most striking result of his study is that EU multilateral aid has no impact on economic growth. A similar result is found for development aid from other sources. His study also gives some support to previous studies showing that aid tends to be harmful for growth in the tropics.

NOTE

A special word of gratitude is due to Monica Olofsson, Jeanie Petersson and Fredrik Wilhelmsson who prepared the final manuscript and Jaya Reddy for excellent proofreading. Special thanks are also due to the Swedish International Development Cooperation Agency, the Crafoord Foundation and the Centre for European Studies at Lund University for their financial assistance.

2. Trade and Specialisation: Changing Patterns in the 1990s?

Joakim Gullstrand and Karin Olofsdotter

INTRODUCTION

Recent years have seen a sharp increase in developing countries' share of world trade. In total, their share of world exports grew from about 25 percent in 1990 to 35 percent in 2002.[1] Moreover, the trade expansion has mainly been in manufactured products, including not only labour-intensive but technologically more advanced as well. This is promising as trade and integration with the world economy are potential engines for growth and development. At the same time, however, it seems as if this process has been uneven and that some developing countries are lagging behind (e.g., World Bank, 2005; UNCTAD, 2005). The purpose of this study is to examine the structure of world trade and specialisation, and its changes in the last decade. The focus on the 1990s is partly due to data availability but, furthermore, to the turbulence of trade and growth performance that many developing countries have witnessed during this decade. Particular attention is given to differences in the determinants of trade across developing countries with respect to income level and geographical location. Besides changes in global patterns, the development of trade structures between developing countries and the European Union is also considered.

This chapter is organised as follows: The first section discusses determinants of trade in general for low-, middle- and high-income countries,[2] and analyses changes in specialisation patterns based on relative factor endowments and trade flows. This part also considers the development of intra-industry trade in low- and middle-income countries. The second section of the chapter focuses on developing countries' trade with the EU. This section looks, in particular, at changes in EU imports from different groups of developing countries according to income level and region. In addition, these countries' export similarities to the EU are considered. The final section summarises the conclusions of the chapter.

SPECIALISATION PATTERNS

The most important explanation for trade between developed and developing countries is differences in comparative advantages. A country will have a comparative advantage if it can produce a good at relatively lower costs than other goods, compared to other countries. The main determinants of comparative advantages, in turn, are a country's endowment of natural resources and factors of production as well as available technology. We start this section by studying how these factors vary across countries at different income levels and how they correlate with trade patterns.[3]

However, factor endowments are not the only driving force behind trade. In fact, a large share of world trade is between countries with similar endowments. This type of trade may be explained by the existence of scale economies in the production process and is associated with trade in similar products between higher income countries. Whether or not the developing countries have increased their participation in this sort of trade in the 1990s is the focus in the last part of this section.

Factor Endowments

As countries grow and accumulate factors of production they may follow a path of development leading them to a new mix of production. This development is included in the Heckscher-Ohlin (HO) model, which states, through the Rybczynski theorem, that capital accumulation increases production of capital-intensive products and decreases the production of labour-intensive products. The 2x2 version (two factors and two goods) of the HO model is, however, rather simplistic and does not provide room for many alternative paths of development. Leamer (1987) extends the simple version of the HO model by using three factors and *n* products, which multiplies the number of development paths. If, for example, two countries accumulate capital but differ in relative abundance of labour and arable land, they may experience different paths of development and end up with different mixes of production. The reason for this is that an additional factor and many goods imply that the world may be divided into several cones of diversification or regions of specialisation that determine the possible output mix for each country.

As we are interested in the path of development for all countries during the 1990s, we base our analysis on the endowment triangle in order to illustrate the relative endowments of three factors in two dimensions (see Leamer, 1987). Each vertex of the triangle represents one of the three factors, while points within the triangle represent a specific combination of them all. Note that a movement on the straight line away from the vertex represents a reduction of the factor in question, whereas along this line the ratio of the other two factors is held constant. The choice of the three factors used to construct the endowment triangle depends on the situation at hand. Leamer (1987) uses physical capital, labour and arable land, but one may also use (as in the example of Deardorff, 2000) physical capital, skilled labour and unskilled labour. The former trinity may be justified since 'physical and human capital tend to accumulate together', while the latter may be justified if one wishes to underline the influence of human capital through policy and culture differences. We start out by following Leamer, and use physical capital (K), labour (L) and arable land. The source and the definition of all the variables are found in the Annex.

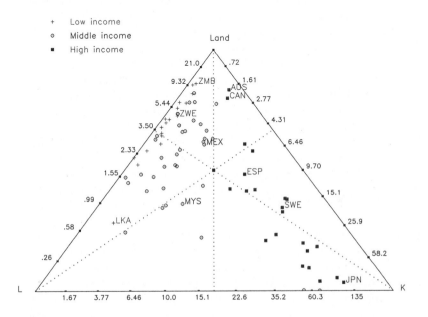

Figure 2.1 Endowment triangle 1990

Figure 2.1 shows the endowment triangle in 1990 for 78 countries. The centre of the triangle represents the total endowment of all countries in this figure (the world hereafter). A straight line from each vertex through the centre divides the triangle into six regions relating to the endowment ratios of the world. Countries in the upper-left and the upper-right regions have a higher ratio of arable land to physical capital and of arable land to labour than the world average. These two regions differ, though, since countries in the former region (e.g. Zambia) have a lower capital-labour ratio than the world, while those in the latter region (e.g. Australia and Canada) have a higher. All the other four regions may be ranked in a similar fashion according to the world endowments. Sweden, for example, is found in the middle-right region together with Spain, and these two have a similar land-labour ratio to Mexico in the upper-left region. But the similarity stops there, since changing our perspective to any other vertex reveals that Sweden is more capital abundant (relative to land or labour) than both Spain and Mexico, while Spain is more capital abundant than Mexico.

A distinct pattern in Figure 2.1 is that most of the high-income countries are located close to the capital vertex, while middle- and low-income countries are located close to the labour and the land vertices respectively. In addition, there is a division of the world along a straight line from the land vertex through the world's endowment point, which reveals that most low- and middle-income countries have less than $17,000 of capital per individual over 15 years of age. This pattern indicates that low-income countries should specialise in labour-intensive agricultural products (e.g. sugar and coffee), while we expect middle-income countries to be net exporters of labour-intensive products (such as clothing, footwear and furniture).

Although most low-income countries are found along a straight line from the vertices of land and labour (indicating a similar amount of capital per individual over 15 and per hectare arable land) we find large differences in land-labour ratios. On the one hand we have Zambia with approximately 15 hectares arable land per individual over 15, and on the other hand we have Sri Lanka with less than one hectare per individual. The diverse range of endowments points of low-income countries implies that they most likely have very different development paths. If we define development as capital accumulation, we expect that a country in the upper-left region will move towards the capital vertex and the middle-right region through the upper-right region. That is, we expect a move from labour-intensive agricultural products to more capital-intensive agricultural products, and thereafter to more capital-intensive manufactures. On the other hand, a country in the middle-left region will move through the lower-left region to the lower-right, i.e. from labour-intensive to more capital-intensive products. Thus, the latter country should specialise in apparel before moving into more capital-intensive goods, while the former is more likely to use agricultural products as a stepping-stone in the development process.[4] However, using this stepping-stone successfully depends on World Trade Organization (WTO) talks and the future market access of low- and middle-income countries in high-income countries.

As the relative position of each country within the endowment triangle is determined by its relative factor endowments, similar expansions of all factors in all countries imply that each country's position will be unchanged. Since capital is an important factor behind per capita income, unchanged country positions mean that no low- or middle-income country will approach the income level of the high-income countries. On the other hand, a much faster accumulation of capital in one country will lead to it moving towards the capital vertex, while the positions of the other countries will remain more or less unchanged.

So what happened during the 1990s? We would like to highlight three important observations by comparing the endowment triangles of 1990 and 2000 (see Figure 2.2). First, we still find the distinct pattern of low-, middle- and high-income countries. Second, we find only a few exceptional movers such as Malaysia, which has moved along a rather straight line towards the capital vertex and is found close to the world capital-labour ratio in 2000. Third, we may discern a clearer division between low- and middle-income countries, since low-income countries are found further away from the world's endowment point. If we rank countries by their distance to the world's endowment point (the highest rank is given to the country with the longest distance), the mean rank of low-income countries rose from 47.16 in 1990 to 48.72 in 2000, while the increase was much smaller for the middle-income countries (from 31.84 to 32.05).[5] More importantly (at least for per capita income differences), the ranking of the distance to the capital vertex rose for low-income countries (from 66.05 to 66.61), while it fell for middle-income countries (from 41.76 to 41.39). That is, middle- and high-income countries tended to become *slightly* more similar during the 1990s, while the distinct position of low-income countries was strengthened.

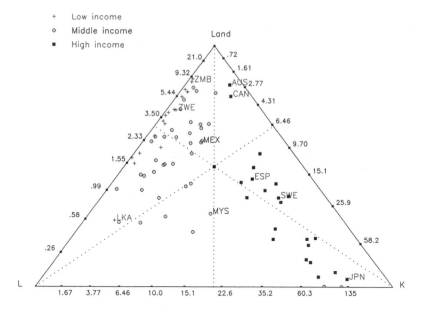

Figure 2.2 Endowment triangle 2000

Although physical and human capital tend to accumulate together, it may be illuminating to substitute human capital for land in the endowment triangle (see Leamer and Lundborg, 1995; Deardorff, 2000). We use the share of the population over 15 that have completed a post-secondary education to divide the total population over 15 into groups of low- and high-skilled individuals, and

Figure 2A.1 in the Annex shows the endowment triangle for 2000. There are several points worth noting. First, the three different income categories are highly concentrated in different regions. Low-income countries are found close to the low-skilled individuals' vertex, while middle-income countries stretch out towards the vertex of high-skilled individuals. Second, countries defined as middle-income countries in the beginning of the period catch up regarding the number of highly skilled individuals per low-skilled individual (note that we do not show the endowment triangle for 1990 in order to conserve space). A straight line from the vertex of physical capital through the endowment point of the world reveals that the world is becoming more skilled since there is approximately 0.05 highly skilled per low-skilled individual in 2000 compared to 0.04 in 1990. At the same time, the number of middle-income countries with a higher skill ratio than the world ratio has increased, and there are also other middle-income countries closing up to the world ratio. The other side of the coin is that low-income countries seem to be falling behind. This observation is supported by the fact that their average ranking regarding distance to the world's endowment point is increasing, while it is falling for both middle- and high-income countries. Third, the world may still be divided into the two parts that persisted during the 1990s, but now more in terms of the amount of physical capital per low-skilled individual. That is, high-income countries hold their positions as highly abundant in physical capital.

Net Trade Patterns

How, then, do the actual patterns of production and trade of developing countries correspond to the theory of comparative advantages? The last section provided a description of factor endowments across countries at different levels of development. Our next step is to ascertain whether these endowment patterns coincide with net trade flows and if countries' net trade has changed over the last decade. As we are interested in paths of development, we particularly want to see if some low- and middle-income countries have experienced a change in their comparative advantages, by going from being net importers to becoming net exporters of more advanced products during the observed period.

In order to study net trade patterns, we use an index of revealed comparative advantages (RCA) that is based on the individual country's trade performance. The RCA approach, which originates from Balassa (1965), makes the assumption that a country's real comparative advantages are 'revealed' by actual trade performance (see Greenaway and Milner, 1993, for a discussion of different measures of RCA). In particular, we define a country's RCA as:

$$RCA_i = \frac{X_i - M_i}{X_i + M_i} \qquad (2.1)$$

where X_i and M_i are the exports and imports of good i, respectively. This index ranges from -1 to +1 where a positive (negative) value implies that the country has a comparative advantage (disadvantage) in the production of good i. Thus, the sign of the RCA index is determined by whether the country is a net exporter or net importer of i. To calculate each country's RCA, we use import and export data from World Trade Analyzer of Statistics Canada and, following Kokko et al. (2005), define six broad product groups according to their use of land, labour, physical capital, energy, human capital and technology (see Annex).

Since we want to identify changes in net trade and comparative advantages in the 1990s we construct figures that represent the RCA of 158 countries in both 1990 and 2000 for each industry group (the number of countries in each figure may differ due to missing values). These are shown for land, labour, physical capital and human capital in Figures 2.3 to 2.6. As each figure has RCA in 1990 on the x axis and RCA in 2000 on the y axis, it can be divided into four quadrants. If a country is found in the lower-left quadrant, this indicates that it has a comparative disadvantage in a particular industry in both years, while a position in the upper-right quadrant implies a comparative advantage. On the other hand, countries in the upper-left or lower-right have evidently witnessed a change in their comparative advantages in the 1990s. Whereas countries in the former have moved from being net importers to being net exporters, the opposite is true if they are found in the latter quadrant.

The overall impression from Figures 2.3 to 2.6 is that revealed comparative advantages are quite stable over time (which is in line with the unchanged country positions in the endowment triangles), since most countries are found either in the lower-left quadrant or the upper-right. Also, the comparative advantages of low- and middle-income countries are mainly found in land- and labour-intensive products while they, on the other hand, seem to have comparative *dis*advantages in human capital- and technology-intensive products.

Turning to the individual figures, we start by noting that the hypothesis that low-income countries specialise in land-intensive products and middle-income countries in labour-intensive products is to some extent corroborated by Figure 2.3 and Figure 2.4. In both years, most of the low-income countries are net exporters of land-intensive products and middle-income countries are clearly overrepresented as net exporters of labour-intensive products. In Figure 2.4 there are some low- and middle-income countries found in the upper-left quadrant as well, indicating that they have moved from being net importers of labour-intensive products to being net exporters. However, for most of these countries, their share of world trade is less than one per mille (with the exception of Mexico and Brunei).

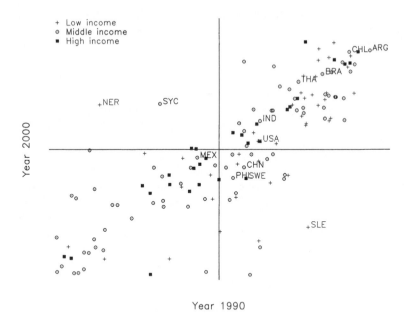

Figure 2.3 Net trade 1990 and 2000, land-intensive products

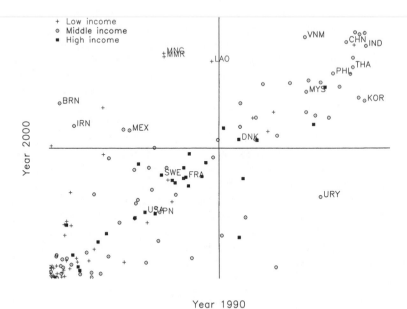

Figure 2.4 Net trade 1990 and 2000, labour-intensive products

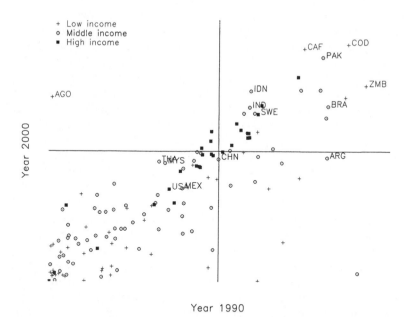

Figure 2.5 Net trade 1990 and 2000, physical capital-intensive products

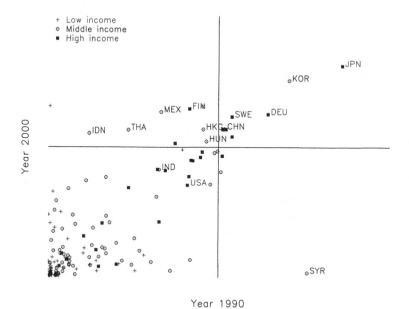

Figure 2.6 Net trade 1990 and 2000, human capital-intensive products

As argued earlier, physical capital accumulation could be seen as a sign of economic development. It was also shown, though, that very few countries were able to substantially increase their capital-labour ratios, relative to high-income countries, in the 1990s. These findings appear to be upheld in Figure 2.5. The only country that has experienced a major positive change in net exports of capital-intensive products is Angola, whereas ten or so developing countries have gone from being net exporters in 1990 to net importers in 2000. Malaysia, earlier identified as an exceptional mover, is still a net importer of capital-intensive products in 2000, although the country's comparative disadvantage seems to be smaller. Otherwise, there does not appear to be a clear pattern across different income groups (even if only a very few high-income countries are found in the very south-west of the figure) and, remarkably, the countries furthest to the north-east are low-income countries. It should be realised, however, that the capital-intensive product group consists of manufactured goods classified by material and includes products such as textiles, mineral manufactures and non-ferrous metals. The position of The Democratic Republic of Congo (COD), for example, can be explained by its heavy reliance on exports of diamonds, a product defined as capital intensive. The impact of natural resources is even more pronounced for energy-intensive goods (figure not shown), as most countries are either net importers or net exporters in both 1990 and 2000. Here, concentrating on larger trade flows (i.e. those above one per mille of world trade), most net exporters are oil producing low- and middle-income countries, while the net importers are, in addition to the US, almost exclusively countries in Europe.

When it comes to the net trade of human capital-intensive products in Figure 2.6, the findings are much clearer. Hence, while most developing countries have a comparative disadvantage in both years, a few, mainly middle-income countries in South Asia (Indonesia, Thailand, Malaysia and Hong Kong), have succeeded in becoming net exporters. The exceptional position of Korea should be noted as a middle-income country that has actually had positive net exports in this line of production during the whole decade. A very similar pattern applies to technology-intensive products (figure not shown) where only some South Asian middle-income countries (and Costa Rica) have gained comparative advantages over the decade. For this product group, only high-income countries are found in the upper-right quadrant.

To sum up, we find that relatively few countries have changed their comparative advantages in the 1990s, a finding supported by for example Lall (1998). With the focus on developing countries, positive movers with human capital- and technology-intensive products (i.e. from being net importers in 1990 to net exporters in 2000) are mainly found in South Asia. As for the low-income countries, almost none has been able to make this movement and only very few have been able to gain comparative advantages in labour-intensive products.

Intra-industry Trade

The preceding discussion revolves round what we call inter-industry specialisation, i.e. specialisation across countries due to differences in endowments or technology. An alternative specialisation opportunity is to specialise within an industry and thereafter exchange a particular variety for another variety of a similar product on the world market, i.e. intra-industry trade (IIT), which may consist of an exchange of vertically or horizontally differentiated products. The former imply that countries with different factor endowments or technologies specialise in different product-quality ranges, while non-homogeneous preferences and income inequalities within countries ensure that there is a demand for both high- and low-quality products in each country.[6] An exchange of horizontally differentiated products is not driven by differences across countries, but by internal, to the firm, economies of scale, the possibility of product differentiation and consumers' 'love for variety'.[7] In this setting, each firm specialises in a unique variety (to avoid competition) and locates its production in one country (to reap economies of scale), and IIT arises since consumers within each country demand unique varieties from other countries.

In this section we give a broad overview of the level and the development of IIT for low- and middle-income countries during the 1990s without distinguishing between horizontal and vertical IIT. The Standard International Trade Classification (SITC, Rev. 2) defines our industries at a three-digit level and IIT at this level of aggregation is measured as overlapping trade (i.e. twice the minimum of exports and imports). A country's share of IIT in total trade is measured as a trade weighted average of IIT shares across industries (see Greenaway et al., 1994).[8] This measure takes any value between zero (no IIT) and one (only IIT). We compare the level of IIT in 1990 with a dynamic measurement of IIT, developed by Brülhart (1994), which shows the share of total trade changes between 1990 and 2000 that consists of intra-industry trade. The dynamic measure (or marginal IIT) may also take any value between zero (trade changes consist of only inter-industry changes) and one (trade changes consist of only IIT).[9]

Figure 2.7 compares the level of IIT in 1990 with the marginal IIT between 1990 and 2000. The static IIT measure reveals that the share of IIT in total trade increases with income. Only a handful of middle-income countries have more than or around 50 percent of IIT in total trade (Hong Kong, Singapore and Hungary). Most high-income countries have more than 50 percent, while middle-income countries are found in the range 25-50 percent and most low-income countries have less than 25 percent of IIT in total trade. This is in line with the notions that the economy of a country becomes more diversified as income rises and that there is more trade among richer countries. Bergstrand (1990) showed, in a model with both supply and demand determinants of horizontal IIT, that bilateral trade flows should become more IIT intensive as per capita income similarity increases (since consumer taste among trading partners become more similar). Furthermore, a higher per capita income *per se* reflects a greater demand for luxury goods (which is often assumed to be more differentiated). This does, however, only explain why horizontal IIT may be more common among richer countries, and several studies (see e.g. Greenaway et al., 1994) have shown that a considerable amount of IIT among high-income countries consists of exchanges of qualities instead of varieties. In this case, human capital, technology differences and R&D may be important factors behind specialisation patterns across the quality dimension.

The picture becomes more diversified when we study marginal IIT. Although several high-income countries are clustered around a marginal IIT of 50 percent (i.e. around half of the increased trade volume consists of an exchange of products stemming from the same three-digit industry), we find a similar development in countries such as Mexico, Hungary, Poland and the Philippines. We also find a handful of low-income countries with a relatively high share of marginal IIT (Cameroon, Guinea Bissau and Haiti), which is in line with the increasing importance of IIT between low- or middle-income countries and high-income countries in, for example, Tharakan (1984) and Gullstrand (2002a). Still, the overall picture is a rather clear division where low-income countries have a low degree of IIT and only a small part of their trade expansion consists of IIT.

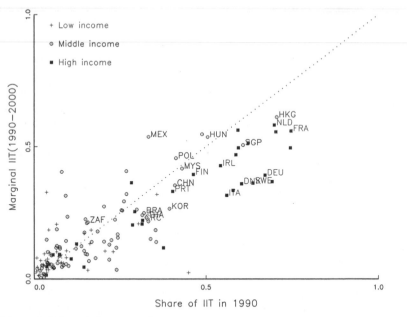

Figure 2.7 Intra-industry trade patterns

EXPORTING TO THE EU

So far, the analysis has concentrated on developing countries' trade and specialisation patterns in the global economy. In this section we give particular attention to developing countries' trade with the EU.[10] On the whole, the group of developing countries managed to increase their share of EU imports from outside countries from 45 percent in 1990 to almost 55 percent ten years later. This amounts to about 20 percent of the developing countries' total exports, which makes the EU one of the most important export markets for the developing world. Then again, significant differences can be observed across different groups of countries.

Starting with EU imports from low- and middle-income countries, there is a general pattern of increasing divergence between the two groups, i.e. while the middle-income group increased their trade share in the 1990s, the low-income group persistently experienced falling shares. The share of extra-EU imports from these income groups is shown in Table 2.1, which contains, in addition to total trade figures, the shares of different product groups for the years 1985 and 2002.

Table 2.1 Share of extra-EU imports from low- and middle-income countries

	Low income		Middle income	
	1985	2002	1985	2002
Land intensive	0.13	0.09	0.48	0.57
Labour intensive	0.01	0.02	0.63	0.78
Physical capital intensive	0.06	0.04	0.43	0.60
Energy intensive	0.04	0.03	0.76	0.60
Human capital intensive	0.005	0.004	0.15	0.46
Technology intensive	0.005	0.001	0.14	0.41
Total trade	0.05	0.02	0.45	0.53

Note: Own calculation using the World Trade Analyzer of Statistics Canada.

Overall, the low-income countries constitute a small share of EU imports and in technology- and human capital-intensive products they account for less than 1 percent in both years. Moreover, their export shares have decreased for all but one product group (labour intensive). Here the decline in land-intensive products is the most outstanding, but there is also a large percentage drop in capital-intensive products. The picture could be less perturbing if absolute trade had increased over the period. Instead, the value, in constant dollars, of the low-income countries' exports to the EU decreased by about 20 percent. The development of the low-income countries thus stands in sharp contrast to that of the group of middle-income countries. These countries accounted for more than half of extra-EU imports in 2002 and gained market access in almost all product groups during the period, the most noteworthy observation being the increased exports of technology-intensive and human capital-intensive products to the EU.

In addition to income levels, it could be interesting to consider the geographical aspect of EU trade and, again, we find large changes over the period. Figure 2.8 shows the share of extra-EU imports from developing countries grouped by region. The falling shares from North Africa and the Middle East, South America and Sub-Saharan Africa are notable, as these three regions accounted for 70 percent of extra-EU imports in the beginning of the period but only about half of that in 2002. Instead, the EU increased imports from the regions East Asia, South Asia and ROW (rest of the world), where the development in trade shares for the latter region can be attributed to some Central and East European countries (see Annex).

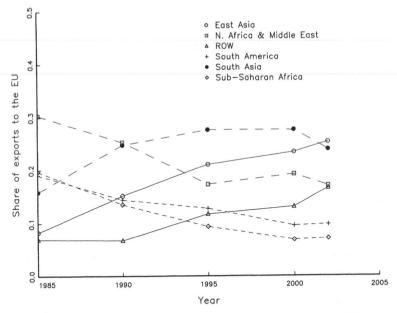

Figure 2.8 Share of low- and middle-income countries' exports to the EU

Table 2.2 shows the development of export shares to the EU for four of the product groups.[11] First, the geographical distribution of EU imports of labour-intensive products seems quite stable over the period, the exception being the increase of export shares for ROW. When it comes to the other product categories, it is interesting to note the difference between East and South Asia. Hence, while the East Asian countries have had large increases in trade shares of physical capital- and technology-intensive products and have retained a high share of human capital-intensive products, the South Asian countries seem to have lost market share, particularly since 1995. The weaker performance of the latter group is probably related to the Asian financial crisis in the late 1990s. The development of the former group, on the other hand, is highly influenced by China, which has remained relatively unaffected by the crisis and has had a very strong export performance.

Table 2.2 Share of extra EU imports from developing countries by region

		East Asia	South Asia	N. Africa & Middle East	Sub-Saharan Africa	South America	ROW
Labour intensive	1985	0.42	0.28	0.15	0.02	0.02	0.12
	1995	0.38	0.28	0.16	0.02	0.02	0.15
	2002	0.38	0.26	0.16	0.02	0.01	0.17
Physical-capital intensive	1985	0.11	0.27	0.10	0.22	0.20	0.11
	1995	0.15	0.26	0.10	0.14	0.15	0.19
	2002	0.20	0.23	0.13	0.11	0.12	0.21
Human-capital intensive	1985	0.46	0.27	0.07	0.03	0.10	0.07
	1995	0.46	0.32	0.05	0.02	0.05	0.11
	2002	0.43	0.18	0.07	0.03	0.04	0.25
Technol. intensive	1985	0.17	0.30	0.17	0.08	0.15	0.13
	1995	0.28	0.46	0.07	0.02	0.05	0.12
	2002	0.31	0.37	0.05	0.02	0.05	0.19

Note: Own calculation using the World Trade Analyzer of Statistics Canada.

The developments of Sub Saharan Africa and South America are comparable to each other, with low and decreasing export shares in labour and human capital, and sharp declines in physical capital and technology. North Africa and the Middle East show similar performance, the difference being the slight improvement of trade share in physical- and human capital-intensive products. Finally, ROW increases in all product groups. Not surprisingly, this boost in exports can be attributed to some transition economies in Central and East Europe, with Poland and Hungary as the largest exporters to the EU in our sample.

The evolution of the developing countries' trade with the EU resembles the changes in global trade flows in the 1990s. Thus, although the developing countries as a group have become more economically integrated with the rest of the world and have managed to increase trade shares, there have been winners and losers. In particular, deteriorating trade shares for low-income countries, mainly in Sub Saharan Africa and North Africa and the Middle East, have also been observed at the global level (World Bank, 2005). When it comes to trade with the EU, however, this development is perhaps more surprising considering the special treatment and focus given to these regions by the EU development and trade policies.

Export Similarities with the EU

We may investigate whether low- and middle-income countries' export profiles become more or less similar to the profile of the EU with the help of a correlation of export shares across three-digit industries. A high correlation implies that a country's export profile is similar to that of the EU (intra plus extra-EU export), while a low or a negative correlation indicates that a country specialises in other industries. In short, a high correlation reveals potential competitors with the EU on the world market. Figure 2.9 shows the export-correlation coefficients (correlation coefficients of export shares across industries between each country and the EU) for 1990 and 2000. The high correlation coefficients of France and Germany reveal that the export profile of the EU is more or less defined by the profiles of these two countries, while Portugal, Denmark, Finland and Ireland stand out with a quite different export profile to the EU as a whole.

The results in Figure 2.9 suggest that the export profile of a number of countries approaches the profile of the EU as a whole, which implies that the EU is facing a higher number of potential competitors on the world market. Mexico, Hungary and Korea, for example, have an export profile in 2000 that is more similar to the EU as a whole than Portugal, Denmark, Ireland, Finland and Greece and have nearly the same correlation coefficient as the Netherlands, Sweden and Italy. Other countries that approach a correlation coefficient of 0.5 are Poland, Thailand, Brazil, China, Hong Kong, Singapore, Malaysia and South Africa.

Also, Figure 2.9 shows a division of the world similar to the other figures. Most low-income countries are clustered around a correlation coefficient close to zero, which implies that their export profiles have no similarities at all to that of the EU. Middle-income countries, however, are more similar and several of them approach the export profile of the EU. The results even suggest that several middle-income countries are more similar to the EU as a whole than many individual EU members.

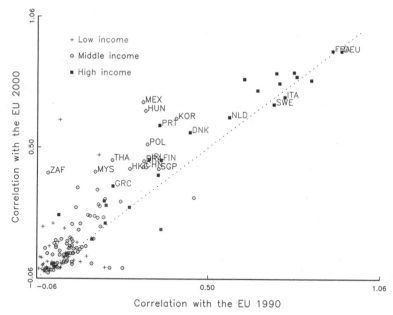

Figure 2.9 Export-profile similarity

CONCLUSION

One would expect the implementation of the WTO agreements, the fragmentation of the production process, and the increased number of regional integration areas in the 1990s to have boosted trade and facilitated labour division across countries. Certainly, there is evidence of an integration process of low- and middle-income countries into the world economy as trade shares have continuously increased. This development, however, does not seem to have brought any fundamental change to the developing countries' comparative advantages. One of the most robust results in this study is the lack of structural changes in the specialisation and trade patterns in the 1990s. There is a distinct division into low-, middle- and high-income countries regardless of the measurement used to analyse these patterns. Thus, low- and middle-income countries remain land and labour abundant at the end of the decade, while most physical capital is still located in high-income countries – a pattern reflected in the trade flows as well.

Nevertheless a number of middle-income countries, mainly in Asia and South America, have become more similar to the high-income group with regard to factor endowments, and have gained comparative advantages in more technology- and skill-based products. On the other hand, low-income countries seem to be moving in the opposite direction as they become more dissimilar to world endowments. Hence, another important result in the chapter is the tendency for growing divergence within the group of developing countries, with low-income countries either lagging behind or showing up as outliers. The increasing gap between low- and middle-income countries is also apparent from the former countries' deteriorating trade shares with the EU. In contrast, middle-income countries have gained market access, and the EU is now facing more competitors on the world market as several middle-income countries' profiles have become more similar to the export profile of the EU.

The findings suggest that trade between developed and developing countries is highly dominated by inter-industry specialisation. The share of IIT in total trade remains low for most developing countries and only a handful of countries have experienced a substantial increase. This implies that welfare gains from trade, particularly in low-income countries, will continue to be accompanied by structural adjustment costs and income distributions effects.[12] These effects are even more likely since a large part of IIT between countries is vertical and driven by country differences in technology and factor endowments (see, e.g., Gullstrand, 2002a; Greenaway et al., 1994).

NOTES

1. Based on own calculations using the World Trade Analyzer of Statistics Canada. For a general description of world trade flows in the 1990s, see also World Bank (2005).
2. We apply the definition used in World Bank (2005), which implies that income rank refers to each country's status in the end of the 1980s.
3. Often a distinction is made between ricardian and endowment-based models where comparative advantages in the former are due to differences in labour productivity. However, as differences in labour productivity depend on the input of additional factors such as physical and human capital, it is possible to take into account technology differences in a HO-based framework (see e.g. Helpman, 1999).
4. For a further discussion about development paths in a three-factor model, see Leamer (1987).
5. We define distance as $d_{wi} = [(x_w-x_i)2 + (y_w-y_i)2]1/2$ between the world, w, and country i.
6. See Falvey and Kierzkowski (1987).
7. See Helpman and Krugman (1985).
8. The share of IIT in total trade is defined as: $B = \Sigma_i 2\min(x_i,m_i) / \Sigma_i(x_i+m_i)$, where x_i and m_i are exports and imports in industry i, respectively. See Gullstrand (2002b) for a comparison of different IIT measures.
9. The marginal IIT measure is defined as: $BA = \Sigma_i w_i B_i A$, where $B_i A=1-[(|\Delta x_i-\Delta m_i|)/(|\Delta x_i|+|\Delta m_i|)]$ and $w_i= [(|\Delta x_i|+|\Delta m_i|)/\Sigma_i(|\Delta x_i|+|\Delta m_i|)]$, and x_i and m_i are exports and imports in industry i.
10. Figures refer to EU15 for the whole period.
11. The developments for land- and energy-intensive products are relatively stable over time, with South America as the main exporter of the former and North Africa and the Middle East of the latter. Noteworthy, though, is the decrease of trade shares for Sub Saharan Africa in land-intensive products from 27 percent in 1985 to 18 percent in 2002.
12. Adjustment costs may stem from labour-market rigidities, and consist of temporary unemployment or reallocation costs (e.g. job search or retraining). IIT (and new trade theory) is associated with lower trade induced adjustment costs of IIT as suggested by the smooth adjustment hypothesis (see Brülhart, 2002).

REFERENCES

Balassa, B. (1965), 'Trade Liberalization and "Revealed" Comparative Advantage', *The Manchester School of Economic and Social Studies*, **33**, 99–123.

Barro, R.J. and J.-W. Lee (2000), 'International Data on Educational Attainment: Updates and Implications', CID Working Paper No. 42.

Bergstrand, J.H. (1990), 'The Heckscher-Ohlin-Samuelson Model, the Linder Hypothesis and the Determinants of Bilateral Intra-Industry Trade', *Economic Journal*, **100**, 1216–1230.

Brülhart, M. (1994), 'Marginal Intra-Industry Trade: Measurement and Relevance for the Pattern of Industrial Adjustment', *Weltwirtschaftliches Archiv*, **130** (3), 600–613.

Brülhart, M. (2002), 'Marginal Intra-Industry Trade: Towards a Measure of Non-Disruptive Trade Expansion', in P.J. Lloyd and H.-H. Lee (eds), *Frontiers of Research in Intra-Industry Trade*, Hampshire and New York: Palgrave Macmillan.

Deardorff, A.V. (2000), 'Patterns of Trade and Growth across Cones', *De Economist*, **148** (2), 141–166.

Easterly, W. and R. Levine (2001), 'What Have We Learned from a Decade of Empirical Research on Growth? It's Not Factor Accumulation: Stylized Facts and Growth Models', *The World Bank Economic Review*, **15**, 177–219.

Falvey, R. and H. Kierzkowski (1987), 'Product Quality, Intra-Industry Trade and (Im)perfect Competition', in H. Kierzkowski (ed.), *Protection and Competition in International Trade*, Oxford: Basil Blackwell.

Greenaway, D., R. Hine, and C. Milner (1994), 'Country-Specific Factors and the Pattern of Horizontal and Vertical Intra-Industry Trade', *Weltwirtschaftliches Archiv*, **130** (1), 77–100.

Greenaway, D. and C. Milner (1993), *Trade and Industrial Policy in Developing Countries: A Manual of Policy Analysis*, London: Macmillan Press.

Gullstrand, J. (2002a), 'Demand Patterns and Vertical Intra-Industry Trade with Special Reference to North-South Trade', *Journal of International Trade and Economic Development*, **11** (4), 429–55.

Gullstrand, J. (2002b), 'Does the Measurement of Intra-Industry Trade Matter?', *Weltwirtschaftliches Archiv*, **138** (2), 317–39.

Helpman, E. (1999), 'The Structure of Foreign Trade', *Journal of Economic Perspectives*, **13** (2), 121–44.

Helpman, E. and P. Krugman (1985), *Market Structure and Foreign Trade: Increasing Returns, Imperfect Competition, and the International Economy*, Cambridge and London: MIT Press.

Kokko, A., T. Mathä, and P. Gustavsson Tingvall (2005), 'European Integration and Trade Diversion: Yeats Revisited', SIEPS Report No. 2005:7.

Lall, S. (1998), 'Exports of Manufactures by Developing Countries: Emerging Patterns of Trade and Location', *Oxford Review of Economic Policy*, **14** (2), 54–73.

Leamer, E. E. (1987), 'Paths of Development in the Three-Factor, n-Good General Equilibrium Model', *Journal of Political Economy*, **95** (5), 961–99.

Leamer, E.E. and P. Lundborg (1995), 'Sweden Competing in the Global Marketplace – A Heckscher-Ohlin View', SNS Occasional Paper No. 68.

Tharakan, P. K. M. (1984), 'Intra-Industry Trade Between the Industrial Countries and the Developing World', *European Economic Review*, **26** (1-2), 213–28.

World Bank (2005), 'Economic Growth in the 1990s: Learning from a Decade of Reform', Washington DC: World Bank.

UNCTAD (2005), 'Growth and Development in the 1990s: Lessons from an Enigmatic Decade', Trade and Development Board.

ANNEX 2

Data Description

Table 2A.1

Country name (ISO-code, Income code, Regional code)

Afghanistan (AFG,L,4) Angola (AGO,L,2) Albania (ALB,M,39) Netherlands Antilles (ANT,M,3) United Arab Emirates (ARE,M,1) Argentina (ARG,M,3) Australia (AUS,H,6) Austria (AUT,H,6) Burundi (BDI,L,2) Belgium (BEL,H,6) Benin (BEN,L,2) Burkina Faso (BFA,L,2) Bangladesh (BGD,M,4) Bulgaria (BGR,M,6) Bahrain (BHR,M,1) Bahamas (BHS,M,3) Belize (BLZ,M,3) Bermuda (BMU,M,6) Bolivia (BOL,M,3) Brazil (BRA,M,3) Barbados (BRB,M,3) Brunei Darussalam (BRN,M,4) Bhutan (BTN,L,4) Central African Republic (CAF,L,2) Canada (CAN,H,6) Switzerland (CHE,H,6) Chile (CHL,M,3) China (CHN,M,5) Côte d'Ivoire (CIV,L,2) Cameroon (CMR,L,2) Democratic Republic of the Congo (COD,L,2) Congo (COG,L,2) Colombia (COL,M,3) Comoros (COM,L,2) Costa Rica (CRI,M,3) Cuba (CUB,M,3) Cayman Islands (CYM,M,3) Cyprus (CYP,H,1) Germany (DEU,H,6) Djibouti (DJI,M,2) Denmark (DNK,H,6) Dominican Republic (DOM,M,3) Algeria (DZA,M,1) Ecuador (ECU,M,3) Egypt (EGY,M,1) Western Sahara (ESH,L,1) Spain (ESP,H,39) Ethiopia (ETH,M,2) Finland (FIN,H,6) Fiji (FJI,M,9) Falkland Islands (Malvinas) (FLK,H,3) France (FRA,H,6) Gabon (GAB,M,2) United Kingdom of Great Britain and Northern Ireland (GBR,H,6) Ghana (GHA,L,2) Gibraltar (GIB,H,6) Guinea (GIN,L,2) Guadeloupe (GLP,H,3) Gambia (GMB,L,2) Guinea-Bissau (GNB,L,2) Equatorial Guinea (GNQ,M,2) Greece (GRC,H,6) Greenland (GRL,H,6) Guatemala (GTM,M,3) French Guiana (GUF,H,3) Guyana (GUY,M,3) Hong Kong Special Administrative Region of China (HKG,M,5) Honduras (HND,M,3) Haiti (HTI,L,3) Hungary (HUN,M,6) Indonesia (IDN,M,4) India (IND,M,4) Ireland (IRL,H,6) Iran (Islamic Republic of) (IRN,M,4) Iraq (IRQ,M,1) Iceland (ISL,H,6) Israel (ISR,H,1) Italy (ITA,H,6) Jamaica (JAM,M,3) Jordan (JOR,M,1) Japan (JPN,H,5) Kenya (KEN,L,2) Cambodia (KHM,L,4) Kiribati (KIR,M,6) Saint Kitts and Nevis (KNA,M,3) Republic of Korea (KOR,M,5) Kuwait (KWT,M,1) Lao People's Democratic Republic (LAO,L,4) Lebanon (LBN,M,1) Liberia (LBR,L,2) Libyan Arab Jamahiriya (LBY,M,1) Sri Lanka (LKA,L,4) Morocco (MAR,M,1) Madagascar (MDG,L,2) Maldives (MDV,M,4) Mexico (MEX,M,3) Mali (MLI,L,2) Malta (MLT,M,6) Myanmar (MMR,L,4) Mongolia (MNG,L,5) Mozambique (MOZ,L,2) Mauritania (MRT,L,2) Mauritius (MUS,M,2) Malawi (MWI,L,2) Malaysia (MYS,M,4) New Caledonia (NCL,H,6) Niger (NER,L,2) Nigeria (NGA,M,2) Nicaragua (NIC,L,3) Netherlands (NLD,H,6) Norway (NOR,H,6) Nepal (NPL,L,4) New Zealand (NZL,H,9) Oman (OMN,M,1) Pakistan (PAK,M,4) Panama (PAN,M,3) Peru (PER,M,3) Philippines (PHL,M,4) Papua New Guinea (PNG,L,6) Poland (POL,M,6) Democratic People's Republic of Korea (PRK,L,5) Portugal

---

Country name (ISO-code, Income code, Regional code)

(PRT,H,6) Paraguay (PRY,M,3) Qatar (QAT,M,1) Réunion (REU,H,2) Romania (ROU,M,6) Rwanda (RWA,L,2) Saudi Arabia (SAU,M,1) Sudan (SDN,L,1) Senegal (SEN,L,2) Singapore (SGP,M,4) Saint Helena (SHN,M,2) Solomon Islands (SLB,L,6) Sierra Leone (SLE,L,2) El Salvador (SLV,M,3) Somalia (SOM,L,2) Saint Pierre and Miquelon (SPM,M,6) Suriname (SUR,M,3) Sweden (SWE,H,154) Seychelles (SYC,M,2) Syrian Arab Republic (SYR,M,1) Turks and Caicos Islands (TCA,M,3) Chad (TCD,L,2) Togo (TGO,L,2) Thailand (THA,M,4) Trinidad and Tobago (TTO,M,3) Tunisia (TUN,M,1) Turkey (TUR,M,1) United Republic of Tanzania (TZA,L,2) Uganda (UGA,L,2) Uruguay (URY,M,3) United States of America (USA,H,6) Venezuela (VEN,M,3) Viet Nam (VNM,M,4) Yemen (YEM,L,1) South Africa (ZAF,M,2) Zambia (ZMB,L,2) Zimbabwe (ZWE,L,2)

Regional codes: North Africa and Middle East (1), Sub Saharan Africa (2), South America (3), South Asia (4), East Asia (5), Rest of the world (6)

In Figures 2.1-2.2, and 2A.1

ARG AUS AUT BEL BEN BGD BOL BRA BWA CAN CHE CHL CHN CMR COL CRI DEU DNK DOM DZA ECU EGY ESP FIN FRA GBR GHA GMB GRC GTM GUY HKG HND HTI HUN IDN IND IRL IRN ISL ITA JOR JPN KEN LKA LSO MEX MLI MOZ MWI MYS NIC NLD NOR NZL PAK PAN PER PHL PRT PRY RWA SEN SGP SLE SLV SWE SWZ SYR TGO THA TTO TUN USA VEN ZAF ZMB ZWE

Note: ISO and regional codes stem from UN Statistics Division (available online). Income codes stem from World Bank (2005). L stands for low-income, M for middle-income (both lower and upper middle), and H for high-income countries.

Table 2A.2

Variables	Definition	Source
Land	Arable land (hectares).	World Development Indicators (2006, The World Bank)
Labour	Population between 15 and 64 years.	World Development Indicators
Physical capital	Stock of physical capital in constant (1995) $US.	Own calculations based on data from World Development Indicators
Human capital	Share of the population over 15 that has completed a post-secondary education.	Barro and Lee (2000)

Note: The capital stock is calculated by the use of a perpetual inventory method where the initial capital stock is computed following Easterly and Levine (2001). Hence, with the assumption of steady state, the initial capital-output ratio, k, can be estimated by $i/(g+d)$, where i is the investment-output ratio, g is the growth rate of real output and d is the depreciation rate. The growth rate is calculated as a weighted average of the country's growth rate in the first ten years for which our investment data is available (starting from 1970), and the world growth rate during the same period (0.064) whereas d is set to 0.7.

Table 2A.3

Product groups (SITC Rev 2)
Energy intensive: 32, 33, 34, 35; Human capital intensive: 53, 55, 76, 78, 79, 88; Labour intensive: 81, 82, 83, 84, 85, 89; Land intensive: 0, 1, 2, 3, 4, 5, 6, 7, 8, 9, 11, 12, 21, 22, 23, 24, 25, 26, 27, 28, 29, 41, 42, 43, 94; Physical capital intensive: 61, 62, 63, 64, 65, 66, 67, 68, 69; Technology intensive: 51, 52, 54, 56, 57, 58, 59, 71, 72, 73, 74, 75, 77, 87, 95

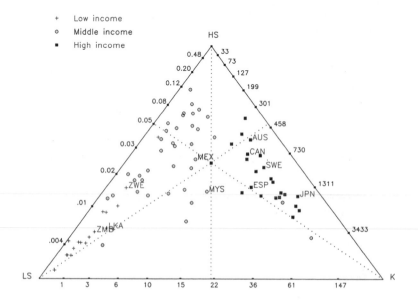

Figure 2A.1 Endowment triangle with human capital 2000

3. Assessing the Effects of EU Trade Preferences for Developing Countries

Maria Persson and Fredrik Wilhelmsson

INTRODUCTION

The European Union has a long history of granting special trade preferences to developing countries, dating back to the Treaty of Rome in 1957 which gave colonies an associated status.[1] Over time, new systems for preferences have been introduced into an increasingly complex pattern and, today, few developing countries lack preferential access of some form to the EU market.

Among possible beneficial effects of trade preferences are increased export volumes, export diversification and the possibility for exporters to charge higher prices. However, there is a widespread view that traditional non-reciprocal preferences have not been able to achieve at least the former two of these goals – a view shared for instance by the European Commission (1996) concerning preferences granted within the Lomé framework. In this chapter, we attempt to see whether this gloomy view of the effects of trade preferences is correct.

More specifically, our goal is to answer two questions: Firstly, have trade preferences affected the value of developing countries' exports to the EU? Secondly, if they have, are there differences between preference systems so that certain groups of developing countries have benefited more than others from EU trade policy? To identify the effects of preferences it is essential to control for the EU enlargements, since they may lead to both trade creation and trade diversion, the latter of which could include decreased exports from developing countries. Therefore, in addition to answering the two main questions, we will also get an estimate of how the effects of preferences have been influenced by the successive EU enlargements.

In order to analyse the trade preferences we construct a detailed database of changes in EU trade preferences. The data are gathered from EU legislation from the 1960s onwards. To estimate the impact of preferences on exports to the EU we apply a specification of the gravity model incorporating recent developments of the model. In the spirit of Bun and Klaassen (2004), the gravity model is augmented with a time trend for each country pair, controlling for the evolution of market access and exporting country openness over the period studied. This is a methodological novelty in the literature on trade preferences and a key to estimating the effects of preferences purged of other factors affecting the evolution of developing countries' exports.

Compared to previous studies this chapter, besides using an improved method, covers a longer period and a wider range of preferences, using the above-mentioned detailed database of EU trade preferences. The sample period is 1960–2002 and the effects of African, Caribbean and Pacific (ACP) preferences (within the Yaoundé and Lomé Conventions), preferences for Mediterranean countries, the Generalised System of Preferences (GSP) and special regimes within the GSP are analysed. Deeper integration, for example Association Agreements with future EU members, is beyond the scope of this chapter.

The chapter is organised as follows. In the second section the EU trade preference schemes relevant to developing countries are briefly described. The third section comments on the previous literature, while the fourth section includes the empirical methodology and the data. The estimation results are analysed in the fifth section and the sixth section concludes the chapter.

TRADE PREFERENCES FOR DEVELOPING COUNTRIES

This section provides a short outline of the rather complex set of trade preferences that the EU has for developing countries. These can broadly be divided into ACP, Mediterranean and GSP preferences. Most of the systems cover much more than trade issues, such as aid and political cooperation, but we will focus strictly on the provisions that are directly trade-related, and particularly on the differences between the systems. For a list of beneficiaries under each system at different times, see Annex 3.

ACP Preferences

The origin of special trade preferences for African, Caribbean and Pacific (ACP) countries lies in the Treaty of Rome signed in 1957, which included provisions for the colonies of EU members to form a free trade area with the EU. Following the independence of most colonies at the beginning of the 1960s, these reciprocal preferences were brought over on a bilateral basis into the Yaoundé Conventions signed in 1963 and 1969. [2]

Following Britain's accession to the EU, the first Lomé Convention was signed in 1975. The Convention provided Yaoundé beneficiaries and mainly former non-Asian British colonies with duty free access on a non-reciprocal basis to the European market for most products except those covered by the Common Agricultural Policy (CAP) (for these products certain preferences were available though). The subsequent Lomé Conventions of 1979, 1984, 1989 and 1995 retained this basic pattern. Since 2000, the ACP relations have been governed by the Cotonou agreement, where ACP countries will continue to receive, for a transitional period, non-reciprocal trade preferences under a WTO waiver. By 2008, these preferences should have been renegotiated into WTO compatible free trade agreements.[3]

Mediterranean Preferences

Countries around the Mediterranean Sea have been involved in different trading arrangements with the EU since the late 1960s and early 1970s, when Tunisia, Morocco, Israel and Egypt signed agreements with the EU. These were followed by Cooperation Agreements signed with the Maghreb (1976) and Mashreq (1977) countries.[4] The bilateral Cooperation Agreements included trade preferences that were non-reciprocal, and gave duty free access for most industrial and many agricultural goods. Since 1995, the Cooperation Agreements have been in the process of being replaced with a new generation of Euro-Mediterranean Association Agreements as part of the Barcelona process's attempts to create a Euro-Mediterranean Free Trade Area by 2010. These agreements include provisions for the transition to free trade.

Generalised System of Preferences

The EU has unilaterally granted almost all developing countries non-reciprocal trade preferences under the GSP since 1971. For long, these preferences took the form of duty free quotas and ceilings, but in 1995 all quantitative restrictions were removed, and preferences were instead granted in the form of tariff reductions, the size of which depended on the *sensitivity* of the product.

In addition to the general arrangements that cover all developing countries, certain groups of countries have also received better preferences within the GSP regime. The least developed countries (LDCs) have been granted more beneficial market access since 1977 and, following the Everything But Arms (EBA) initiative in 2001, may now export all goods except arms and ammunition duty and quota free to the EU. For countries affected by the production and trafficking of illicit drugs, there has been a special arrangement with additional benefits (sometimes called the *drug regime*) since 1991.

Pyramid of Privilege

It has been customary in the literature to talk of a 'pyramid of privilege' to describe the relationship between the systems in terms of the trade benefits they offer, with ACP countries on top having the most wide-ranging benefits, and countries only able to use the GSP at the bottom (see Figure 3.1).[5]

It is worth saying a few words about the relationship between each of the systems. Starting from the top of the pyramid, the main difference regarding trade provisions between the Yaoundé and Lomé Conventions is the fact that the former preferences unlike the latter were formally reciprocal. However, in reality there were strong limitations to the reciprocity that was demanded by the Yaoundé countries (Young 1972). Therefore, even though these systems might have different effects due to, for instance, the time period when they were granted and the number of developing countries involved, it should be valid to compare the other preferential systems with the ACP system as a whole when it comes to the characteristics of the preferences.

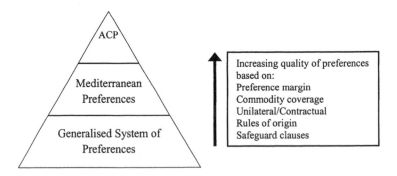

Figure 3.1 Pyramid of privilege

The trade preferences for Mediterranean countries were designed to be similar to the ACP preferences, but two important exceptions to this were textiles and clothing and agricultural products covered by the CAP, where ACP countries were given better access to the EU market.

Comparing the ACP preferences with those granted under the GSP, a first important difference is that both the preference margin and the commodity coverage are wider for ACP countries. Secondly, ACP preferences are contractual which makes market access more certain.[6] Thirdly, rules of origin are more generous, and allow e.g. full cumulation of origin within the ACP group (Inama 2002).[7] Lastly, Lomé preferences have less restrictive safeguard clauses (McQueen 1998).

Finally, looking at the differences between Mediterranean and GSP preferences one may note that Mediterranean countries, like ACP countries, have the advantage that their preferences are not only contractual, but also wider in scope and depth than those of the GSP.

So, to summarise, for at least a long time the ACP countries had the best access to the EU market of the developing countries in our sample, followed by Mediterranean countries, and only those countries that did not have any other preferential access could be expected to actually use their GSP preferences.[8] In the 1990s, the pyramid became harder to define since the Mediterranean countries started to sign free trade agreements with the EU, at the same time as preferences for especially the least developed countries improved within the GSP system. Hence, over time, as the trade provisions changed, the pyramid changed with them, and it is not so obvious today where different systems should be placed.

As an overall assessment of the quality of preferences under different systems, Figure 3.1 continues to be valid though. Hence, we expect the effects to be biggest for ACP preferences, smaller for Mediterranean preferences and more modest for GSP preferences. Special sub-regimes for LDCs and drug-producing countries within the GSP system are expected to have a larger effect than having only general GSP preferences, but it is not entirely straightforward to make hypotheses about the size of these effects compared with those of the ACP and Mediterranean preferences.

PREVIOUS STUDIES

Though quite a lot has been written about the EU's system of trade preferences for developing countries, there have not been many *ex post* studies.[9] One of the first in the gravity tradition is Sapir (1981) who uses yearly cross-sectional Ordinary least squares (OLS) regressions of a gravity model for 1967–1978 to estimate the effect of the GSP regime, where the reference is north-north trade. He finds a significant and positive effect for 1973 and 1974, corresponding to 48 percent gross trade creation. Oguledo and MacPhee (1994) use a similar method for 1976, and find a statistically significant effect for GSP, Mediterranean and Lomé preferences. The Lomé effect is larger than the Mediterranean effect, which in turn exceeds that of the GSP. Also using the gravity model, but estimated with OLS on three-year averages for 1973–92, Nilsson (2002) finds a significant and positive effect for most though not all years for GSP and Lomé, and that the effect of the latter is larger. The Mediterranean preferences are mostly insignificant.

None of these studies seems to have used an appropriate method, since cross-sectional regressions of the gravity model do not fully control for country heterogeneity, which leads to biased estimates due to omitted variables. The cross-section or pooled cross-section is, in fact, a restricted version of the more general panel model and these restrictions should be tested before implementation (Mátyás 1997).

An example of a study that does incorporate the recent developments in the gravity literature is that of Péridy (2005) who estimates the effect of Mediterranean preferences for 1975–2001 in a sample of OECD and some developing countries, with various panel data methods and OLS for comparison. The Mediterranean dummy is highly significant in all cases, and with similar magnitudes in all specifications (except OLS). The corresponding gross trade creation is 20–27 percent of actual exports. Carrère (2004) studies the effects of regional trade agreements in Africa with a proper panel specification, and even though she does not explicitly discuss the effects of EU trade preferences on developing countries, she includes a dummy variable to control for ACP preferences. The results indicate that these preferences have had a significant and very large effect on ACP exports.[10] The sample used stretches from 1962 to 1996 and includes basically all available countries. Finally, concerning EU imports Soloaga and Winters (2001) find, using a gravity model, evidence of significant trade diversion occurring between 1980–82 and 1995–96, i.e. during a period when the EU experienced three rounds of enlargements.

EMPIRICAL METHODOLOGY AND DATA

Methodological Considerations

In order to estimate the effect of EU preferences on exports from developing countries at the same time as controlling for EU enlargements, we use a formulation of the gravity model including time trends as in Bun and Klaassen (2004). The gravity model has frequently been used to estimate the effects of preferential trade agreements but without the inclusion of time trends.[11] The latter provide an instrument to control for country-pair specific factors that vary over time, for example transportation costs. Other factors that are not specific to country-pairs but rather to exporting countries, and that are controlled for by time trends are variations in competitiveness and supply capacity.[12] Besides these factors, the time trends capture some of the variations in exporting countries' market access, which may vary among importing countries. Preferences are, indeed, intended to increase market access, but there are several other important factors besides tariffs that affect market access that should not be ascribed to preferences. Mayer and Zignago (2005) find that market access has changed significantly over time as a result of factors other than tariff liberalisation; hence failing to control for the evolution of exporting countries' market access might bias the results.

One drawback of including country-pair time trends is that they could pick up parts of the effects of preferential liberalisation if these effects are gradual. Since it has been argued that traditional fixed effects estimation only measures the short-run effects of trade liberalisations (see Egger 2004), this should not be a serious problem. Some authors (e.g., Carrère 2006) include real exchange rates to control for the evolution of competitiveness over time, but we have opted not to do so due to the large number of missing observations.

To avoid bias resulting from country heterogeneity we include country-pair fixed effects, as well as time effects, to control for factors common to all country-pairs that vary over time. Thus, the estimated model is:

$$\ln M_{ijt} = \alpha + \beta X_{ijt} + \gamma_1 EU_{it} + \gamma_2 EU_{it} * GSP_{jt} + \gamma_3 EU_{it} * Yaounde_{jt} +$$
$$\gamma_4 EU_{it} * MED_{jt} + \gamma_5 EU_{it} * GSP_{jt} * Yaounde_{jt} +$$
$$\gamma_6 EU_{it} * GSP_{jt} * Lome_{jt} + \gamma_7 EU_{it} * GSP_{jt} * Lome_{jt} * LDC_{jt} +$$
$$\gamma_8 EU_{it} * GSP_{jt} * LDC_{jt} + \gamma_9 EU_{it} * GSP_{jt} * Drug_{jt} +$$
$$\gamma_{10} EU_{it} * GSP_{jt} * MED_{jt} + \mu_{ij} * t + u_{ijt}$$
$$i \in EU_{15}$$

$$(3.1)$$

where the error term u_{ijt} can be decomposed into country-pair and time fixed effects and a normally distributed error term; $u_{ijt} = \mu_{ij} + \lambda_t + \varepsilon_{ijt}$. M_{ijt} is imports to European country i from exporting developing country j at time t, and the vector $\mathbf{X}$ includes the main explanatory variables real GDP and population of both countries in natural logarithms. $\mu_{ij} * t$ is a set of country-pair time trends; EU is a dummy variable equal to one if country i is a member of the EU at time t and $Yaoundé$, $Lomé$, GSP, LDC, $Drug$ and MED are dummy variables taking the value one if country j is granted preferential access to the EU market under the given preference scheme (described above) at time t. Since some preference groups are overlapping, we also include all possible interactions of the main preference dummy variables in order to distinguish the impact of preferences on various country groups. In cases where, for all observations, all countries within a preference system also have preferences under the GSP, the relevant dummies are only included as interactions – this applies to Lomé, Drug and LDC countries. Finally, all preference dummies are interacted with the EU dummy to make sure that the preference effect is measured only when country i is actually a member of the EU at time t. This also implies that the residual reference group consists of countries that are not members of the EU and countries not receiving any preferences at time t.

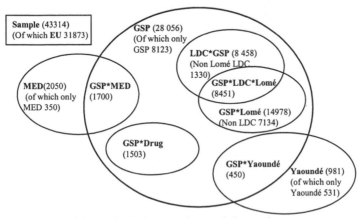

Note: Number of observations in the regression sample in parentheses.

Figure 3.2 Preference systems in the regression sample

Figure 3.2 illustrates the relationship between the dummy variables and the number of observations for each group. To simplify the picture the EU dummy variable has been omitted.

Data

The focus of this study is on exports to the EU from developing countries. Therefore, the sample of countries is limited to EU15 countries and developing countries over the period 1960–2002. The panel is unbalanced with 43 314 bilateral observations. The sample of 109 developing country exporters excludes countries with a deeper form of integration with the EU,[13] formerly planned economies in Central and Eastern Europe and major oil exporting countries.[14] Trade in the formerly planned economies has gone through a major reorientation as a result of the transition to a market economy and incorporation into the EU, so, in the absence of appropriate variables to correct for these changes in trades they are excluded to reduce the risk of omitted variable bias. The reason for excluding major oil exporters is that the structure of their trade is likely to differ from that of other developing countries and that they are less influenced by EU trade policies. A comprehensive list of the included countries and preferences granted to them by the EU is found in Annex 3.

When it comes to the actual data, the variables of main interest, i.e. the dummy variables for different preferences, come from a database of preferential trade agreements created for this chapter. The database is based on the original legal texts in the *Official Journal of the European Communities*, and great care has been taken to ensure that each country is listed as a beneficiary under a certain arrangement only for those years when it has actually been able to use these arrangements (the starting year is hence e.g. not the date of the formal signing of the agreements but rather the actual entry into force of the agreement, or in some cases the premature entry into force of the trade provisions). Unlike what has been usual in the literature, the database also covers a wide range of preferences, including sub-regimes within the GSP.

The data on the other gravity variables are extracted from the following sources: Nominal imports in US$ from DOTS (IMF 2002 and 2005a); population, real GDP in constant 2000 US$ and US GDP-deflator from World Development Indicators (World Bank 2005).[15] The nominal imports have been converted to real imports using the GDP deflator of the US.

RESULTS

This section will start with some preliminary observations regarding the data. The estimation results are then analysed, following which the aggregate effects for country groups are calculated and commented on.

Preference Receiving Countries' Exports to the EU

Table 3.1 contains some basic data on exports to the EU from the main preference groups. Despite an increasing number of positive trade flows from developing countries to the EU over the time period studied, the share of preference-receiving countries in total EU (15) imports has decreased. This alone cannot be taken as evidence that preferences have had little or no effect. Nevertheless, it indicates that developing countries' exports to the EU have increased less than could be expected given the general evolution of EU imports. Real exports to the EU from most preference groups have increased though, as has the number of *observed* trade flows.

Table 3.1 EU imports from selected groups of developing countries[a]

Country group[b]	Variable (3 year average)	1960–1962	1971–1973	1981–1983	1991–1993	2000–2002
ACP	Real exports[c]	9 687	17 333	14 867	17 333	22 333
	Share of EU imports (%)[d]	3.15	2.21	1.76	1.06	0.94
	Observations (3 years)	486	1 110	1 782	2 391	2 386
GSP[e]	Real exports	34 300	55 900	55 500	111 000	206 333
	Share of EU imports (%)	11.14	7.11	6.57	6.85	8.73
	Observations (3 years)	1 371	2 217	3 110	4 018	4 053
MED	Real exports	4 780	7 047	11 400	17 600	27 967
	Share of EU imports (%)	1.54	0.90	1.35	1.09	1.19
	Observations (3 years)	181	205	241	294	294
Drug	Real exports	3 727	5 530	4 580	6 317	8 377
	Share of EU imports (%)	1.21	0.71	0.54	0.39	0.35
	Observations (3 years)	306	389	412	417	420
LDC	Real exports	4 233	8 743	5 483	7 480	11 800
	Share of EU imports (%)	1.38	1.11	0.65	0.46	0.50
	Observations (3 years)	229	607	997	1475	1539

Notes: [a] EU defined as EU members as of 2000. Imports to (West) Germany are not included before 1971.
[b] Defined as countries receiving preferences in 2000 and in our regression sample.
[c] Real exports in million US$.
[d] Note that imports from other EU countries form part of the total imports to an EU country.
[e] GSP includes ACP, MED, Drug and LDC countries.

Estimation Results

The results of the estimation of Equation 3.1 above are shown in Table 3.2. Since the method of including bilateral time trends is new in this literature, we include the results of regressions both with and without bilateral time trends. The GDP coefficients for importing and exporting countries are positive and highly significant in both specifications. However, including the time trends reduces the coefficients, which is what we would expect if the GDP variable partly explains the trends in a country's trading relations. The population of the exporting country has no significant effect on trade in the time trend specification, but a significantly positive effect in the specification without time trends. In contrast, EU countries with a large population import significantly less from developing countries in both specifications.

Table 3.2 Gravity model estimates

Dependent variable ln(real imports)	(1) With time trend		(2) Without time trend	
Variables	Coeff.	P-value	Coeff.	P-value
GDP(i)	0.643	0.000	1.272	0.000
POP(i)	-1.527	0.000	-0.660	0.027
GDP(j)	1.230	0.000	1.420	0.000
POP(j)	-0.549	0.300	0.613	0.000
EU	-0.239	0.000	-0.295	0.000
EU*GSP	0.035	0.323	0.344	0.000
EU*Yaoundé	-0.035	0.471	-0.142	0.007
EU*GSP*LDC	0.155	0.039	0.348	0.000
EU*GSP*Drug	-0.025	0.561	0.185	0.000
EU*MED	-0.083	0.188	0.435	0.000
EU*GSP*Yaoundé	0.254	0.000	0.108	0.104
EU*GSP*Lomé	0.231	0.000	-0.088	0.013
EU*GSP*LDC*Lomé	-0.139	0.094	-0.688	0.000
EU*GSP*MED	0.182	0.029	-0.408	0.000
Country-pair time trend	Yes		No	
Country-pair fixed effect	Yes		Yes	
Time fixed effect	Yes		Yes	
Observations	43 314		43 314	
Country-pairs	1520		1520	

Note: Natural logarithms of real GDP and population. P-values are based on robust standard errors, since diagnostic tests indicate that both heteroskedasticity and autocorrelation are present in the data.

Comparing the two specifications with and without time trends in Table 3.2, it is obvious that inclusion of time trends has a large impact on the estimates and the decomposition of the trade effects of preferences. The inclusion of time trends is important to control for country-pair factors that are not constant over the rather long period studied (1960–2002), since failing to control for factors affecting trade might bias the results. On the other hand, time trends can capture some of the effects of trade preferences if the effect is gradual. Hence, the model with time trends is likely to underestimate the true effect of preferences, while failure to control for the time trends would bias the results in an unknown direction. Therefore, we prefer a conservative estimation strategy implying a possible downward bias to our estimates.

A common result in both models is that countries joining the EU, *ceteris paribus*, experience a fall in imports from developing countries. However, the conclusions that can be drawn about the coefficients of EU*GSP, EU*Yaoundé and EU*MED differ greatly depending on whether time trends are included or not. Hence, it is not possible to compare the other coefficients of the specifications directly since they are only included as interactions. Our preferred specification is the one with bilateral time trends, so we will focus on the results from that.

Looking at the results, one can start by noting that having only GSP preferences does not significantly increase exports, and neither does having only Yaoundé or Mediterranean preferences. This means that preferences granted in the 1960s and at the beginning of the 1970s did not increase the receiving countries' exports. Countries that are granted additional preferences under the drug regime do not have an extra effect above the GSP effect, but for countries that have GSP, also getting Yaoundé, LDC, Lomé or Mediterranean preferences *does* have a significant extra effect.[16] Strictly speaking, the Yaoundé and some Mediterranean countries first have preferences under their respective schemes, and then receive GSP preferences. Consequently, the correct interpretation regarding these countries is presumably that preferences only start to have an effect later in the period (i.e. 1972 when the GSP dummy starts being 1) or in the case of Mediterranean preferences that it is the more recent Cooperation Agreements that actually have an effect. For countries with GSP and LDC preferences there is a non-significantly smaller effect of also being in the Lomé Convention.[17]

Lastly, as mentioned above, the negative EU dummy shows that joining the EU has a negative effect on imports from developing countries, but since new EU members also implement EU trade preferences, which may have a positive impact on imports from developing countries, the total effect of EU enlargements should be analysed using the EU dummy in combination with the relevant preference dummy variables.

Effects on Specific Country Groups

While the estimation results above are interesting in their own right, what we really want to be able to say something about is the aggregate effect of preferences and EU enlargements on different groups of developing countries based on what preference regimes they are a party to. Such an aggregation is shown in Table 3.3. Note that Table 3.3 does not include the *EU effect*, and that it is based on the time trend specification.

The key conclusion from Table 3.3 is that all country groups, with the exception of countries exporting to the EU under the drug regime or under the general arrangements of the GSP, have benefited significantly from getting preferences. For example, countries with GSP and Yaoundé preferences have experienced an export increase corresponding to almost 29 percent of actual exports. On the other hand, countries with GSP and Mediterranean preferences have had gross trade creation of over 14 percent of actual exports, even though the effect strictly speaking is not significant at the 5 percent level since the p-value is 0.058.

Table 3.3 Estimated aggregate effects of preferences

Preferences received	Coeff.	P[a]	%[b]	Definition
GSP	0.035	0.323	3.56	GSP
GSP & Yaoundé	0.254	0.000	28.92	GSP + Yaoundé + GSP*Yaoundé
GSP & LDC but not Lomé	0.190	0.019	20.92	GSP + GSP*LDC
GSP & Drug	0.010	0.857	1.01	GSP + GSP*Drug
GSP & MED	0.134	0.058	14.34	GSP + MED + GSP*MED
GSP & Lomé but not LDC	0.266	0.000	30.47	GSP + GSP*Lomé
GSP & LDC & Lomé	0.282	0.000	32.58	GSP + GSP*Lomé + GSP*LDC + GSP*LDC*Lomé

Notes: [a] P-values from a Wald test that the sum of the coefficients indicated in the last column equal zero.
[b] The percentage increase of exports (gross trade creation) is given by $(e^{coef}-1)*100$. To save space 'EU' has been omitted, but all variables are interacted with the EU dummy.

So, in most cases, *ceteris paribus*, getting preferences has increased developing countries' exports. What can be said about the magnitudes of the effects? Generally, these follow expectations very nicely. Groups of countries that have some form of ACP preferences, and hence are at the top of the pyramid of privilege, do have the largest positive effects: Lomé countries appear somewhat more favoured than Yaoundé countries. As expected, the positive effects for Mediterranean countries are smaller, but still significant, while for countries that only enjoy GSP status there are no significant effects.

Looking more closely at the results, one interesting conclusion is that those countries that cannot use Lomé preferences, but can use the special preferences for least developed countries within the GSP, have actually had a larger effect than Mediterranean countries. This may seem surprising, but it does fit the comment, made in the second section above, that it is difficult to correctly place LDC preferences in the pyramid of privilege since these preferences change over time – as do Mediterranean preferences. Specifically, the possibly larger effects of the Barcelona process are not captured by the EU*GSP*MED dummy since it is coded as 1 from the 1970s.

All in all, however, our results do seem to confirm not only that preferences can have an export-increasing effect, but also that the magnitude of these effects are consistent with the quality of the preferences that are available. In other words, ACP preferences (Lomé or Yaoundé) have the largest effects, Mediterranean preferences have smaller but still significant effects, but those countries that only get a preference margin in relation to developed countries (without preferential trade agreements with the EU), i.e. countries only having GSP, have not been able to use these preferences to increase exports significantly.

Compared with results obtained earlier in the literature, our conclusions are similar to those in Oguledo and MacPhee (1994), even though they find much larger effects than we do. Our results also confirm Nilsson's (2002) conclusion that ACP preferences have had the largest effects, but unlike him we cannot find a significant effect associated with the general GSP, while we do find that Mediterranean preferences have increased these countries' exports. Note that we find a significant and quite large effect associated with the special regime for LDCs within the GSP, which might explain why Nilsson, who does not differentiate between different regimes in the GSP, finds a positive GSP effect. Again, Nilsson's effects are larger than ours.

Concerning Mediterranean preferences, our results are very much in line with those of Péridy (2005), who uses a method more similar to ours: he finds that preferences have led to a gross trade creation of 20–27 percent of actual exports, while our figure is somewhat lower at around 14 percent. Considering that we include Mediterranean preferences from the end of the 1960s onwards, while Péridy's study only starts at 1975, this difference seems reasonable.

On the other hand, our estimates of the effects of ACP preferences are much smaller than those in Carrère (2004). The main differences between our study and Carrère's are the country sample and the estimation technique. We are only concerned with exports to EU countries, while she uses a much larger sample including South–South and North–North trade. Also, our study applies standard fixed effects while she uses a Hausman and Taylor (1981) approach.

Besides showing that preferences can and do have large effects that differ between countries, another interesting result of our estimations is the negative and highly significant coefficient for the EU dummy. As noted above, the correct interpretation of this is that countries *joining* the EU, all else equal, decrease their imports from developing countries, i.e. there is evidence of significant trade diversion. With our method, we cannot say whether countries that are already EU members decrease their imports from developing countries when the union is enlarged, since dummy variables in the fixed effects model will capture the effect of changing status. So, what we capture is the effect of enlargement on *new* members' imports. Our result of a negative effect supports the findings by Soloaga and Winters (2001).

To evaluate the full impact of the EU and its trade policy on developing countries' exports the estimated coefficient of the EU dummy variable should be added to the results in Table 3.3. If this is done, the joint effect of EU enlargements and trade preferences will be insignificant for all preference systems, except GSP and *Drug* for which the effect is negative, since the negative effect of EU-enlargements dominates the effect of preferences. As stated above, the EU dummy variable indicates the effect of accession to the EU on average over the studied period and should not be confused with the effects of preferences, shown in Table 3.3, that are conditioned on the size of the EU.

CONCLUSIONS

We have estimated a gravity model on a large sample of EU and developing countries over the period 1960 to 2002 to assess the effects of trade preferences offered by the EU, while taking into account the potential effect of EU enlargements. Using a new database of EU trade preferences created for this chapter, and incorporating recent methodological developments in the gravity literature, we have been able to show that not only can trade preferences in general increase exports from developing countries, but the size of the gross trade creation is also in line with expectations. ACP countries that have benefited under the Lomé and Yaoundé Conventions, and which have been described as being on top of the 'pyramid of privilege', have actually seen the largest export-increasing effects, with levels of gross trade creation at around 30 percent of actual exports. Mediterranean countries, theoretically somewhat less preferred than ACP countries, have had smaller but still substantial effects: increases of around 14 percent of exports. Countries at the bottom of the pyramid of privilege, those only having access to the GSP, have not had any significant increases of their exports, even though the group of least developed countries that receive additional benefits within the GSP have seen substantial effects. Besides the effects for least developed countries, which as far as we know have not been estimated *ex post* elsewhere, these results are in line with more recent contributions to the literature on trade preferences. Our estimated effects are generally smaller than those that have been estimated in a cross-sectional setting, but similar to those obtained by panel data methods.

In addition to the positive effect of getting preferences, our estimations also show that countries *becoming* members of the EU start to import less from developing countries. This is an effect that has not been looked at much before, even though there are earlier studies suggesting that the EU does have a trade-diverting effect.

To offer some comments on these results, a first important point to make is that preferences have actually had an effect, even though many commentators, looking mostly at shares of EU imports, have concluded that they are of little value. To reconcile these different views, it is crucial to understand that our results say that when taking a lot of other factors that influence trade into account, including the negative impact of EU enlargements, trade preferences have had a positive effect, even though these other factors have had large and negative effects. For instance, the correct interpretation for ACP countries and

LDCs for whom EU import shares certainly have declined, is that their disappointing trade record would have been *even worse* without preferences.

The second point to make is that our method does not allow us to see, for example, whether ACP countries gain their positive effects at the expense of other developing countries, i.e. whether the effects are due to trade diversion. Certainly, this would seem plausible.

Thirdly, our study offers evidence on the effects of preferences and EU enlargements seen over the whole period. It is likely that the effects of preferences have diminished over time, considering the general dismantling of trade barriers that has taken place and that would erode the preference margin. Further research on this development, as well as on the evolution of the enlargement effect over time, would be interesting.

A fourth and final comment, and perhaps the most important one from a policy perspective, is that our results suggest that developing countries may suffer large drawbacks every time the EU is enlarged. Since the end of this study's time period, ten new countries have become members of the EU, and more are waiting to enter the union in the near future. If all of these show the same decline when it comes to importing goods from developing countries, the resulting trade diversion, reducing developing countries' exports, could be large, and it may not be enough to just offer preferences to balance these negative effects.

NOTES

A previous version of the chapter was presented at the ETSG annual meeting in Dublin 2005 and at Lund University. We would like to thank Yves Bourdet, Åsa Eriksson, Joakim Gullstrand, Karin Olofsdotter, Viktor Tanaka and Joakim Westerlund for helpful comments and suggestions. Fredrik Wilhelmsson gratefully acknowledges financial support from *Sparbanksstiftelsen Färs & Frosta* and *Stiftelsen för främjande av ekonomisk forskning vid Lunds Universitet*.

1. For simplicity, this chapter will consistently use the term EU even though the formally correct term would at times be EEC or EC. However, no confusion should arise.
2. For an excellent account of the relations between EU and ACP countries, see Grilli (1993).
3. Lomé preferences do not fulfil the obligations under which the so-called Enabling Clause allows developed countries to grant trade preferences to developing countries (see e.g. Abass 2004). This explains the need to renegotiate the preferences into WTO-compatible FTAs.
4. Since this chapter restricts its attention to preferences available to countries that are not current or probable future members of the EU, the sample of Mediterranean countries contains Algeria, Morocco and Tunisia (Maghreb countries); Egypt, Jordan, Syria and Lebanon (Mashrek countries) and Israel. In practice, Algeria, as a major oil exporter, disappears from our sample.
5. See e.g. Grilli (1993).
6. Note though that preferences for LDCs under Everything But Arms are granted for an unlimited time period, which makes this difference smaller (see e.g. Brenton 2003).
7. This may in fact be one of the major explanations why LDCs that are eligible for duty free access under the EBA continue using otherwise less beneficial Lomé-style preferences under the Cotonou agreement (Brenton 2003).
8. Note that certain preference systems overlap: see Figure 3.2.

9. There are more *ex ante* studies using various forms of partial or general equilibrium models to simulate the effects of preferences: see e.g. Baldwin and Murray (1977), Karsenty and Laird (1987), Ianchovichina et al. (2002), Cernat et al. (2003) and Yu and Jensen (2005).
10. Carrère's (2004) estimates indicate that the increase in ACP countries' exports resulting from the preferences is 129 percent or 62 percent depending on which variables are included in the regression.
11. See Greenaway and Milner (2002) for a discussion of the application of the gravity model to preferential trade agreements.
12. A more flexible definition in the importer*time and exporter*time dimension including country by time fixed effects in line with Baltagi et al. (2003) is possible, but as argued by Bun and Klaassen (2004), the present model is more flexible in the cross-section dimension.
13. Countries that became members of the EU 2004, and Bulgaria, Romania and Turkey.
14. As defined in Direction of Trade Statistics (DOTS) by the IMF (2005).
15. GDP data for Germany is taken from IMF (2005b).
16. The relevant dummies are EU*GSP*Drug, EU*GSP*Yaoundé, EU*GSP*LDC, EU*GSP*Lomé and EU*GSP*MED.
17. The relevant dummy is EU*GSP*Lomé*LDC.

REFERENCES

Abass, A. (2004), 'The Cotonou Trade Régime and WTO Law', *European Law Journal*, **10** (4), 439–62.

Baldwin, R.E. and T. Murray (1977), 'MFN Tariff Reductions and Developing Country Trade Benefits under the GSP', *The Economic Journal*, **87** (345), 34–46.

Baltagi, B., (2001), *Econometric Analysis of Panel Data*, 2nd edition, Chichester, UK and New York, US: John Wiley & Sons, Ltd.

Baltagi, B.H., P. Egger and M. Pfaffermayr (2003), 'A Generalized Design for Bilateral Trade Flow Models' *Economics Letters*, **8** (3), 391–97.

Brenton, P. (2003), 'Integrating the Least Developed Countries into the World Trading System: The Current Impact of European Union Preferences under "Everything But Arms"', *Journal of World Trade*, **37** (3), 623–46.

Bun, M.J.G. and F.J.G.M. Klaassen (2004), 'The Euro Effect on Trade is not as Large as Commonly Thought', Tinbergen Institute Discussion Paper 2003-086/2, Amsterdam: Tinbergen Institute.

Carrère, C. (2004), 'African Regional Agreements: Impact on Trade with or without Currency Unions', *Journal of African Economies*, **13** (2), 199–239.

Carrère, C. (2006), 'Revisiting the Effects of Regional Trade Agreements on Trade Flows with Proper Specification of the Gravity Model', *European Economic Review*, **50** (2) 223–47.

Cernat, L., S. Laird, L. Monge-Roffarello and A. Turrini (2003), 'The EU's Everything But Arms Initiative and the Least-developed Countries', WIDER Discussion Paper 2003/47, Helsinki: United Nations University, World Institute for Development Economics Research.

Egger, P. (2004), 'Estimating Regional Trading Block Effects with Panel Data', *Review of World Economics*, **140** (1), 151–66.

European Commission (1996), 'Green Paper on Relations between the European Union and the ACP Countries on the Eve of the 21st Century: Challenges and Options for a New Partnership', European Commission Green Papers, COM(96)570.

Grilli, E.R. (1993), *The European Community and the Developing Countries*, Cambridge, UK and New York, US: Cambridge University Press.

Greenaway, D. and C. Milner (2002), 'Regionalism and Gravity', *Scottish Journal of Political Economy*, **49** (5), 574–85.

Hausman, J. and Taylor, W. (1981), 'Panel Data and Unobservable Individual Effects', *Econometrica*, **49** (6), 1377–98.

Ianchovichina, E., A. Mattoo and M. Olarreaga (2002), 'Unrestricted Market Access for Sub-Saharan Africa: How Much is it Worth and Who Pays?', *Journal of African Economies*, **10** (4), 410–32.

Inama, S. (2002), 'Market Acess for LDCs. Issues to Be Addressed', *Journal of World Trade*, **36** (1), 85–116.

International Monetary Fund (2002), 'Direction of Trade Statistics Historical', CD-rom IMF, Washington, DC.

International Monetary Fund (2005a), 'Direction of Trade Statistics', CD-rom, IMF, Washington, DC.

International Monetary Fund (2005b), 'International Financial Statistics', on-line, http://ifs.apdi.net/imf, 2005-10-14.

Karsenty, G. and S. Laird (1987), 'The GSP, Policy Options and the New Round', *Weltwirtschaftliches Archiv*, **123** (2), 262–95.

Mátyás, L. (1997), 'Proper Econometric Specification of the Gravity Model', *The World Economy*, **20** (3), 363–68.

Mayer, T. and S. Zignago (2005), 'Market access in Global and Regional Trade', CEPII Working paper 2005-02, Paris: Centre d'Etudes Prospectives et d'Informations Internationales.

McQueen, M. (1998), 'Lomé Versus Free Trade Agreements: The Dilemma Facing the ACP Countries', *The World Economy*, **21** (4), 421–43.

Nilsson, L. (2002) 'Trading Relations: Is the Roadmap from Lomé to Cotonou Correct?', *Applied Economics*, **34** (4), 439–52.

Official Journal of the European Communities, various issues.

Oguledo, V.I. and C.R. MacPhee (1994), 'Gravity Models: A Reformulation and an Application to Discriminatory Trade Arrangements', *Applied Economics*, **26** (2), 107–20.

Péridy, N. (2005), 'The Trade Effects of the Euro-Mediterranean Partnership: What Are the Lessons for ASEAN Countries?' *Journal of Asian Economics*, **16** (1), 125–39.

Sapir, A. (1981), 'Trade Benefits under the EEC Generalized System of Preferences', *European Economic Review*, **15** (3), 339–55.

Soloaga, I. and L.A. Winters (2001), 'Regionalism in the Nineties: What Effect on Trade?', *North American Journal of Economics and Finance*, **12** (1), 1–29.

World Bank (2005), 'World Development Indicators', CD-rom, The World Bank, Washington, DC.

Young, C. (1972), 'Association with the EEC: Economic Aspects of the Trade Relationship', *Journal of Common Market Studies*, **11** (2), 120–35.

Yu, W. and T.V. Jensen (2005), 'Tariff Preferences, WTO Negotiations and the LDCs: The Case of the "Everything But Arms" Initiative', *The World Economy*, **28** (3), 375–405.

ANNEX 3   BENEFICIARY COUNTRIES UNDER PREFERENTIAL TRADING REGIMES

Table 3A.1 Beneficiary countries under preferential trading regimes.

Country	GSP			MED	ACP	
	General	*LDC*	*Drug*		*Yaoundé*	*Lomé*
Albania	1992-2000					
Angola	1972	1997				1987
Argentina	1972					
Bahamas	1972					1976
Bahrain	1972					
Bangladesh	1973	1977				
Barbados	1972					1976
Belize	1972					1982
Benin	1972	1977			1964-1975	1976
Bhutan	1973	1977				
Bolivia	1972		1991			
Botswana	1972	1977-1997				1976
Brazil	1972					
Burkina Faso	1972	1977			1964-1975	1976
Burundi	1972	1977			1965-1975	1976
Cambodia	1972	1993				
Cameroon	1972				1964-1975	1976
Cape Verde	1972	1981				1977
Central African Republic	1972	1977			1964-1975	1976
Chad	1972	1977			1964-1975	1976
Chile	1972					
China	1980					
Colombia	1972		1991			
Comoros	1972	1981				1977
Congo, Dem. Rep.	1972	1993			1964-1975	1976
Congo, Rep.	1972				1965-1975	1976
Costa Rica	1972		1992			
Côte d'Ivoire	1972				1964-1975	1976
Djibouti	1972	1981				1978
Dominica	1972					1979
Dominican Republic	1972					1992
Ecuador	1972		1991			
Egypt	1972			1974		
El Salvador	1972		1992			
Equatorial Guinea	1972	1981				1976
Eritrea	1995	1995				1993
Ethiopia	1972	1977				1976
Fiji	1973					1976
French Polynesia	1972					
Gabon	1972				1964-1975	1976

Country	GSP General	LDC	Drug	MED	ACP Yaoundé	Lomé
Gambia	1972	1977				1976
Ghana	1972					1976
Grenada	1972					1976
Guatemala	1972		1992			
Guinea	1972	1977				1976
Guinea-Bissau	1972	1981				1976
Guyana	1972					1976
Haiti	1972	1977				1992
Honduras	1972		1992			
India	1972					
Israel				1971		
Jamaica	1972					1976
Jordan	1972		1978			
Kenya	1972				1971-1975	1976
Kiribati	1980	1988				1980
Laos	1972	1977				
Lebanon	1972		1978			
Lesotho	1972	1977				1976
Liberia	1972	1993				1976
Macao, China	1972					
Madagascar	1972	1993			1964-1975	1976
Malawi	1972	1977				1976
Malaysia	1972					
Maldives	1972	1977				
Mali	1972	1977			1964-1975	1976
Mauritius	1972				1972-1975	1976
Mongolia	1991					
Morocco	1972		1970			
Mozambique	1972	1990				1986
Namibia	1991					1990
Nepal	1972	1977				
New Caledonia	1972					
Nicaragua	1972		1992			
Niger	1972	1977			1964-1975	1976
Pakistan	1972		2002			
Panama	1972		1992			
Papua New Guinea	1972					1977
Paraguay	1972					
Peru	1972		1991			
Philippines	1972					
Rwanda	1972	1977			1964-1975	1976
Samoa	1973	1977				1976
Sao Tome and Principe	1972	1981				1977
Senegal	1972	2002			1964-1975	1976
Seychelles	1972	1981-1989				1977
Sierra Leone	1972	1983				1976

Country	GSP			MED	ACP	
	General	LDC	Drug		Yaoundé	Lomé
Singapore	1972-1999					
Solomon Islands	1979	1993				1979
Sri Lanka	1972					
St. Kitts and Nevis	1972					1984
St. Lucia	1972					1979
St. Vincent and the Grenadines	1972					1980
Sudan	1972	1977				1976
Suriname	1972					1977
Swaziland	1972					1976
Syria	1972			1978		
Tanzania	1972	1977			1971-1975	1976
Thailand	1972					
Togo	1972	1983			1964-1975	1976
Tonga	1973	1981-1997				1976
Trinidad and Tobago	1972					1976
Tunisia	1972			1970		
Uganda	1972	1977			1971-1975	1976
Uruguay	1972					
Vanuatu	1980	1993				1981
Vietnam	1972					
Yemen	1991	1991				
Zambia	1972	1993				1976
Zimbabwe	1981					1981

Note: The years indicate the *actual* entry into force of accession to the various systems; this may differ substantially from the formal date of signing (and in some cases from the actual entry into force of the whole system: e.g. within the frameworks of ACP and Mediterranean Preferences, trade provisions often start to apply before the rest of the agreements). When two dates are included, the second signifies the last year of receiving preferences. Consistently, a date of entry into force from January 1 to June 30 is translated into the same year, while a date of entry into force from July 1 to December 31 is counted from the next year. Since the preferences under the Arusha Agreement were quite similar to the ones in the Yaoundé Convention, countries benefiting from this (Kenya, Tanzania and Uganda) are listed as Yaoundé countries.

Source: Various issues of the Official Journal of the European Communities 1964–2002.

4. Comparative Effects of EU and US Trade Policies on Developing Country Exports

Lars Nilsson

INTRODUCTION

Developed countries have provided developing countries with preferential market access via trade policies in the form of unilateral trade preference schemes, non-reciprocal agreements or bilateral free trade agreements (FTAs) since the early 1970s. The European Union (EU) and the United States (US), which are the two largest importers of goods from developing countries, absorbing more than 40 percent of their total exports in 2003, have several such arrangements in place.

All but a few developing countries are covered by the respective EU and US generalised system of preferences (GSP). Furthermore, 50 least developed countries (LDCs)[1] are eligible for access to the EU market without any restrictions[2] under the EU's so-called Everything but Arms (EBA) initiative.[3] In addition, 77 African, Caribbean and Pacific (ACP) countries are eligible for preferences under the EU's Cotonou Agreement. The US provides around 40 African countries with further preferences under its African Growth and Opportunity Act (AGOA). The US also offers countries in Latin America and in the Caribbean special preferences under its Andean Trade Preference Act (ATPA) and Caribbean Basin Initiative (CBI), respectively.

The coverage of countries under the EU and US schemes differ and some countries are granted no preferences. In most cases, regardless of whether their exports are destined for the EU or the US market, developing countries can choose which preferential trade regime to export under. It may therefore be more appropriate to compare the EU and US imports from developing countries on the whole, rather than analysing the effects of particular EU and US preference schemes.

A number of studies have analysed the effects of either EU or US trade preference schemes,[4] while studies quantitatively comparing the effects of the EU and US trade policy on developing country exports appear to be rare.[5] Based on the World Bank's definition of developing countries,[6] this study analyses the relative effects on developing country exports of EU and US trade policies in a gravity model setting. The results shed some light on the combined effects of EU trade policy on developing country exports vis-à-vis those of the US, irrespective of trade preference scheme applied.

The study is organised as follows: the second section provides the main features of the EU and US preference schemes for developing countries. The third section defines developing countries per income category and describes their exports to the EU and US. The fourth section outlines the methodology and discusses the empirical results. The fifth section summarises the main findings and makes some concluding remarks.

EU AND US TRADE POLICIES TOWARDS DEVELOPING COUNTRIES

The EU's GSP

In 1971, the European Community (EC) introduced its first GSP scheme. It has been modified on several occasions since and the EU adopted a revised scheme in June 2005 which runs from 1 January 2006 until the end of 2008. The main change in the new scheme is a reduction from five to three GSP provisions. Product coverage under the general scheme will increase from 6900 to about 7200 products by adding mainly agricultural and fishery products. Non-sensitive products (slightly less than half of the products covered) enjoy duty-free access, while sensitive products (mainly agricultural products, but also textile, clothing and apparel, carpets and footwear) benefit from a tariff reduction of 3.5 percentage points of *ad valorem* duties compared to the most favoured nation (MFN) tariff and a 30 percent reduction of specific duties (with a few exceptions).[7] For textiles and clothing, the reduction is 20 percent of the *ad valorem* MFN duty rate.[8]

Besides this expanded general scheme, a new 'GSP Plus' scheme is introduced for especially vulnerable countries with special development needs. It replaces former GSP sub-schemes for countries that recognise labour rights and environmental standards and helps them combat drug production and trafficking. The scheme allows for duty-free entry to the EU market of the goods covered by the general GSP scheme.[9] The EBA, which gives the 50 LDCs duty free access to the EU for all products, except arms and ammunition, remains unchanged.

The new GSP scheme also introduces changes to the graduation mechanism. The former criteria (share of preferential imports, development index and export-specialisation index) have been replaced with a single straightforward criterion, namely the share of the Community market expressed as a share of preferential imports. The share is 15 percent in general, but 12.5 percent for textiles and clothing, split into two sections. The EU restricts its GSP scheme to some beneficiaries by removing or excluding preferences for countries such as Brazil, China, India, Indonesia, Pakistan, Russia and Thailand.[10] It is predicted that 80 percent of China's exports will 'graduate' from the GSP under the new scheme.

The Cotonou Agreement

The Cotonou Agreement between the EC and the 79 ACP countries was signed on 23 June 2000. It entered into force in April 2003 and replaced previous Lomé Conventions, the first of which dates back to 1975.[11] Under the Cotonou Agreement's trade pillar, the ACPs benefit from non-reciprocal trade preferences for the period 2001–2007.[12] Products originating in ACP countries are exempted from EU customs duties. Preferences for agricultural products are differentiated. Tropical products which do not compete with European products enter the EU market duty free. Temperate products face an exemption or reduction of customs duties, while fruits and vegetables are subject to seasonal restrictions. Other agricultural products face quantitative restrictions or are excluded from preferential treatment. For certain products (bananas, beef and veal, and sugar), the EU provides special market access via so-called commodity protocols. In 2008 at the latest, the unilateral preferences under the Cotonou Agreement are to be replaced by WTO-compatible reciprocal economic partnership agreements (EPAs) between the EU and individual ACP countries or groups of countries.[13]

Other EU Preferential Trading Schemes for Developing Countries

The World Bank classifies the former candidate countries in Central and Eastern Europe, with the exception of Slovenia, as developing countries.[14] Before EU membership their trade relations with the EU were governed by the so-called Europe Agreements, which aimed to progressively establish an FTA between the EU and the respective country. EU trade relations with another candidate country, Turkey, are governed by a customs union for industrial products (including processed agricultural products).[15] In addition, the EU has a number of bilateral or regional FTAs with other developing countries, offering them additional market access on top of the GSP preferences. For instance, trade is an essential component of the Euro Med Partnership, which ultimately aims to deepen regional integration in the Mediterranean region and to establish a Euro-Mediterranean FTA by 2010. Bilateral FTAs have also been established with for example Chile, Mexico and South Africa.

The EU has also introduced Autonomous Trade Measures (ATMs) for the countries of the Western Balkans (Albania, Bosnia and Herzegovina, Croatia (a candidate country as of summer 2004), the former Yugoslav Republic of Macedonia (a candidate country as of winter 2005), Montenegro and Serbia). The ATMs are similar to the EBA in that they provide for duty- and quota-free access for all products from the beneficiary countries, but with the exception of quotas for baby-beef, some fish products and wine. Live bovine animals, beef and prepared fish are excluded and there are tariff quotas for sugar. In the case of Albania, Croatia and the former Yugoslav Republic of Macedonia, the trade measures are contractual and reciprocal since the signing of each country's Stabilisation and Association Agreement.

The US GSP, AGOA and Other Preferential Trading Schemes

The US GSP scheme has been in operation since 1976. The latest renewal of the scheme took place in 2002 validating it through 2006. It provides for duty-free access to the US market for about 4600 products, with an additional 1800 products for the least developed beneficiaries. Products eligible for GSP treatment include selected manufactures and semi-manufactures and selected agricultural, fishery and primary industrial products not otherwise duty free. Certain articles, such as textiles, watches, footwear, handbags, luggage and work gloves, are excluded.

The granting of duty-free access to eligible products is subject to 'competitive-need limitations', which impose ceilings on GSP benefits for each product and country. A country loses its GSP eligibility with respect to a product if 'competitive-need limits' are exceeded.[16] However these are automatically waived for the GSP beneficiaries that are designated (by the US) as LDCs. A country may be 'graduated' from the US GSP if its per capita income exceeds the threshold level of income set for high-income countries by the World Bank, or through discretionary removal when a country is no longer deemed to be a developing country.

The African Growth and Opportunity Act (AGOA) was introduced in 2000 and is valid until 2015. It is available to all sub-Saharan African (SSA) countries and extends the product coverage of the GSP, particularly in the field of textiles and clothing, by adding some 1800 products to the regular GSP product coverage. All AGOA-designated countries are granted duty-free treatment for all products currently eligible under the GSP programme. About two-thirds of the AGOA beneficiaries are subject to so-called apparel eligibility, qualifying their exports for duty-free and quota-free treatment for eligible articles.[17] Furthermore, the AGOA eliminates the GSP 'competitive-need limitations' for its beneficiaries. The President determines annually whether sub-Saharan African countries are, or remain, eligible for AGOA benefits based on their progress in meeting certain criteria. These criteria include establishment of a market-based economy, rule of law, elimination of barriers to US trade and investment, implementation of economic policies to reduce poverty, protection of internationally recognized worker rights, and establishment of a system to combat corruption. Additionally, countries cannot engage in violations of internationally recognized human rights, or support acts of international terrorism and activities that undermine US national security or foreign policy interests.

The Caribbean Basin Initiative (CBI), introduced in 1983, covered 24 countries in the Caribbean and provided more extensive product coverage than the GSP. It was substantially expanded in 2000 through the US-Caribbean Basin Trade Partnership Act (CBTPA), which introduced apparel preferences into the scheme.

The Andean Trade Preference Act (ATPA) was enacted in 1991 for the benefit of Bolivia, Colombia, Ecuador and Peru. The programme provides duty-free access to the US market for approximately 5600 products. The ATPA was renewed in 2001 under the new title of Andean Trade Promotion and Drug Eradication Act, the main change being the extension of duty-free access to apparel and footwear.

Overall, compared to US trade policy, EU trade policy vis-à-vis developing countries generally offers a greater product scope, a wider country coverage and higher preference margins. All other things being equal, one would expect EU trade policy towards developing countries to have larger effects on these countries' exports than US trade policy.

Developing Country Exports to the EU and the US

The World Bank considers gross national income (GNI) the best single indicator of economic capacity and progress.[18] It has defined per capita income thresholds and uses the term developing countries for low-income countries, lower-middle income countries and upper-middle income countries.[19] Annex Table 4A.1 shows that 157 countries are categorized by the World Bank as developing countries, of which 61 are low-income, 59 are lower-middle income and 37 are upper-middle income countries.[20]

All low-income and lower-middle income countries, but North Korea and the West Bank and Gaza, are eligible for the EU's GSP scheme and all United Nations (UN) defined LDCs are beneficiaries of the EU's EBA initiative.[21] According to the World Bank's definition, 17 low-income countries are not ranked as LDCs by the UN, while six lower-middle income countries are. All of the 79 ACP countries are considered to be developing countries, except for the Bahamas which the World Bank classifies as a high-income country. Many Caribbean ACPs are ranked as upper-middle income countries as are most of the developing countries with which the EU has bilateral FTAs.

All of the US AGOA beneficiaries, all the countries subject to the ATPA and 20 of the 24 US CBI beneficiaries are listed as developing countries in Annex Table 4.A.1. Excluded countries are either classified as high-income countries or are not found in World Bank statistics. The number of low-income and lower-middle income countries subject to US MFN treatment or less is about 25.

EU and US Imports from Developing Countries

Table 4.1 below lists EU and US imports from the developing countries. It shows that the EU imports about as much from the developing countries as the US does over the period. EU imports from low-income countries amount to about 10 percent of its total imports from developing countries. Around 60 percent of EU imports come from lower-middle income countries while the remaining 30 percent come from upper-middle income countries. The volume of EU imports from developing countries is fairly constant over the study period.

The volume of US imports from low-income countries is slightly lower than the EU's and so are its imports from lower-middle income countries. On the other hand, US imports from upper-middle income countries are larger than corresponding EU imports. Total US imports from developing countries decrease over the period, primarily as a result of a decrease in the volume of imports from the upper-middle income countries.

Table 4.1 EU and US imports from developing countries, 2001–2003 (€ billion)

Developing Country	EU			US		
	2001	**2002**	**2003**	**2001**	**2002**	**2003**
Low-income	49.3	46.7	46.1	39.2	36.6	39.3
Lower-middle income	291.2	287.2	298.9	242.4	248.1	237.9
Upper-middle income	165.0	162.5	168.1	233.4	220.6	195.5
Total	505.5	496.4	513.1	515.0	505.3	472.7

Note: All figures are expressed in constant 2001 euros.

Source: Own calculations.

The distribution of exports from the developing countries is skewed. Ten low-income countries account for a little less than 80 percent of the group's exports to the EU (see Table 4.2). Three of these countries are beneficiaries of the standard EU GSP scheme (India, Vietnam and Pakistan), four are ACP countries and signatories to the Cotonou Agreement (Nigeria, Côte' d'Ivoire, Cameroon and Ghana) and three are eligible for the EBA (Bangladesh, Angola and Congo (Dem. Rep.)). In the case of the US, ten low-income countries account for about 90 percent of the group's exports to the US. Five of these countries export under GSP preferences (India, Bangladesh, Pakistan, Cambodia and Equatorial Guinea), three are covered by the AGOA (Nigeria, Angola and Congo) and Nicaragua is a beneficiary of the CBI while Vietnam does not have any preferences on the US market.

The pattern is similar for lower-middle income countries. The ten largest exporters to the EU market account for more than 80 percent of the group's total exports to the EU. Exports are dominated by China and Russia, which together account for 45 percent of total exports to the EU from lower-middle income countries.[22] The share of the ten largest lower-middle income countries on the US market is just below 90 percent, and is heavily dominated by China, which accounts for more than half of all exports from this group of countries to the US market.

Among the upper-middle income countries, the (at the time) candidate countries for EU accession dominate. The top ten exporters account for about 90 percent of all exports from the upper-middle income countries, and three former candidate countries – today members of the EU – account for close to half of that flow. Among the upper-middle income countries, Mexico, with a share of more than 60 percent, is the largest exporter to the US market. The ten largest exporters within this group of countries claim a share of 97 percent of the group's total exports to the US market.

Table 4.2 Top ten low-income (LI), lower-middle income (LMI) and upper-middle income (UMI) exporters to the EU and US, average 2001–03 (% of their total exports to the EU and the US in constant 2001 euros)

Developing Countries	LI/LMI/UMI	To EU	EU pref.	To US	US pref.
India	LI	27.0	GSP	31.2	GSP
Nigeria	LI	12.1	ACP	22.5	AGOA
Vietnam	LI	9.2	GSP	7.0	–
Bangladesh	LI	7.0	EBA	6.1	GSP
Pakistan	LI	6.0	GSP	6.6	GSP
Côte d'Ivoire	LI	4.9	ACP	1.1	GSP
Angola	LI	3.7	EBA/ACP	9.4	AGOA
Cameroon	LI	3.4	ACP	–	–
Ghana	LI	2.2	ACP	–	–
Congo (Dem Rep)	LI	2.1	EBA/ACP	–	–
Cambodia	LI	–	–	3.0	GSP
Nicaragua	LI	–	–	1.8	CBI
Congo	LI	–	–	1.4	AGOA
Equatorial Guinea	LI	–	–	1.7	GSP
TOTAL	LI	77.6	–	91.8	–
China	LMI	28.2	GSP	54.6	–
Russia	LMI	16.5	GSP	3.1	GSP
Turkey	LMI	7.4	CU	–	–
Brazil	LMI	6.0	GSP	6.9	GSP
South Africa	LMI	5.2	BA/GSP	1.8	GSP
Algeria	LMI	5.0	BA/GSP	–	–
Thailand	LMI	3.9	GSP	6.5	GSP
Romania	LMI	3.5	BA	–	–

Table 4.2 (continued)

Developing Countries	LI/LMI/UMI	To EU	EU pref.	To US	US pref.
Indonesia	LMI	3.4	GSP	4.3	GSP
Philippines	LMI	2.4	GSP	4.6	GSP
Iraq	LMI	–	–	2.1	GSP
Colombia	LMI	–	–	2.6	ATPA
Dominican Republic	LMI	–	–	1.8	CBI
TOTAL	LMI	81.5	–	88.3	–
Poland	UMI	17.0	BA	–	–
Czech Republic	UMI	16.2	BA	–	–
Hungary	UMI	15.0	BA	1.3	GSP
Malaysia	UMI	8.7	BA	11.3	–
Saudi Arabia	UMI	7.6	BA	7.2	–
Libya	UMI	6.3	BA	–	–
Slovakia	UMI	5.9	BA	–	–
Mexico	UMI	3.9	GSP	62.6	NAFTA
Argentina	UMI	3.5	GSP	1.6	GSP
Chile	UMI	2.9	GSP	2.0	GSP
Venezuela	UMI	–	–	7.6	GSP
Costa Rica	UMI	–	–	1.5	CBI
Trinidad and Tobago	UMI	–	–	1.5	CBI
Gabon	UMI	–	–	0.8	AGOA
TOTAL	UMI	87.0		96.6	

Note: Explanations for the abbreviations under EU pref. and US pref. are given in the note to Annex Table A4.1.

Source: Own calculations.

ESTIMATING THE EFFECTS OF EU VS. US TRADE POLICY ON DEVELOPING COUNTRY EXPORTS

The Gravity Model

The gravity model has been extensively used to estimate a range of issues such as the effects of trade preference schemes, regional trading blocs, customs unions, exchange-rate regimes etc.[23] It has constantly gained in popularity and use partly as a result of improved theoretical underpinnings.[24] The work of Anderson and van Wincoop (2003) is widely seen as the standard reference for the theoretical foundation of the gravity model. Based on the assumptions of each country producing only one good, identical homothetic consumer preferences approximated by a CES function, market clearance and symmetric trade costs, Anderson and van Wincoop (2003) derive a gravity model expressed as follows:

$$X_{ij} = \frac{Y_i Y_j}{Y_w} \left(\frac{t_{ij}}{P_i P_j} \right)^{(1-\sigma)} \tag{4.1}$$

Equation 4.1 states that bilateral trade X between countries i and j is determined by the product of their respective national incomes Y over world income Y_w and the level of the absolute trade barrier t_{ij} between them relative to the product of the price indices P_i and P_j, which are referred to as 'multilateral resistance variables'. The main novelty, compared to previously derived and applied gravity models, is that trade in this version of the gravity model depends not only on the bilateral trade barrier between two countries, but also on the relation between this bilateral trade barrier and the average level of trade barrier each of the countries faces in world trade.

This result has empirical implications which are consistent with the literature on empirical applications of the gravity model. For example, Mátyás (1997) argued that a gravity model should be estimated along the dimension of the importer, the exporter and time in order to be correctly specified. Egger and Pfaffermeyer (2003) note that Mátyás' specification is a restricted version of its more general counterpart, which also includes time-invariant bilateral or country-pair effects. As proposed by Anderson and van Wincoop (2003) and Feenstra (2003), applied by Rose and van Wincoop (2001), and in line with the suggestions by Mátyás (1997) and Egger and Pfaffermeyer (2003), the unobservable 'multilateral resistance' term $(P_i P_j,)$ mentioned above can be modelled empirically through the introduction of exporting country-specific binary variables.[25] These binary variables account for all time-invariant national factors that affect the developing countries' exports. The gravity model applied here is estimated over the 2001–03 period, which is why the multilateral resistance each country faces can be assumed to be a constant country characteristic.

The version of the gravity model used in this study is specified in (natural) logs below.

$$X_{ijt} = \alpha + \beta_1 \left(GNI_{it} \times GNI_{jt} \right) + \beta_2 DIST_{ij} + \beta_3 EUIMP_i + \beta_4 EUCOL_j + \\ \sum \gamma_k DEVEXP_{kj} + \lambda_t + \varepsilon_{ijt} \tag{4.2}$$

The GNI variables provide a measure of economic mass which combines the effects of potential demand of the importing country i and potential supply of the exporting country j.[26] A greater economic mass is expected to influence trade positively. The variable for geographic distance, $DIST_{ij}$, is a measure of transport and transaction costs. Transport costs are related to distance, while transaction costs reflect better information and smaller cultural differences when countries are adjacent. A greater distance is expected to influence trade negatively. An importing country binary variable, EUIMP,[27] is introduced to distinguish EU imports from US imports from the developing countries as is a binary variable controlling for EU colonial ties with the developing countries, EUCOL.[28] DEVEXP denote exporting country-specific binary variables and λ_t is a time dummy.

The right-hand-side variables of the gravity model above provide a relationship with developing country exports that could be considered as 'normal' for developing countries integrated into the world trade system. In this study, US imports from developing countries are used as 'counterfactual' trade flows. The binary variable for EU imports indicates whether EU imports from the developing countries are above this benchmark level.[29]

EU import data is from COMEXT while US import figures derive from the IMF's Direction of Trade Statistics. Income data (GNI) have been obtained from the World Bank's World Development Indicators.[30] Distances in kilometres have been computed as straight lines between capitals (the EU capital is set to be Brussels) and come from the US Department of Agriculture.[31] Finally, e is a log normally distributed error term and α, β_i, γ_k, and λ_t are parameters to be estimated.

Zero- or missing-value observations in the trade data amount to some 4 percent of the observations. Income data (for exporting countries) are missing in 9 percent of the cases. Only five countries – the Marshall Islands, Micronesia, Palau, St Vincent and the Grenadines and Serbia and Montenegro (in the case of exports to the US) – have income figures available while exports are zero or missing. No particular attempt is therefore made to deal with the zero- or missing-value observations in the trade data.[32]

Results for EU Imports from All Developing Countries (Table 4.3 – Columns 1 and 3)

Equation 4.2 is estimated for the average cross-section of 2001–03 and in a time-series for the same time period. The ordinary least squares regression results are found in Table 4.3. The explanatory power of the model is excellent, with the included variables explaining 85–90 percent of the variation of exports from developing countries. There is not much difference between the cross-section and the time-series regression. The coefficients for income and distance have the expected sign and are significant at the 1 percent level. The results indicate that the effects of EU trade policy towards developing countries are significant and greater relative to US trade policy. The coefficient for the binary variable denoting overall EU imports from developing countries (EUIMP) is positive and significant at the 5 percent level in the cross-section regression and at the 1 percent level in the time-series regression. The size of the coefficients is basically the same in the two regressions. The same result holds for the coefficients of the binary variable for EU colonial ties (EUCOL).

Results for EU Imports from Developing Countries Per Income Group (Table 4.3 – Columns 2 and 4)

Table 4.3 shows the comparative effects of EU and US trade policy towards developing countries broken down into effects on exports from (i) low-income (LI) countries, (ii) lower-middle income (LMI) countries and (iii) upper-middle

Table 4.3 Gravity model regression results of EU and US Imports from developing countries, 2001–2003

Estimation method	Cross-section 2001–03 (average)		Time-series 2001–03	
Column	1	2	3	4
Economic mass				
$(GNI_i \times GNI_j)$	1.10***	1.13***	1.05***	1.08***
	4.38	*4.69*	*9.62*	*10.29*
Distance (*DIST*)	-1.37***	-1.36***	-1.39***	-1.38***
	-10.38	*-10.50*	*-22.29*	*-22.57*
EU imports (*EUIMP*)	0.44**		0.45***	
	2.54		*5.55*	
Low-income (LI)	–	0.70**	–	0.78***
	–	*2.23*	–	*5.08*
Lower-middle income (LMI)	–	0.26	–	0.23**
	–	*1.33*	–	*2.53*
Upper-middle income (UMI)	–	0.62**	–	0.65***
	–	*2.16*	–	*4.81*
EU Colonial ties (*EUCOL*)	0.63**	0.50*	0.66***	0.49***
	2.51	*1.81*	*5.32*	*3.70*
Year 2002	–	–	0.02	0.03
	–	–	*0.28*	*0.33*
Year 2003	–	–	0.18**	0.19**
	–	–	*2.06*	*2.18*
Constant	-33.61**	-35.09***	-31.01***	-32.56***
	-2.54	*-2.76*	*-5.36*	*-5.84*
Adjusted R^2	0.85	0.85	0.89	0.90
Number of obs.	276	276	812	812

Note: All variables are in logs. The log value of the binary variables takes on the values 1 and 0, respectively. The *t*-statistics in italics are estimated with robust standard errors. The coefficients for the exporting country-specific binary variables (DEVEXP) are not reported. ***, ** and * denote statistical significance at the 1, 5 and 10 percent level.

income countries (UMI). The sign, size and significance of the coefficients for economic mass and distance remain practically the same as in the regressions on the effects of overall EU exports above. The coefficients for low-income countries are positive and statistically significant at the 5 percent level in the cross-sectional regression, and at the 1 percent level in the time-series regression. The same holds for the coefficients for the upper-middle income countries, while in the case of the lower-middle income countries the coefficient is positive but insignificant in the cross-sectional regression, and positive and significant at the 5 percent level in the time-series regression. The effects of EU colonial ties are positive and significant at conventional levels in both regressions, but the effects are smaller compared to the regression on the overall effects of EU trade policy (Table 4.3. – columns 1 and 3). The time dummy is insignificant in 2002 but positive and significant in 2003. Interacting the binary variable for EU trade policy with the time dummy does not yield any significant result. The relative impact of EU trade policy vis-à-vis US trade policy on developing country exports therefore appears to be constant over the period.

Gross-Trade-Creating Effects of the EU Trade Policy

The results indicate that overall EU trade policy has been more successful in generating exports from developing countries compared to US trade policy towards the same set of countries. The coefficients of the binary variables for EU imports provide a measure of EU trade policy success relative to US trade policy. Table 4.4 shows the coefficients converted into estimates of gross trade creation (GTC) as a percentage of total EU imports from developing countries.[33] The figures show that, overall, EU trade policy on average has generated some 35 percent more exports from developing countries over the 2001–03 period compared to US trade policy. The result is mainly explained by effects on exports from low-income countries (GTC of 50 percent to 55 percent). The difference in effect is also rather strong for the upper-middle income countries; EU trade policy is estimated to have generated some 45 per cent more exports

Table 4.4 Comparative effects of EU trade policy vs. US trade policy vis-à-vis developing countries, 2001–2003 (gross trade creation)

Estimation method	Cross section 2001–03 (average)	Time-series 2001–03
EU imports (EU)	35.6	36.2
Low-income countries (LI)	50.3	54.2
Lower-middle income countries (LMI)	(22.9)	20.5
Upper-middle income countries (UMI)	46.2	47.8

Note: The figure in parentheses is based on statistically insignificant estimates.

Source: Own calculations based on the regression results displayed in Table 4.3.

compared to US trade policy. The effects are weakest for the lower-middle income countries, where EU trade policy has generated approximately 20 per cent more exports, albeit the cross-sectional regression indicates that this result is insignificant.

DISCUSSION

The results above indicate that the EU's trade policy for the poorest countries, in the form of the EBA and the Cotonou Agreement, has increased exports to the EU relatively more compared to developing countries' exports to the US under predominantly the GSP and the AGOA (cf. Table 4.2). This result is not surprising in light of the deep and broad character of these schemes. In the 1990s, before the introduction of the EBA, GSP sub-schemes were introduced in the framework of the general GSP arrangement which provided for access to the EU market that went beyond the regular EU and US GSP schemes.

The results also point to positive effects of EU trade policy compared to US trade policy on exports from lower-middle income countries (albeit statistically insignificant in the cross-sectional regression). This indicates that there is less of a difference between EU and US treatment of exports from the main developing countries that primarily access the EU and US markets under the respective GSP scheme. As a generalisation, one could say that the difference between the EU and US GSP schemes is less than the difference between the EU's EBA initiative and Cotonou Agreement on the one hand and the US GSP and AGOA on the other, as indicated by the results for the low-income countries above.

The main exporters to the EU market among the upper-middle income countries are the former candidate countries in Central and Eastern Europe, with which the EU had far-reaching bilateral trade agreements progressively leading to liberalised trade with the EU in the run-up to membership. Mexico dominates exports to the US among the countries in this group. Compared to the overall effects of EU trade policy on developing country exports, it appears as if these agreements have been quite successful in facilitating exports. The estimates of GTC lie in the range of 45 percent. However, excluding the then candidate countries for EU membership as well as Mexico from the sample does not alter the result, which thus appears to be relatively robust.

Finally, the variable EU Colonial ties (EUCOL) denotes that all EU imports are affected by an EU member state's former colonial relationship and not only the developing country's exports to this particular member state. This ought to lead to an overestimation of the effects of colonial ties as data for the EU is given at the aggregate EU-15 level.

Relation to Other Studies

Haveman and Schatz (2003) note that the EU trade policy provides deep and broad programs, but that the US (and Japanese) programs, although broad, are significantly less deep. They estimate that EU preference programs increased exports from LDCs by about 45 percent in the year 2000, as compared to 10 percent in the case of the US, and that LDC exports to the US would increase by some 150 percent should the US dismantle its tariff on products from LDCs.[34,35] The difference in trade-generating effect between the EU and US schemes is estimated to be around 35 percent in Haveman and Schatz (2003). This is by and large in line with the results obtained in this study, which finds the effects of the EU trade policy to be about 50 percent greater for low income countries, the bulk of which are LDCs, compared to the overall effects of US trade policy on developing country exports. Bourdet and Nilsson (1997) analysed the impact of EU and US GSP schemes over the 1976–92 period and found that the merits of the EU and American GSP schemes in terms of their effects on exports from developing countries differed markedly. The volume of exports that could be attributed to the EU GSP scheme was significantly larger than the volume attributed to the US scheme. The difference in gross trade-generating effects between the two schemes was in the range of 40 percent in favour of the EU.[36] A further comparison of the EU and US schemes suggested that the EU scheme was less beneficial to strongly export-oriented countries and more beneficial to less competitive developing countries.

Finally, the literature on the effects of preference erosion (see e.g. Francois et al. (2005) and OECD (2005)) commonly finds relatively greater negative effects of EU trade liberalisation on preferences-dependent developing countries' exports compared to other preference donors, thereby confirming the relative importance of EU preferences.

The somewhat higher relative effects on developing country exports of EU trade policy vis-à-vis US trade policy found in this study, compared to previous studies, supports the notion that the difference in access for developing country exports to the EU and US markets has widened since early 2000 through the introduction of the EBA. However, as noted above, the effect of individual preference schemes are not examined in this study and hence, there is no statistically significant support for this empirically.

SUMMARY AND CONCLUSION

A descriptive comparison of the EU and US preferential trading arrangements shows that EU trade preferences for developing countries are in general more advantageous in scope and depth than corresponding US schemes. The empirical results of the analysis show that EU trade policy towards developing countries has generated significantly more exports compared to US policies vis-à-vis the same countries. The effects are relatively larger for the poorest group of developing countries, which is dominated by LDCs that enjoy the most preferential access to the EU market through the Cotonou Agreement and the EBA initiative. The result holds both for cross-sectional and time-series regressions.

Developed countries have committed themselves to introducing duty- and quota-free access for goods from LDCs.[37] To date, only the EU has lived up to these promises through the introduction of its EBA initiative. This analysis indicates that EU trade policy towards the poorest developing countries in relative terms has increased exports significantly more than US trade policy, thereby strengthening arguments for the introduction of an EU-like trade policy by other developed countries as well.

NOTES

The opinions expressed in this chapter are the author's own and do not necessarily reflect any views of the European Commission. Thanks to Claudio Gasparini and Dominique Sabatte for providing trade statistics and to Jacques Gallezot, Anne van Bruggen and colleagues in DG Trade and DG Taxation and Customs Union for useful comments.

1. As defined by the United Nations, see http://www.un.org/special-rep/ohrlls/ohrlls/default.htm.
2. Duties on fresh bananas were reduced by 20 percent annually starting on 1 January 2002 and eliminated on 1 January 2006. Duties on rice were reduced by 20 percent on 1 September 2006, and will be reduced by 50 percent on 1 September 2007 and by 80 percent on 1 September 2008 and eliminated at the latest by 1 September 2009. Duties on sugar were reduced by 20 percent on 1 July 2006, and will be reduced by 50 percent on 1 July 2007 and by 80 percent on 1 July 2008 and eliminated at the latest by 1 July 2009.
3. The EBA is formally part of the EU's GSP.
4. See e.g. Brenton and Ikezuki (2004), Nilsson (2002) and Page and Hewitt (2002).
5. Exceptions are Bourdet and Nilsson (1996) and Haveman and Schatz (2003). GAO (2001) and Stevens and Kennan (2004) provide qualitative comparisons of mainly EU and US trade policies vis-à-vis developing countries while Kommerskollegium (2005) carries out a qualitatively comparative analysis of the trade policies of the EU, the US, Canada and Japan.
6. Low-income countries, lower-middle income countries and upper-middle income countries.
7. Tariffs are suspended if preferential treatment results in (ad valorem) duties of 1 percent or less, or in specific duties of €2 or less.
8. This concerns mainly products in chapters 50–63 of the Harmonised System (HS).
9. To be eligible, beneficiaries must meet a number of criteria including ratification and effective application of key international conventions on sustainable development and good governance, and demonstrate that their economies are dependent and vulnerable. Poor diversification and dependence are defined as meaning that the five largest sections of a beneficiary's GSP-covered exports to the Community must represent more than 75 percent of its total GSP-covered exports. GSP-covered exports from that country must also represent less than 1 percent of total EU imports under GSP.
10. See Council Regulation (EC) No 2501/2001, Annex I.
11. The Lomé Convention was in turn preceded by Yaoundé Conventions I and II.
12. South Africa is a signatory to the Cotonou Agreement but its membership of the ACP Group is qualified (Protocol 3 on South Africa attached to the Cotonou Agreement). The provisions of the Trade, Development and Cooperation Agreement between the EC and South Africa take precedence over the provisions of the Cotonou Agreement. Cuba belongs to the ACP group of countries but is not a signatory to the Cotonou Agreement.
13. The Agreement is under the cover of a WTO waiver approved at the Doha Ministerial Meeting, which will expire on 31 December 2007. See WTO document WT/MIN(01)/15 of 14 November 2001.
14. These countries are all new member states of the EU as of 1 May 2004 except for Bulgaria and Romania, which became members of the EU on 1 January 2007.
15. Agricultural and coal and steel products are not covered by the customs union.

16. A beneficiary country loses GSP eligibility for a product if, during the previous calendar year, US imports of a GSP article from that country account for 50 percent or more of the value of total US imports of that product, or exceed a certain dollar value. Legislation reauthorizing GSP in 1996 set the dollar limit at $75 million for 1996 with an annual increase of $5 million for each subsequent calendar year.

17. Qualifying articles include: apparel made of US. yarns and fabrics; apparel made of sub-Saharan African (regional) yarns and fabrics, subject to a cap; apparel made in a designated lesser-developed country of third-country yarns and fabrics, subject to a cap; apparel made of yarns and fabrics not produced in commercial quantities in the United States; certain cashmere and merino wool sweaters; and eligible handloomed, handmade, or folklore articles; and ethnic fabrics.

18. This stance is based on the stable relationship found between a summary measure of well-being, such as poverty incidence and infant mortality on the one hand and economic variables including per capita GNI on the other, even though it recognises that GNI does not in itself constitute or measure welfare or success in development.

19. The thresholds are updated every year to incorporate the effect of inflation and thus remain constant in real terms over time.

20. Tuvalu is not included in World Bank statistics. It is classified by the United Nations as an LDC.

21. The UN's Economic and Social Council uses the following criteria to identify LDCs: (i) a low-income criterion, based on a three-year average estimate of the gross domestic product (GDP) per capita (under $750 for inclusion and above $900 for 'graduation'); (ii) a human resource weakness criterion, and (iii) an economic vulnerability criterion, To be added to the list, a country must satisfy all three criteria. To 'graduate', a country must meet the thresholds for two of the three criteria in two consecutive reviews. However, countries with a population above 75 million are excluded. Following the latest review in 2003, the number of LDCs now equals 50.

22. Note that Russia does not enjoy full preferences under the EU's GSP.

23. See Greenaway and Milner (2002) for an overview of gravity models and regional free trade areas.

24. See e.g. Anderson and Wincoop (2003) and Evenett and Keller (2002) and the literature cited therein.

25. Alternatively, Anderson and van Wincoop (2003) suggest using (complex) non-linear estimation techniques.

26. Equation 4.1 implies that the coefficient for income is restricted to unity. Allowing for non-tradable goods in the model following Anderson (1979), this restriction is relaxed and the parameter $\beta 1$ can be estimated.

27. Note that with trade flows in only one direction (exports from developing countries), the introduction of country-pair specific effects along importer and exporter dummies is not possible.

28. These variables denote former European Union member country colonial relationships that ended during or after the Second World War, see the CIA's World Fact book (www.cia.gov).

29 Note that the results do not provide any information about the absolute effects of EU or US trade preferences.

30. The data have been converted to constant 2001 euros using yearly averages of the euro dollar exchange and the euro GDP deflator as provided by the ECB (http//:www.ecb.int).

31. http://www.wcrl.ars.usda.gov/cec/moregen.htm.

32. Trade and/or income data is missing for the following countries: In 2001 – Afghanistan, American Samoa, Cuba, Iraq, North Korea, Libya, Marshall Islands, Mayotte, Micronesia, Myanmar, Northern Mariana Islands, Palau, Somalia, St Vincent and the Grenadines and Tuvalu. In 2002, data is also missing for Equatorial Guinea and Zimbabwe and in 2003 for Belize, Oman, Saudi Arabia and Suriname.

33. The figures are derived in the following way. Actual EU imports from developing countries are divided by the base of the natural logarithm (e) raised to the power of the coefficients of the relevant binary variables in Table 4.2. This provides estimates of the factors by which EU imports from developing countries have increased relative to US imports from the same countries as a result of trade policy. Subtracting the latter from actual trade yields estimates of

gross trade creation. The GTC figures reveal how much smaller trade would have been if the EU had had a US-like trade policy.
34. Haveman and Schatz (2003) estimate that the elimination of remaining EU trade barriers to LDC exports would lead to a 2.6 percent expansion in EU imports from LDCs.
35. One should, however, note that the underlying statistical significance of the estimates of Haveman and Schatz (2003) are unclear as their regression statistics are not reported.
36. The figure is based on an average of the yearly GTC estimations, all of which are not statistically significant.
37. Trade ministers stated at Doha in 2001; – 'We commit ourselves to the objective of duty-free, quota-free market access for products originating from LDCs' (WTO (2001), Doha WTO Ministerial Declaration, WT/MIN(01)/DEC/1) and the December 2005 Hong Kong Ministerial Declaration states that '... Members declaring themselves in a position to do so, agree to implement duty-free and quota-free market access for products originating from LDCs...'. Annex F of the declaration further states that '...Members facing difficulties [...] shall provide duty-free and quota-free market access for at least 97 per cent of products originating from LDCs, defined at the tariff line level, by 2008...' (WTO (2005), Hong Kong WTO Ministerial Declaration, WT/MIN(05)/DEC).

REFERENCES

Anderson, J.E. (1979), 'A Theoretical Foundation for the Gravity Equation', *American Economic Review*, **69** (1), 106–116.

Anderson, J.E. and E. van Wincoop (2003), 'Gravity with Gravitas: A Solution to the Border Puzzle, *American Economic Review*, **93** (1), 170–92.

Bourdet, Y. and L. Nilsson (1997), 'Trade Preferences and Developing Countries' Exports: A Comparative Study of the EU and US GSP Schemes', mimeo, Lund University, Lund.

Brenton, P. and T. Ikezuki (2004), 'The Initial and Potential Impact of Preferential Access to the U.S. Market under the African Growth and Opportunity Act, World Bank Policy Research Working Paper 3262.

Egger, P and M. Pfaffermayr (2003), 'The Proper Panel Econometric Specification of the Gravity Equation: A Three-way Model with Bilateral Interaction Effects', *Empirical Economics*, **28**, 571–80.

Evenett, S. J. and W. Keller (2002), 'On Theories Explaining the Success of the Gravity Equation', *Journal of Political Economy*, **110** (2), 281–316.

Feenstra, Robert C. (2003), *Advanced International Trade: Theory and Evidence*, Princeton, NJ: Princeton University Press.

Francois, J., B. Hoekman and M. Manchin (2005), 'Preference Erosion and Multilateral Trade Liberalization', CEPR Discussion Paper No. 5153.

GAO (2001), 'Report to the Chairman, Subcommittee on Trade, Committee on Ways and Means, House of Representatives, International Trade – Comparison of U.S. and European Union Preference Programs', GAO-01-647, June.

Greenaway, D. and C. Milner (2002), 'Regionalism and Gravity', *Scottish Journal of Political Economy*, **49** (5), 574–85.

Haveman, J.D. and H.J. Schatz (2003), 'Developed Country Trade Barriers and the Least Developed Countries: The Economic Result of Freeing Trade', Working Paper No. 2003.7, Public Policy Institute of California.

Kommerskollegium/National Board of Trade (2005), 'A Comparative Analysis of the Trade Policies of the European Union, the United States, Canada and Japan', http://www.kommers.se.

Mátyás, L (1997), 'Proper Econometric Specification of the Gravity Model', *The World Economy*, **20** (3), 363–68.

Nilsson, L. (2002), 'Trading Relations: Is the Roadmap from Lomé to Cotonou Correct?' *Applied Economics*, **34**, 439–52.

OECD (2005), 'Trade Preference Erosion: Potential Impacts', TD/TC/WP(2004)30/REV1.

Office of the United States Trade Representative (1999), 'U.S. Generalized System of Preferences Guidebook', Washington, DC.

Office of the United States Trade Representative (2004), 'U.S. Generalized System of Preferences Guidebook', ADDENDUM, Washington, DC.

Page, S. and A. Hewitt (2002), 'The New European Trade Preferences: Does Everything but Arms (EBA) Help the Poor?' *Development Policy Review*, **20** (1), 91–102.

Rose, A.K. and E. van Wincoop (2001), 'National Money as a Barrier to International Trade: The Real Case for Currency Union', *American Economic Review,* **91** (2), 386–90.

Stevens, C. and J. Kennan (2004), 'Comparative Study of G8 Preferential Access Schemes for Africa', Institute for Development Studies.

UNCTAD (2001), 'Duty and Quota Free Market Access for LDCs: An Analysis of Quad Initiatives', UNCTAD/DITC/TAB/Misc.7.

UNCTAD (2002), 'Generalized System of Preferences: Handbook on the Scheme of the European Community', UNCTAD/ITCD/TSB/Misc.25/Rev.2.

UNCTAD (2003), 'Trade Preferences For LDCs: An Early Assessment of Benefits and Possible Improvements', UNCTAD/ITCD/TSB/2003/8.

ANNEX 4

Table 4A.1: List of low-income countries and middle-income countries and EU and US trade preferences applying to them

Country	Income	LDC/ EBA	ACP	EU GSP	US GSP	AGOA	ATPA	CBI
Afghanistan	LI	x		x	x			
Albania	LMI			ATM	x			
Algeria	LMI			x/BA				
American Samoa	UMI			x				
Angola	LI	x	x	x	x	x		
Antigua Barbuda	UMI		x	x	x			x
Argentina	UMI			x	x			
Armenia	LMI			x	x			
Azerbaijan	LMI			x				
Bangladesh	LI	x		x	x			
Barbados	UMI		x	x	x			x
Belarus	LMI			x				
Belize	UMI		x	x	x			x
Benin	LI	x	x	x	x	x		

Country	Income	LDC/ EBA	ACP	EU GSP	US GSP	AGOA	ATPA	CBI
Bhutan	LI	x		x	x			
Bolivia	LMI			x	x		x	
Bosnia & H.	LMI			ATM	x			
Botswana	UMI		x	x	x	x		
Brazil	LMI			x	x			
Bulgaria	LMI			BA	x			
Burkina Faso	LI	x	x	x	x	x		
Burundi	LI	x	x	x	x			
Cambodia	LI	x		x	x			
Cameroon	LI		x	x	x	x		
Cape Verde	LMI	x	x	x	x	x		
C. African R.	LI	x	x	x	x			
Chad	LI	x	x	x	x	x		
Chile	UMI			x/BA-03	x			
China	LMI			x				
Colombia	LMI			x	x		x	
Comoros	LI	x	x	x	x			
Congo, D.R.	LI	x	x	x	x	x		
Congo, R.	LI		x	x	x	x		
Cook Islands	LMI		x	x				
Costa Rica	UMI			x	x			x
Côte d'Ivoire	LI		x	x	x			
Croatia	UMI			ATM/BA	x			
Cuba	LMI		x	x				
Czech R.	UMI			BA	x			
Djibouti	LMI	x	x	x	x	x		
Dominica	UMI		x	x	x			x
Dominican R.	LMI		x	x	x			x
Ecuador	LMI			x	x		x	
Egypt	LMI			BA/x	x			
El Salvador	LMI			x	x			x
Eq. Guinea	LI	x	x	x	x			
Eritrea	LI	x	x	x	x			
Estonia	UMI			BA	x			
Ethiopia	LI	x	x	x	x	x		
Fiji	LMI		x	x	x			
Gabon	UMI		x	x	x	x		
Gambia	LI	x	x	x	x	x		
Georgia	LMI			x	x			
Ghana	LI		x	x	x	x		
Grenada	UMI		x	x	x			x
Guatemala	LMI			x	x			x
Guinea	LI	x	x	x	x	x		
Guinea-Bissau	LI	x	x	x	x	x		
Guyana	LMI		x	x	x			x

Country	Income	LDC/ EBA	ACP	EU GSP	US GSP	AGOA	ATPA	CBI
Haiti	LI	x	x	x	x			x
Honduras	LMI			x	x			x
Hungary	UMI			BA	x			
India	LI			x	x			
Indonesia	LMI			x	x			
Iran	LMI			x				
Iraq	LMI			x	x			
Jamaica	LMI		x	x	x			
Jordan	LMI			BA/x	x			
Kazakhstan	LMI			x	x			
Kenya	LI		x	x	x	x		
Kiribati	LMI	x	x	x	x			
Korea, D.R.	LI							
Kyrgyz R.	LI			x	x			
Lao PDR	LI	x		x				
Latvia	UMI				x			
Lebanon	UMI			BA/x	x			
Lesotho	LI	x	x	x	x	x		
Liberia	LI	x	x	x				
Libya	UMI			x				
Lithuania	UMI				x			
Macedonia, FYR	LMI			ATM/BA				
Madagascar	LI	x	x	x	x	x		
Malawi	LI	x	x	x	x	x		
Malaysia	UMI			x				
Maldives	LMI	x		x				
Mali	LI	x	x	x	x	x		
Marshall Islands	LMI		x	x				
Mauritania	LI	x	x	x	x	x		
Mauritius	UMI		x	x	x	x		
Mayotte	UMI			x				
Mexico	UMI			x/BA	NAFTA			
Micronesia	LMI		x	x				
Moldova	LI			x	x			
Mongolia	LI			x	x			
Morocco	LMI			BA/x	x			
Mozambique	LI	x	x	x	x	x		
Myanmar	LI	x		x				
N. Mariana Isl	UMI			x				
Namibia	LMI		x	x	x	x		
Nauru	LMI		x	x				
Nepal	LI	x		x	x			
Nicaragua	LI			x				x
Niger	LI	x	x	x	x	x		

Country	Income	LDC/ EBA	ACP	EU GSP	US GSP	AGOA	ATPA	CBI
Nigeria	LI		x	x	x	x		
Niue	LMI		x	x				
Oman	UMI			x	x			
Pakistan	LI			x	x			
Palau	UMI		x	x				
Panama	UMI			x	x			x
Papua N. Guinea	LI		x	x	x			
Paraguay	LMI			x	x			
Peru	LMI			x	x		x	
Philippines	LMI			x	x			
Poland	UMI			BA	x			
Romania	LMI			BA	x			
Russia	LMI			x	x			
Rwanda	LI	x	x	x	x	x		
Samoa	LMI	x	x	x	x			
São Tomé & Pr.	LI	x	x	x	x	x		
Saudi Arabia	UMI			x				
Senegal	LI	x	x	x	x	x		
Serbia & Mont.	LMI			ATM				
Seychelles	UMI		x	x	x	x		
Sierra Leone	LI	x	x	x	x	x		
Slovakia	UMI			BA	x			
Solomon Isl.	LI	x	x	x	x			
Somalia	LI	x	x	x	x			
South Africa	LMI		x	BA/x	x	x		
Sri Lanka	LMI			x	x			
St Kitts-Nev	UMI		x	x	x			x
St Lucia	UMI		x	x	x			x
St Vincent	UMI		x	x	x			x
Sudan	LI	x	x	x				
Suriname	LMI		x	x	x			
Swaziland	LMI		x	x	x	x		
Syria	LMI			x				
Tajikistan	LI			x				
Tanzania	LI	x	x	x	x	x		
Thailand	LMI			x	x			
Timor-Lesté	LI	x	x	x				
Togo	LI	x	x	x	x			
Tonga	LMI		x	x	x			
Trinidad & Tob.	UMI		x	x	x			x
Tunisia	LMI			BAx	x			
Turkey	LMI			CU	x			
Turkmenistan	LMI			x				
Tuvalu		x	x	x	x			

Country	Income	LDC/ EBA	ACP	EU GSP	US GSP	AGOA	ATPA	CBI
Uganda	LI	x	x	x	x	x		
Ukraine	LMI			x				
Uruguay	UMI			x	x			
Uzbekistan	LI			x	x			
Vanuatu	LMI	x	x	x	x			
Venezuela	UMI			x	x			
Vietnam	LI			x				
W. Bank & Gaza	LMI							
Yemen, R.	LI	x		x	x			
Zambia	LI	x	x	x	x	x		
Zimbabwe	LI		x	x	x			
No. of countries	158	50	78	147	124	37	4	18

Notes: LI denotes low-income countries, LMI denotes lower-middle income countries and UMI denotes upper-middle income countries. Economies are divided among income groups according to 2003 GNI per capita, calculated using the World Bank Atlas method. Low-income countries have a per capita income of $765 or less, lower-middle income countries fall in the range of a per capita income of $766–3035, while upper-middle income countries have a per capita income of $9386 or more. LDCs are defined according to the UN and are beneficiaries of the EU's Everything but Arms (EBA) Initiative.

ACP denotes the African, Caribbean and Pacific countries under the Cotonou Agreement. EU GSP and US GSP denote the Generalised System of Preferences of the EU and US, respectively. AGOA signifies the US African Growth and Opportunity Act (countries are listed only if they have been eligible for the AGOA for the full period 2001–2003), ATPA the US Andean Trade Preference Act and CBI the US Caribbean Basin Initiative. ATM stands for the Autonomous Trade Measures the EU has introduced for the countries of the Western Balkans, BA represents a bilateral agreement, including preferential trade provisions, between the EU and the country concerned (association agreement, cooperation agreement, Europe agreement or other) and CU indicates a customs union. NAFTA denotes the North American Free Trade Area.

The classification concerns the countries' preferential trading status with the EU and the US over the 2001–03 period.

Sources: Council Regulation (EC) No 2501/2001 of 10 December 2001 (http://ec.europa.eu/trade/issues/global/gsp/legis/index_en.htm). World Bank data and statistics (http://www.worldbank.org/data/), Office of the United States Trade Representative 1999 and 2004, UNCTAD 2002 and the United Nations (http://www.un.org/special-rep/ohrlls/ldc/list.htm).

5. Is the Middle East and North Africa Region Achieving its Trade Potential?

Ludvig Söderling

INTRODUCTION

Improving growth and tackling high unemployment rates are among the greatest challenges for Middle East and North African (MENA) countries. These challenges will no doubt need to be addressed by a broad mix of macroeconomic and structural reforms. This chapter studies one important aspect of this challenge, namely the scope for enhancing international trade. Further trade liberalization and trade facilitation in the MENA region is important for at least three broad reasons. First, to improve economic performance in a durable manner, it is crucial to accelerate productivity growth. Increased trade openness can contribute to productivity growth by means of a more efficient allocation of resources, technology transfers, access to a wider range of inputs, competitive pressure, and scale effects. Second, to ensure external sustainability and sufficient demand, growth needs to be largely export-driven. Several MENA countries are exposed to external vulnerabilities that would be substantially mitigated by strong export growth. In addition, given the small size of local markets, it is questionable whether domestic demand could constitute viable engines of growth. Finally, most MENA countries are in need of economic diversification, since they are often dependent on either commodity or agricultural exports. Increased diversification would protect MENA countries against terms of trade shocks or climatic vagaries. In addition, increased diversification is directly associated with improved productivity (see, e.g., Feenstra et al., 1999 and Berthélemy and Söderling, 2001). In this regard, international trade can be an important factor in encouraging product diversification.

This study attempts to quantify the scope for increasing MENA countries' external trade in the near-to-medium term. The analysis uses a gravity model of bilateral trade, incorporating important recent theoretical developments by Anderson and van Wincoop (2003). The model is applied to a panel dataset covering some 90 countries over the period 1990–2002 and about 90 percent of total world trade. The gravity model predicts a global benchmark level of bilateral trade based on a number of characteristics of the countries involved.

Deviations from the benchmark provide a measure of the potential to increase trade between particular countries. While the exact magnitude of such estimates should be treated with a degree of caution, they can provide guidance as to (a) what the prospects are of significantly increasing trade over the near-to-medium term; and (b) which countries present the greatest untapped potential for increasing trade.

Particular attention will be given to the impact of integration efforts between the (pre-2004 accession) European Union (EU) and a number of Southern and Eastern Mediterranean countries (hereinafter referred to as Mediterranean countries), which began in earnest in the mid-1990s with the Barcelona process. The Barcelona process aims at an eventual Euro-Mediterranean free trade zone. In this context, the main instruments used are bilateral association agreements with the European Union (AAEUs), supported by grants under the MEDA program, and complemented by loans from the European Investment Bank (EIB). An AAEU came into force first with the Palestinian Authority (1997), followed by agreements with Tunisia[1] (1998), Morocco (2000), Israel (2000), Jordan (2002), Egypt (2004), and Algeria (2005). Lebanon signed its agreement in 2002 (awaiting ratification by all EU member states). Negotiations were concluded with Syria in 2003. This study focuses on six MENA countries: Algeria, Egypt, Jordan, Morocco, Syria, and Tunisia. In particular, Morocco and Tunisia will be analyzed in some detail in view of their further advances within the Barcelona process and given their export composition, which makes them more likely to benefit from trade integration than other countries in the sample. The Palestinian Authority and Lebanon were excluded owing to data limitations.

The relevant questions are whether the Barcelona process has resulted in a closer integration between Mediterranean countries and the EU and, if so, whether this has been achieved at the cost of undue concentration of trade toward the EU. We will suggest that the result of the Barcelona process has been uneven and that there is still room for most countries in the sample to enhance their integration with the EU. Nevertheless, the analysis will also point to significant underexploited export markets outside the EU (notably the United States) with which MENA countries could increase trade.

ANALYTICAL FRAMEWORK

The Model

The underlying model is based on Anderson and van Wincoop (2003). Each country is assumed to produce a fixed quantity of a unique bundle of goods. On the demand side, consumers around the world choose between goods from different countries, which are imperfectly substitutable following a constant elasticity of substitution (CES) function. Accordingly, the consumer in country j maximizes the utility function

$$U_j(c) = \left(\sum_i \beta_i^{(1-\sigma)/\sigma} c_{ij}^{(\sigma-1)/\sigma} \right)^{\sigma/(\sigma-1)} \qquad (5.1)$$

subject to the budget constraint

$$\sum_i p_{ij} c_{ij} = y_j \qquad (5.2)$$

where c_{ij} is consumption by country j of goods from country i, i.e. country j's real imports from country i (including country j's 'imports' to itself, see below), β_i is a positive distribution parameter,[2] σ is the elasticity of substitution between goods from different countries (assumed greater than 1), p_{ij} is the price of the good from country i in country j, and y_j is nominal income in country j. The bilateral import price p_{ij} depends on the producer price and on trade costs (including transportation costs, tariffs, and other trade barriers broadly defined) so that $p_{ij} = p_i t_{ij}$ ($t_{ij} > 1$), with p_i and $t_{ij} - 1$ denoting producer prices and trade costs, respectively.

Denoting nominal imports from country i to country j by $x_{ij} = p_i c_{ij}$, the solution to the optimization problem is

$$x_{ij} = \left(\frac{\beta_i p_i t_{ij}}{P_j} \right)^{(1-\sigma)} y_j \qquad (5.3)$$

where P_j is a consumer price index of country j given by

$$P_j = \left(\sum_i \left(\beta_i p_i t_{ij} \right)^{(1-\sigma)} \right)^{1/(1-\sigma)} \qquad (5.4)$$

Imposing market clearance (i.e. $y_i = \sum_j x_{ij}$), Anderson and van Wincoop (2003) show that the gravity equation can be expressed as

$$x_{ij} = \frac{y_i y_j}{y_w} \left(\frac{t_{ij}}{\Pi_i P_j} \right)^{(1-\sigma)} \qquad (5.5)$$

where y_w is global income and Π_i is a price index for the exporting country, similar to the one for the importing country, the P_j. The presence of Π_i and P_j in the denominator of equation 5.5 implies that what matters for trade is not the *absolute* level of bilateral trade barriers (t_{ij}), it is bilateral barriers *relative* to the overall price indices. This has major consequences for the estimation and interpretation of gravity equations, generally overlooked in empirical applications prior to the publication of Anderson and van Wincoop's paper. Interpretation issues will be discussed below. From an estimation point of view, the presence of Π_i and P_j implies that exporter and importer dummies should be included in the regression.[3] Unlike Anderson and van Wincoop (2003) we are not imposing the restriction that trade barriers are symmetric (i.e. $t_{ij} = t_{ji}$). This implies that two dummies need to be estimated for each country – one exporter and one importer dummy.[4] While there are theoretical arguments for imposing symmetry – Anderson and van Wincoop (2003) conclude that it is necessary in order to ensure a unique equilibrium – it has been criticized as too restrictive and unrealistic (Helpman et al., 2004). Furthermore, Baltagi et al. (2003) provide empirical evidence indicating that a more general specification of the gravity equation is preferable.[5]

In logs, and adding a time dimension, the gravity model to be estimated is thus

$$\ln x_{itj} = \text{constant} + a_1 \ln y_{it}y_{jt} + a_2 \ln t_{ijt} + \gamma_i + \lambda_j + \tau_t + \varepsilon_{ijt} \qquad (5.6)$$

where γ_i and λ_j are exporter and importer fixed effects, controlling for Π_i and P_j, respectively, τ_t is a time dummy, and ε_{ijt} is a white noise disturbance term. Following Coe and Hoffmaister (1998) and Coe, Subramanian, and Tamirisa (2004) the time dummy is included to control for time-specific events, including global shocks and changes in global income, price levels, and exchange rates over time.[6] Nominal income y_{it} is approximated by nominal GDP. Equation 5.5 would imply that a_1 is equal to 1, but this can be relaxed by allowing for nontradable goods in the model (as in Anderson, 1979).[7] Hence, the approach taken here is to estimate a_1 rather than restricting it to unity. The coefficient a_2 is equal to $(1 - \sigma)$.

The bilateral trade resistance term is of particular interest and can be further developed. The following specification is used

$$\ln t_{ijt} = \delta \ln d_{ij} + \mu Landl_{ij} + \phi Adj_{ij} + \varphi Col_{ij} + \nu Lang_{ij} + \\ \pi PrimX_{it} + \theta Border_{ij} + \eta_{ij} \qquad (5.7)$$

where d is distance, *Landl* is the number of landlocked countries in the pair (i.e. 0, 1, or 2), *Adj, Col, Lang,* and *Border* are dummies for, respectively, adjacent countries, countries with colonial ties, countries sharing a common language, and trade across borders, as opposed to trade within the same country (i.e. i $\neq$ j).

PrimX is a dummy for commodity exporters interacted with a commodity price index (i.e. equal to zero for non-commodity exporters and the log of the commodity price index for commodity exporters). η_{ij} is a country pair-specific effect, fixed or random.[8] The latter is a measure of remaining bilateral trade resistance, deriving from tariff and nontariff barriers and any unobservable factors that could have an impact on bilateral trade. These bilateral effects will be the focus of this study.

The *Border* dummy, used in several studies to measure the home bias or border effect, is not of particular interest for the present study, and is included in the specification for the moment simply to acknowledge its existence. Estimating the border effect requires *intra*-national trade (i.e. production sold on the domestic market) to be included in the regressions. However, under the assumption that within-country trade is not structurally different from international trade, once account has been taken of the border effect, there is no reason why excluding these observations from the analysis would introduce any particular bias in the estimations. Indeed, excluding intra-national trade avoids potential biases related to problems measuring within-country trade and within-country distance.[9] Therefore, in what follows, only international trade will be included in the regressions. This implies that the border effect can not be discerned from any other effect captured by the constant in the regression. For this chapter this is not a concern, given the definition of trade potential used here (see below).

Estimating Trade Potentials

Estimations of trade potentials are associated with a weakness, emphasized by Egger (2002), who criticizes the method of estimating trade potentials as the difference (or ratio) between predicted and actual trade. In a correctly specified cross-country (or pooled panel) regression any comparison between predicted and actual trade would be pointless, since residuals should be white noise. Any systematic deviation of actual trade from predicted trade should be interpreted as deriving from omitted variables, which could introduce a bias in the estimation results, if such variables are correlated with the other explanatory variables. Egger (2002) suggested using out-of-sample estimates of trade potentials. Another possibility is to use panel data and introduce country-pair-specific effects, thereby explicitly taking account of omitted unobservable effects. Both approaches will be applied here.

For our purposes, bilateral trade potentials (exports or imports) are defined as the difference between actual trade and the level of trade that would prevail if the particular country-pair-specific effects η_{ij} had been equal to the global average. As η_{ij}s are normalized to average zero, the trade potential is calculated as

$$\text{`predicted' trade} - \text{actual trade} = \left(e^{-\eta_{ij}} - 1\right) * x_{ijt}. \tag{5.8}$$

Equation 5.8 does not allow for a study of the evolution of trade potentials over time, since by construction η_{ij} is time-invariant. To address this issue, we shall complement the analysis by using out-of-sample calculations of trade potentials. More specifically, when studying the change in Mediterranean countries' trade performance vis-à-vis the EU over time, the gravity equation is estimated excluding EU-Mediterranean trade. The results from this equation are subsequently fitted to EU-Mediterranean data and compared with actual trade levels. Without denying the importance of openness to imports, the analysis will focus on the export side, to avoid repetition and to save space.

The interpretation of the estimated trade potentials warrants some discussion. Π_i and P_j in the denominator of equation 5.5 can be expressed as (see Anderson and van Wincoop, 2003, for details)

$$\Pi_i = \left(\sum_j \left(\frac{t_{ij}}{P_j} \right)^{1-\sigma} \theta_j \right)^{1/(1-\sigma)} \tag{5.9}$$

and

$$P_j = \left(\sum_i \left(\frac{t_{ij}}{\Pi_i} \right)^{1-\sigma} \theta_i \right)^{1/(1-\sigma)} \tag{5.10}$$

where θ_i is country i's share in global income. Equation 5.9 expresses Π_i as an average of the exporting country's bilateral trade costs relative to its trading partners' overall price levels, weighted by the economic size of those partners. Hence, Π_i can be considered as a measure of the exporting country's access to global export markets. Similarly, P_i can be seen as a measure of the importing country's openness to imports. In other words, the inclusion of importer and exporter dummies implies that the unobserved bilateral trade costs terms (η_{ij}) are estimated after controlling for both the exporter's and the importer's overall degree of global trade integration. Hence, the trade potential can be interpreted as the gain (or loss) in trade between two countries that would occur if their bilateral trade barriers (after controlling for distance etc.) were brought to the global integration-adjusted average. This allows for a realistic interpretation of trade potentials, controlling for different countries' progress in trade liberalization, their institutional and human capacities, country size etc. The absolute value of the Ps can not be interpreted, and the model therefore does not provide any information about the impact on bilateral trade of a general improvement in a country's overall trade capacity or degree of openness.[10] Hence, the gravity model presented here is useful for studying trade patterns, rather than absolute global volumes. In view of this, an alternative interpretation is to consider the trade potentials as a measure of bilateral trade discrimination. The bilateral trade potential between Country A and Country B is the difference between the actual level of trade and the level that would prevail if neither country discriminated (broadly defined) against the other.[11]

There is a caveat associated with the way trade potentials are calculated here. Equations 5.9 and 5.10 imply that the effect on trade of a decrease in bilateral trade costs (e.g. by the creation of a free trade area) can not be analyzed in isolation, given the general equilibrium effects such measures have on all multilateral resistance terms. For example, a sharp reduction in t_{ij} will have a direct impact on Π_i and P_j and an indirect impact on all Ps around the world. This impact will be greater, the greater are the shares of countries i and j's income in total world income. This consideration is somewhat complicated to deal with, since it would imply explicitly estimating all global price indices and making assumptions on the elasticity of substitution σ, which is unknown. However, in the present application, where we will consider limited reductions in bilateral trade costs between a number of small countries and a few of their trade partners, the general equilibrium effects are likely to be small and will hence be ignored.[12] It should, however, be recognized that doing so will slightly exaggerate potentials to increase bilateral trade with a given country (although not necessarily trade overall).

EMPIRICAL RESULTS

Estimation Issues

When estimating gravity models, a solution must be found to deal with zero-value observations. Using linear estimation techniques requires taking logs of the data, which obviously is not possible for zero-value observations. Gravity model applications often deal with this issue by omitting zero-value observations. However, this truncates the joint distribution of the data, which introduces an estimation bias. This bias can potentially be sizeable, given that bilateral trade data typically include a large number of zero observations, particularly when developing countries are included. Other methods include replacing zero-value observations by an arbitrary small number (see e.g. Wang and Winters, 1992), or using nonlinear estimation techniques. Coe, Subramanian, and Tamirisa (2004) advocate the latter and show that dropping zero observations can have a significant impact on estimation results. We take two alternative approaches. The first uses a random effects (RE) Tobit model, which includes information from the zero-value observations. Estimating the RE Tobit model using the full dataset turned out to be somewhat impractical from a computational point of view and three-year averages (1991–93, 1994–96, 1997–99, and 2000–2002) were used instead, to reduce the size of the database.

To complement the first method, an alternative approach was also taken, consisting of two steps. First, the full panel (i.e. 1990–2002) was fitted to an RE Tobit model, excluding exporter and importer dummies. The fitted values from this regression were then used to replace zero-value observations. In the second step, standard linear techniques were used. This approach resembles the method of replacing zero-value observations by small numbers, but takes away the arbitrariness in the exact value of these small numbers. Three models are used in the second step: RE, fixed effects (FE) and Hausman and Taylor (HT). A shortcoming of the random effects model is that it requires η_{ij} to be uncorrelated with the explanatory variables in the model, or else estimation results will be inconsistent. FE, on the other hand, is equivalent to introducing country-pair-specific dummies, which wipes out the effect from any time-invariant variables, such as distance and all the dummies. This would make the interpretation of estimated trade potentials uninteresting for trade policy, since these potentials would include the effects of uncontrollable factors, notably distance. Although the Hausman test suggests that the RE model is indeed the preferred model, one may still suspect that η_{ij} could be correlated with economic mass or distance (Péridy, 2004, found that to be the case). Hence, HT estimates are also reported as a complement. The HT method is a multi-step procedure that allows for correlation between η_{ij} and some of the explanatory variables (see Hausman and Taylor, 1981 for details).

Results

Table 5.1 displays the results from the RE Tobit model, in addition to the linear RE, FE, and HT regressions. Regression 2 is an RE Tobit regression excluding trade between Mediterranean countries and EU countries, to be used for out-of-sample predictions of trade potentials with the EU. All variables, except the primary exporter dummy interacted with commodity prices are significant at the 1 percent level, with the expected sign and reasonable magnitudes. The coefficient on economic mass (0.51) is substantially lower than the unity value implied by the bare-bone Anderson and van Wincoop (2003) model in equation 5.5. However, it is in line with Coe, Subramanian, and Tamirisa (2004), who find that the coefficient for economic mass declined from about 0.8 in the late 1970s to around 0.5 in the 1990s, using nonlinear techniques on panel data. In regressions 3–5, the coefficient on economic mass increases to 0.66, confirming Coe, Subramanian, and Tamirisa's (2004) findings that regression results are somewhat sensitive to the method used to deal with zero observations. It turns out, however, that trade potentials are not. We will consider the RE Tobit model the preferred model to be used for calculations of trade potentials, but all relevant tables and figures are reproduced in the Annex using regression 5 as the basis for calculations.[13] Regression 5 uses the two-step method with the HT regression in the second step, allowing for any potential correlation between the country-pair effects and economic mass and distance. While the magnitudes of the estimated trade potentials vary somewhat between the different methods, the overall findings do not.[14]

Table 5.1 Estimations of the gravity equation

	RE Tobit (1)	RE Tobit (2)	FE (3)	RE (4)	HT (5)
Economic mass: ln(GDPi*GDPj)	0.51***	0.51***	0.66***	0.66***	0.66***
Distance	-1.37***	-1.36***	---	-1.31***	-1.52***
Common language	0.66***	0.69***	---	0.71***	0.58***
Adjacent	0.37***	0.43***	---	0.23***	-0.11
Landlocked	-4.39***	-4.22***	---	-4.81***	-2.31***
Primary exporter × commodity price	0.03	-0.06	0.07	0.07	0.07
Colony	0.73***	0.69***	---	0.62***	0.73***
Constant	14.79***	14.7***	-2.76***	11.65***	11.65***
Number of observations	28 363	27 692	92 995	92 995	92 995
Number of groups	7 455	7 287	7 521	7 521	7 521
Sigma U (pooled v/s RE)	1.28***	1.29***			
Hausman test FE v/s RE			---	$\chi2(14) =$ 0.2	
Time dummies	yes	yes	yes	yes	yes
Importer and exporter dummies	yes	yes	---	yes	yes
Includes EU-Med. trade	yes	no	yes	yes	yes

Note: Dependent variable, nominal bilateral imports. Regression 3 is estimated with heteroscedasticity consistent error terms *, **, and *** indicates significance at the 10, 5, and 1 percent level, respectively. Time, country, and bilateral effects are not reported.

Source: Author's calculations.

Overview of Mediterranean Countries' Export Performance

In-sample estimates (using equation 5.8) of the most important export potentials and cases of over-exporting are reported for each Mediterranean country in Table 5.2. Export potentials are expressed as a percentage of GDP of the relevant Mediterranean country, unless otherwise indicated. This is a more relevant measure than actual trade as a percentage of predicted trade when it comes to identifying large untapped markets. However, the latter measure would be more appropriate in analyzing the degree of integration among a particular group of countries, since trade potentials in absolute terms are dependent on the size of the countries involved. For this reason, trade will in

Table 5.2 Estimated export potentials (percent of GDP unless otherwise indicated)

	Algeria		Egypt		Jordan		Morocco		Syria		Tunisia	
	Country	%	Country	%	Country	%	Country	%	Country	%	Country	%
EU												
Total export potential[a]		-21.6		-0.1		3.5		4.5		-12.3		-13.8
Unweighted avg.		495.7		169.1		47.7		103.0		276.0		167.4
Non-EU												
Top export potentials												
	Saudi Arabia	0.3	Israel	0.2	Israel	5.0	US	0.9	Iran	0.3	US	0.8
	Australia	0.1	Iran	0.1	US	3.3	Switzerland	0.2	Japan	0.2	Japan	0.2
	Colombia	0.0	China	0.1	Estonia	0.5	Egypt	0.1	US	0.2	Switzerland	0.1
	Malaysia	0.0	Japan	0.1	Canada	0.2	Hong Kong	0.1	China	0.1	Hong Kong	0.1
	Syria	0.0	Switzerland	0.0	Egypt	0.1	Korea	0.1	Korea	0.1	Korea	0.1
Top 5 over-export destinations												
	US	-4.5	India	-0.2	India	-2.6	India	-0.9	UAE	-1.7	Libya	-1.5
	Brazil	-2.4	Saudi Arabia	-0.1	Saudi Arabia	-1.2	Japan	-0.5	Turkey	-1.2	India	-0.5
	Turkey	-1.9	US	-0.1	UAE	-1.2	Mexico	-0.2	Saudi Arabia	-0.8	Turkey	-0.3
	Canada	-1.7	Turkey	-0.1	China	-0.4	Libya	-0.2	Kuwait	-0.4	Algeria	-0.2
	Indonesia	-0.3	Singapore	-0.1	Pakistan	-0.4	New Zealand	-0.2	Algeria	-0.3	Iran	-0.2

Notes: Export potentials are calculated based on average data for 2000–2002.
[a] Actual/predicted exports.

Source: Author's calculations.

some cases also be analyzed as a percentage of predicted trade. Negative export potentials indicate exports beyond model predictions.

For the moment, the EU is presented only as a group. The first row of in Table 5.2 presents the total amount of over- or under-exports to the EU as a share of GDP. This is conceptually different from the second row, which shows the unweighted average of Mediterranean countries' actual to predicted export ratio with each individual EU country. The latter is a more relevant measure of integration with the EU.

Table 5.2 shows most Mediterranean countries' total exports to the EU surpassing model predictions. Jordan is a notable exception, with exports attaining only one half of the benchmark for the EU on average. Egypt's total over-exports to the EU are relatively small despite a high average ratio of actual to predicted exports. This is due to the fact that Egypt tends to over-export to smaller countries while under-exporting to most large EU countries. As we will show below, Egypt has seen a relative decline in its exports to the EU over the 1990s. Algeria and Syria, both predominantly hydrocarbon exporters, over-export significantly to the EU. Morocco exports broadly at par with model predictions, while Tunisia overtrades on average. Trade with the EU will be analyzed more in detail below.

The US figures prominently as a major untapped export market for Jordan, Morocco, Syria, and Tunisia, while Algeria and Egypt over-export to the United States. The apparent weak integration of most Mediterranean countries with the United States is in line with Péridy (2004), who found MENA countries' trade with the United States far below potential, especially in the Maghreb. In the case of Jordan, the estimated trade potential is likely exaggerated since trade with the United States has increased sharply in the last few years of the studied period, which is not taken into account by the in-sample estimates of export potentials in equation 5.8. Given the significant untapped export market in the United States, the recent US–Middle East free trade initiative is encouraging. The initiative involves Egypt, Tunisia, Algeria, Saudi Arabia, Kuwait, Yemen, and Bahrain, all of which have concluded Trade and Investment Framework Agreements (TIFAs) as a first step toward a free trade agreement (FTA) with the United States. Jordan concluded an FTA with the United States in 2002, as the first Middle Eastern country, followed by Morocco in 2004. Other important untapped non-EU markets include Japan and a number of other Asian countries. Regarding countries in the region, Israel unsurprisingly presents a significant untapped market, in particular for Jordan but also for Egypt. Egypt, Israel, and the United States recently signed an agreement allowing certain Egyptian exports with a minimum level of Israeli contents tariff-free entry into the United States. This agreement is expected to significantly increase trade between Egypt and Israel, and support Egyptian textiles exports to the United States. Syria's trade potential vis-à-vis Israel could not be evaluated for lack of data, but is likely to be substantial. On the over-export side, India and Turkey emerge as major trading partners for most Mediterranean countries.

Mediterranean Countries' Integration with the EU

Despite the fact that the EU's trade policies are uniform across member states, Mediterranean countries' export performances vary significantly across the EU. Furthermore, there is no clear pattern regarding which EU countries tend to be more or less integrated with the MENA region. A case in point is the difference between Morocco's and Tunisia's trading patterns, where the former under-exports significantly to France and over-exports to the United Kingdom, while the opposite is true for the latter. Evidently, conventional tariff and nontariff barriers only explain part of the Mediterranean countries' trade performance with the EU. Further analysis is therefore warranted. In this regard, trade composition may matter, and will be analyzed based on disaggregate data from the UN's COMTRADE database. In addition, given the ongoing integration efforts within the Barcelona process, the analysis should include a time dimension. Hence, we calculate out-of-sample estimates of EU-Mediterranean trade potentials, which are allowed to vary over time.

Figure 5.1 suggests that the Mediterranean-EU integration process has yielded mixed results. Tunisia, the first country within the sample to have implemented an AAEU, appears to have benefited on balance. In particular, its export performance to France, Italy, Belgium, and Spain improved substantially during 1991–2002, more than making up for a loss vis-à-vis Germany. In the same period, the United Kingdom changed from Tunisia's largest EU export potential to being in line with model predictions. Morocco, the only other sample country to implement an AAEU within the studied period, has seen a surge in exports vis-à-vis the United Kingdom and Spain, while losing ground with most other EU countries. The latter may to an extent be attributed to repeated droughts, which could have skewed results by suppressing agricultural exports to the EU for reasons unrelated to trade policy. The export performance has been generally favorable for Algeria and, to a lesser extent, Syria. However, it is difficult to attribute this to any integration efforts, in view of the fact that both countries' exports are still completely dominated by oil and gas. Jordan continues to export very little to the EU (a total of just over $170 million in 2002 according to the IMF's *Direction of Trade Statistics, DOTS.*) Meanwhile Egypt has clearly become less integrated with the EU during the 1990s.

While the difference in export performance to the EU could be partly explained by varying degrees of commitment to the Barcelona process, it is also likely that the economic structure matters. Table 5.3 exposes stark differences in the Mediterranean countries' export composition. Commodities play a less central role in Morocco and Tunisia, whose exports are concentrated in reasonably high value-added manufacturing. Electronics have emerged as a major export category in both countries, attaining around 15 percent of total exports in 2002 in both cases. However, it is textiles that stick out as a major determinant of Tunisia's and Morocco's export performance to the EU. As Figure 5.2 shows, both countries' textiles trade is characterized by substantial

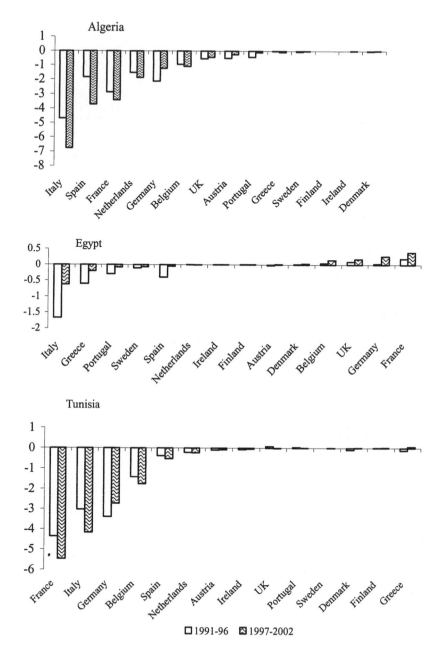

Figure 5.1 Export potentials to the EU (percent of GDP)

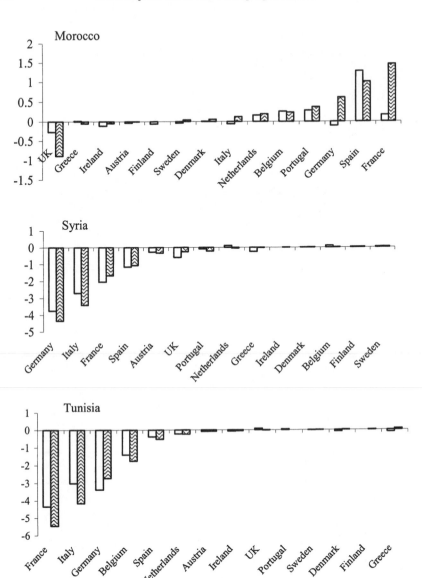

Note: Negative export potentials indicate exports beyond model predictions.

Source: Author's calculations.

Figure 5.1 (continued)

Table 5.3 Composition of Mediterranean countries' exports to the EU

| | Sector | Share of commodity exports (percent) | | export growth (% of total growth) |
		1995	2002	1995-2002
Net oil exporters				
Algeria	Hydrocarbons	96	97	98
	Other	4	3	2
Syria	Hydrocarbons	–	93	–
	Other	–	7	–
Net oil importers				
Egypt, Arab Rep.	Hydrocarbons	37	39	-21
	Textiles	27	16	-117
	Metal goods	15	15	-10
	Agriculture	9	8	-21
	Cotton	4	7	21
	Other	8	16	48
Jordan	Salts	56	43	-104
	Pharmaceuticals	1	22	81
	Metal goods	0	9	33
	Textiles	12	7	-30
	Agriculture	14	6	-46
	Other	17	12	-34
Morocco	Textiles	31	40	50
	Agriculture	32	20	7
	Electronics	3	17	32
	Fertilizer	9	3	-4
	Chemicals	5	3	2
	Footwear	2	3	5
	Other	19	14	8
Tunisia	Textiles	50	50	52
	Electronics	9	15	34
	Hydrocarbons	10	10	8
	Footwear	5	6	11
	Fertilizer	5	3	-3
	Agriculture	4	3	2
	Other	18	12	-3
Memorandum items				
:hed goods as share of textile exports (%)				
Egypt		22	30	
Jordan		61	95	
Morocco		86	94	
Tunisia		95	93	

Note: The signs on contributions to export growth are inverted for Egypt and Jordan, since COMTRADE shows a decline in exports to the EU by these countries between 1995 and 2002.

Source: COMTRADE and author's calculations.

imports of intermediate goods from a few countries and export of finished goods to those same countries. This suggests that outsourcing and/or intra-firm trade has played an important role in explaining Morocco's and Tunisia's trade performance. This type of intra-firm trade is particularly pronounced in Tunisia's trade with France, Italy, Germany, and Belgium, which also are the countries to which Tunisia over-exports by far the most. Similarly, Morocco's improved export performance to the United Kingdom and Spain reflects a sharp increase in intra-textiles trade: exports of finished textile goods to the United Kingdom and Spain were multiplied by 18 and 26 respectively in nominal terms between 1995 and 2002. However, although France is Morocco's largest trading partner in textiles, it is also the most underexploited export market. This is not as contradictory as it may seem, in light of the fact that Morocco's textiles exports to France are still lower than Tunisia's despite the latter country's much smaller size. The dominant role of intra-firm trade is important; Berthélemy (2005) shows that international fragmentation of production is an important determinant of increased economic diversification.

The central role of textiles for Tunisia's and Morocco's exports is a cause of concern for the medium term, given the recent expiration of the Multifiber Agreement (MFA), which will inevitably expose the sector to increasing competition, especially from China.[15] At the same time, the importance of intra-textiles sector trade points to the existence of well-established ties with a number of EU countries, possibly including direct ownership of Tunisian and Moroccan textiles firms. Such ties are unlikely to unravel overnight, giving these countries additional time to adjust.

The question remains why Morocco's and Tunisia's geographical pattern of integration with the EU is so different. Migration comes to mind as a potentially important factor that could facilitate the formation of business networks and other ties likely to enhance trade. Migration could not be included in the model due to data limitations but descriptive data could provide a basis for qualitative evidence. Tunisia's largest 'over-traders' in the EU also tend to be the countries with the largest Tunisian immigrant population, although in Morocco's case, the correlation is less clear. Further research could be useful in this area. It may also be interesting to analyze bilateral foreign direct investment patterns, to determine to what extent these may influence bilateral trade flows.[16]

Egypt's trade pattern with the EU is entirely different from Morocco's and Tunisia's. Overall, Egypt's current export composition appears less susceptible to trade creation with the EU than that of Morocco and Tunisia. Although Egypt is a slight net oil importer, hydrocarbons still represents a major share of exports. Egypt's textiles exports to the EU have fallen dramatically since the mid-1990s and manufactured goods are in relatively low value-added sectors, such as metal goods.

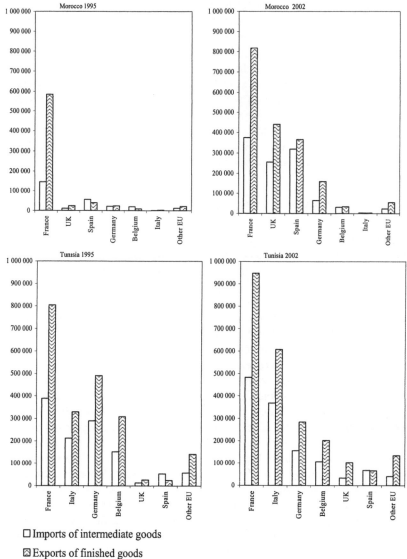

☐ Imports of intermediate goods

◪ Exports of finished goods

Sources: COMTRADE, author's calculations.

Figure 5.2 Morocco and Tunisia: Textiles trade with the EU ($US thousands)

None of the intra-textile sector trade described above is evident in Egypt. In fact, Egypt's textiles exports to the EU are predominantly intermediate inputs, in addition to raw cotton. About three-quarters of textile exports to the EU are directed to Italy, France, Germany, and the United Kingdom, i.e. the same countries that export intermediate textile inputs to Tunisia and Morocco. Although the data do not permit tracing the exact flows of commodities, one might speculate that hub-and-spoke effects are present. A possible example would be a European firm which imports intermediate inputs from Egypt, provides a design, and outsources to Tunisian and Moroccan firms for assembly of the final product, rather than locating the entire production chain within Mediterranean countries. However, the scope of such hub-and-spoke effects is likely limited by virtue of the fact that Egyptian textile exports to the EU are relatively small (some $200 million in 2002, compared with a combined $2.5 billion imports of intermediate textile goods by Tunisia and Morocco).

CONCLUSIONS AND DISCUSSION

The preceding analysis points to the existence of significant untapped export markets for the Mediterranean countries, both within and outside the EU. The United States emerges as possibly the most important untapped market. In this regard, Algeria and Egypt are exceptions, since they both over-export to the United States. In any case, the success of recent integration efforts with the United States, including Jordan's and Morocco's free trade agreements, could prove crucial for Mediterranean countries' future trade performance.

Mediterranean integration efforts with the EU have yielded mixed results. Algeria and Syria both over-export to the EU, but given the still-complete dominance of oil and gas exports, this can hardly be attributed to trade policy. In fact, the lack of growth in nontraditional exports from these countries suggests considerable scope for further integration. Meanwhile, Jordan's exports to the EU remain far below model predictions, and Egypt has seen its degree of integration with the EU fall significantly over the past decade. Morocco's exports to the EU are broadly at par with predicted levels, while, on average, Tunisia over-exports to the EU. Nevertheless, although the impact of the Barcelona process since its inception in the mid-1990s seems to have been modest in general, it appears to have had a significant effect in individual cases. This is most clearly observed for Tunisia, which has significantly improved its export performance vis-à-vis France, Italy, Belgium, and Spain. Similarly, Morocco's export record to the United Kingdom and Spain has improved substantially since the beginning of the Barcelona process.

This outcome is not entirely surprising. Only Tunisia and (later) Morocco implemented AAEUs during the period under study, which likely explains their relative progress in integration with the EU. However, it does not explain the wide difference in the two countries' trade performance among EU countries. A plausible explanation for this disparity is that a reduction in trade barriers first induces trade with countries where networks have already been established, and hence a certain amount of fixed costs have already been covered. This explanation appears particularly relevant for Tunisia, where trade has expanded most with countries with which intra-textile trade relations had already been established before the trade liberalization began. Nevertheless, Morocco's experience shows that it is feasible to also build new trade relations to increase exports.

Substantial export potentials remain within the EU for all countries except Algeria and Syria, and only small potentials remain for Tunisia. For Algeria and Syria, the near-to-medium-term challenge has less to do with trade patterns than with diversifying their export bases. As long as virtually all exports consist of oil and gas, trade policy can only do so much to increase exports. More important seems to be broad-based structural reforms – including trade liberalization – aimed at improving overall productivity and flexibility, thereby providing an environment conducive to private business initiatives. Jordan, in contrast, under-exports to virtually all EU countries, suggesting the importance of stepped-up integration efforts across the board. The other Mediterranean countries could benefit from targeting selected EU countries: Morocco could significantly increase its exports by targeting France and Germany. The results also suggest that Morocco's increasing integration with Spain is appropriate given its significant remaining export potential to that country. Egypt could make gains by targeting France, Germany, and the United Kingdom.

Morocco's and Tunisia's experiences suggest that the Barcelona process and the AAEUs have not created any serious distortions, in view of the fact that both countries over-export to a large number of non-EU countries while under-exporting to several EU countries (about one-third for Tunisia, most for Morocco). In Tunisia's case, however, there are signs that its focus on the EU is beginning to reach its limits, and recent efforts to liberalize trade on a multilateral basis are thus welcome. In both countries, market diversification and product diversification will likely become increasingly important as the full effects of the elimination of the MFA are felt.

NOTES

The views expressed in this chapter are those of the author and should not be interpreted as those of the International Monetary Fund.

1. Tunisia signed the AAEU in 1995 and began implementing its provisions in 1996, i.e. two years ahead of ratification by all parties.
2. $\beta_i^{(1-\sigma)/\sigma}$ can be interpreted as the number of goods within the bundle produced by country i.
3. It is also possible to explicitly account for the price indices as in Anderson and van Wincoop (2003). However, the procedure is rather involved, since the Πs and Ps are unobservable, and σ is unknown.
4. Under the assumption of symmetric trade costs, the gravity equation becomes

$$x_{ij} = \frac{y_i y_j}{y_w} \left(\frac{t_{ij}}{P_i P_j} \right)^{(1-\sigma)}$$ in which case only one dummy per country is needed, since the relevant

index is assumed to be the same whether the country imports or exports.

5. In addition to separate importer and exporter dummies and asymmetric bilateral fixed effects, they also include importer and exporter dummies interacted with a time trend in their preferred model.
6. Ideally, in a panel setting, trade and income should be measured in real terms but bilateral trade deflators are not available.
7. Moreover, trade in the model would refer to all trade while bilateral trade data include trade in goods only.
8. Note that asymmetry allows $\eta_{ij} \neq \eta_{ji}$.
9. Rose and van Wincoop (2001) also use only international trade in a gravity equation based on the same Anderson and van Wincoop model as in this chapter.
10. The ratio of international trade costs to intra-national trade costs could provide a measure of a country's level of global trade integration. However, this is beyond the scope of this study, which excludes intra-national trade for reasons mentioned above.
11. In this context, supply constraints are not considered as binding, an assumption that appears plausible in view of the high unemployment rates in conjunction with the fact that the countries in question have access to international capital markets and/or have high levels of reserves. One caveat, however, concerns the supply of specialized skilled labor: as trade becomes more diversified, the labor force's skill set will also need to be increasingly diversified.
12. Such general equilibrium effects turned out to be substantial in Anderson and van Wincoop (2003), but they simulated the impact of a total elimination of borders between the United States, Canada, and other member countries of the Organization for Economic Cooperation and Development (OECD).
13. The equivalent regression excluding EU–Mediterranean trade (unreported) is used for out-of-sample estimates in Annex Figure 5A.1. Basing the calculations on regression 4 instead of regression 5 produces very similar results
14. Similarly, Helpman, Melitz, and Rubinstein (2004) argue that there may be an additional source of bias, deriving from a firm-level selection process determining whether or not to enter a given export market. Preliminary results from the two-step Heckman procedure (unreported), which corrects for this type of sample selection bias, generally yield trade potentials of larger magnitudes, while the pattern and the overall story do not change.
15. Until January 1, 2005, the MFA gave several MENA and other countries' textile exports preferential access to the EU.
16. One may also speculate that Tunisia's overtrade with France and Italy may be exaggerated at the expense of other countries, since some exports to these countries may subsequently be distributed to other countries in the EU. However, this explanation appears less convincing in view of the fact that Tunisia also overtrades significantly with Germany and Belgium, while Morocco overtrades with the UK and undertrades with France and Spain.

REFERENCES

Anderson, J.E. (1979), 'A Theoretical Foundation for the Gravity Equation', *American Economic Review*, **69**, (1) 106–16.

Anderson, J.E. and E. van Wincoop (2003), 'Gravity with Gravitas: A Solution to the Border Puzzle', *American Economic Review*, **93** (1), 170–92.

Baltagi, B., P. Egger and M. Pfaffermayr (2003), 'A generalized design for bilateral trade flow models', *Economic Letters*, **80** (3), 391–97.

Berthélemy, J.-C., (2005), 'Commerce International et Diversification Economique', *Revue d'Economie Politique*, **115** (5), 591–612.

Berthélemy, J.-C. and L. Söderling (2001), 'The Role of Capital Accumulation, Adjustment and Structural Change for Economic Take-off: Empirical Evidence from African Growth Episodes', *World Development*, **29** (2) 323–43.

Coe, D.A. Subramanian and N. Tamirisa (2004), 'The Missing Globalization Puzzle', unpublished, International Monetary Fund.

Coe, D. and A. Hoffmaister (1998), 'North-South Trade: Is Africa Unusual?', IMF Working Paper 98/94, Washington: International Monetary Fund.

Egger, P. (2002), 'An Econometric View on the Estimation of Gravity Models and the Calculation of Trade Potentials,' *World Economy*, **25** (2), 297–312.

Feenstra, R.C., D. Madani, T.-H. Yang and C.-Y. Liang (1999), 'Testing Endogenous Growth in South Korea and Taiwan', *Journal of Development Economics*, **60** (2), 317–41.

Hausman, J. and W. Taylor (1981), 'Panel Data and Unobservable Individual Effects', *Econometrica*, **49** (6), 1377–98.

Helpman, E., M. Melitz and Y. Rubinstein (2004), 'Trading Partners and Trading Volumes', available on the web at http://post.economics.harvard.edu/faculty/helpman/papers.html.

Péridy, N. (2004), 'The New U.S. Trans-Ocean Free Trade Initiatives: Estimating Export and FDI Potentials from Two Dynamic Panel data Models', paper presented at European Trade Study Group Conference, September 2004, University of Nottingham, UK.

Rose, A. and E. van Wincoop (2001), 'National Money as a Barrier to International Trade: The Real Case for Currency Union', *American Economic Review*, **91** (2), 386–90.

Wang, Z.K. and A. Winters (1992), 'The Trading Potential of Eastern Europe', *Journal of Economic Integration*, **7** (2), 113–36.

ANNEX 5

Estimated Trade Potentials and Export Potentials to the European Union

The following results are obtained using Regression 5 in Table 5.1. They should be compared to the results in Table 5.2 and Figure 5.1.

Table 5A.1 Estimated export potentials (percent of GDP unless otherwise indicated)

	Algeria		Egypt		Jordan		Morocco		Syria		Tunisia	
	Country	%	Country	%	Country	%	Country	%	Country	%	Country	%
EU												
Total export potential		-15.4		-0.5		4.7		3.9		-11.9		-8.0
Actual/predicted exports												
Unweighted average		187.8		155.3		34.8		85.1		231.7		107.6
Non-EU												
Top 5 export potentials												
	Egypt	0.2	Israel	0.2	Israel	11.2	US	1.1	US	0.2	US	1.2
	India	0.2	China	0.1	US	5.0	Switzerland	0.3	Japan	0.2	Japan	0.3
	China	0.1	Switzerland	0.0	Egypt	0.6	Egypt	0.1	Iran	0.2	Switzerland	0.2
	Saudi Arabia	0.1	Japan	0.0	Canada	0.2	Hong Kong	0.1	China	0.1	Canada	0.1
	Australia	0.1	Canada	0.0	Turkey	0.2	Korea	0.1	Norway	0.1	Czech Rep	0.0
Top 5 over-export destinations												
	US	-3.9	US	-0.3	India	-2.5	India	-0.9	UAE	-1.5	Libya	-1.4
	Brazil	-2.3	India	-0.2	UAE	-1.1	Japan	-0.5	Turkey	-1.0	India	-0.4
	Turkey	-1.7	Korea	-0.1	Saudi Arabia	-0.9	Libya	-0.2	Saudi Arabia	-0.7	Turkey	-0.2
	Canada	-1.5	Saudi Arabia	-0.1	China	-0.4	New Zealand	-0.2	Kuwait	-0.3	Iran	-0.1
	Korea	-0.1	Singapore	-0.1	Pakistan	-0.4	Mexico	-0.2	Algeria	-0.3	Algeria	-0.1

Note: Export potentials are calculated based on average data for 2000–2002.

Source: Author's calculations.

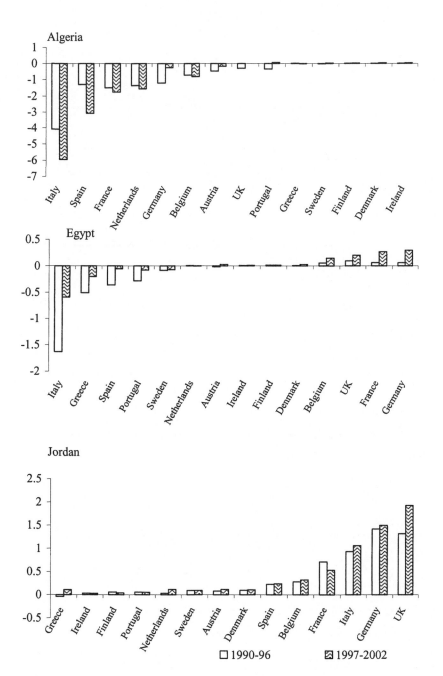

Figure 5A.1 Export potentials to the EU (percent of GDP)

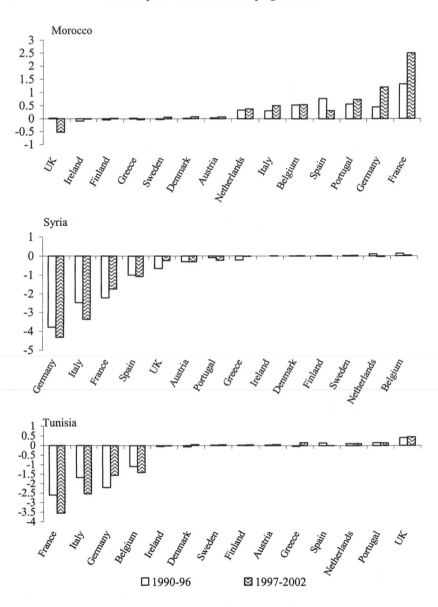

Note: Negative export potentials indicate exports beyond model predictions.

Source: Author's calculations.

Figure 5A.1 (continued)

Data

The database covers 93 countries (see Table 5A.2 below) over the period 1990–2002 (unbalanced panel).

Table 5A.2 Variable definitions

Variable	Definition	Source
Bilateral trade	Bilateral imports in current US dollars	IMF: Direction of Trade Statistics
Economic mass	Product of importer and exporter country GDP in current US dollars	IMF: World Economic Outlook database
Distance	Geographical distance between the importer and exporter country	Andrew Rose, 2002, 'Do We Really Know that the WTO Increases Trade?', NBER Working Paper 9273. Database available on A. Rose's website at http://faculty.haas.berkeley.edu/arose/
Common language	Dummy equal to 1 if the the importer and exporter country share a common language, zero otherwise	Rose (2002)
Adjacent	Dummy equal to 1 if the the importer and exporter country share a border, zero otherwise	Rose (2002)
Landlocked	Number of landlocked countries in the country pair, i.e. 0, 1, or 2.	Rose (2002)
Primary exporter	Dummy equal to 1 if the exporter country exports mainly primary commodities, zero otherwise.	Coe and Hoffmaister, 1998. See Table 5A.3.
Commodity price	Price index for fuel and non-fuel commodities	IMF: Global Data Source for 1992–2002, extended backward to 1990/91 using the change in the price of crude oil (dated Brent, source: IMF's Commodity Price System)
Colony	Dummy equal to 1 is either trading partner ever colonized the other, zero otherwise	Rose (2002)

Table 5A.3 Country coverage and exporters of primary commodities

Country	Primary exporter	Country	Primary exporter
Algeria	Yes	Korea	No
Argentina	No	Kuwait	Yes
Armenia	Yes	Latvia	No
Australia	No	Libya	No
Austria	No	Lithuania	No

Table 5A.3 (continued)

Country	Primary exporter	Country	Primary exporter
Bahrain	Yes	Malawi	Yes
Bangladesh	No	Malaysia	No
Belgium	No	Mauritania	Yes
Benin	No	Mauritius	No
Bolivia	Yes	Mexico	No
Brazil	No	Morocco	No
Bulgaria	No	Netherlands	No
Cameroon	No	New Zealand	No
Canada	No	Nigeria	Yes
Chile	Yes	Norway	No
China	No	Oman	Yes
Colombia	No	Pakistan	No
Costa Rica	No	Panama	No
Côte d'Ivoire	Yes	Paraguay	No
Czech Rep.	No	Peru	No
Denmark	No	Philippines	No
Ecuador	No	Poland	No
Egypt	No	Portugal	No
El Salvador	No	Qatar	Yes
Estonia	No	Russia	Yes
Ethiopia	Yes	Saudi Arabia	Yes
Finland	No	Senegal	No
France	No	Singapore	No
Georgia	Yes	Slovenia	No
Germany	No	South Africa	No
Ghana	Yes	Spain	No
Greece	No	Sudan	Yes
Guatemala	No	Sweden	No
Guinea	Yes	Switzerland	No
Honduras	Yes	Syria	Yes
Hong Kong	No	Tanzania	Yes
Hungary	No	Thailand	No
India	No	Tunisia	No
Indonesia	No	Turkey	No
Iran	Yes	UAE	Yes
Ireland	No	Uganda	Yes
Israel	No	UK	No
Italy	No	Uruguay	No
Japan	No	US	No
Jordan	No	Venezuela	Yes
Kazakhstan	Yes	Zambia	Yes
Kenya	No		

6.   The EU and South Africa: Trade and Diversification

Lennart Petersson

INTRODUCTION

A foreign policy challenge faced by South Africa after its transition to democracy was the formalisation of its relationship with its largest trading partner, the European Union (EU). The EU played a leading role in trying to reverse apartheid and was therefore committed to supporting the democratisation process in South Africa. In 1994, the EU Council of Ministers lifted all remaining sanctions and adopted the 'package of immediate measures' to facilitate South Africa's reintegration into the global economy and to contribute to the country's reconstruction and development. The package included the extension of the Generalised System of Preferences (GSP) for industrial products and a number of development and technical support measures.

In October 1994, South Africa formally accepted the EU invitation to engage in negotiations. In October 1999, after five years of negotiations, the European Union (EU) and the Republic of South Africa ratified the Trade, Development and Cooperation Agreement (TDCA), which has been partially applied since 1 January 2000. The agreement has two components, the more prominent relating to the creation, after a transitional period, of a Free Trade Area (FTA) between the EU and South Africa (EU-SA FTA). Cooperation agreements and substantial financial assistance constitute the second component.

This chapter will focus on the structural dynamics of South Africa's exports to the EU market and the role of inter- and intra-industry specialisation in expanding product groups. The main issue is whether trade liberalisation has produced a sustainable export growth and diversification into non-traditional products or been limited to an increase in traditional exports.

The chapter is organised as follows: first, the EU-SA FTA agreement and South Africa's trade policy are described and arguments in favour of export diversification are discussed. Then, the structural dynamics and specialisation of South Africa's trade with the EU since the early 1990s are analysed according to the factor intensity of different commodity groups. Cumulative export experience functions are used to separate trade into traditional and non-traditional accelerating export industries from those of moderate export growth. The next section analyses the role of intra-industry and marginal intra-industry specialisation and trade and quality differentiation in the process of export diversification. The last section concludes and summarises the chapter.

THE EU-SA FREE TRADE AREA AGREEMENT

Initially, the new South African government sought admission to the Lomé Convention, based on non-reciprocal trade concessions. With respect to trade, the outcome of this agreement between the EU and the African, Caribbean and Pacific (ACP) countries led, however, to some dissatisfaction. Trade preferences granted for decades seemed to have done little to help expand and diversify ACP exports and turned out to be WTO-incompatible. The Cotonou Agreement, signed in 2000, introduced major changes with preferential market access commitments to be made on the basis of reciprocity as part of a comprehensive package of trade-related measures and EU assistance. The terms are to be negotiated in the context of so-called Economic Partnership Agreements that are to be concluded by 1 January 2008. In this regard, the outcome of the negotiations between the EU and South Africa, as a possible model for other development agreements, has become of prime interest in the wider perspective of the relationship between the EU and the ACP countries (Davis 2000: 6, Lee 2002: 86).

The negotiation process for the new trade partnership started officially in June 1995. In its negotiation directives the EU proposed a so-called 'twin-track approach' including qualified membership of the Lomé Convention and negotiations for a bilateral FTA agreement (Eurostep 2000a: 8). In April 1997 South Africa became the 71st member of the Lomé Convention on a qualified basis, limited to political participation in the institutions of the Convention and eligibility for tenders for projects in the ACP countries (Europstep 2000b: 6, Lee 2002: 87). The EU-SA bilateral Trade, Development and Cooperation Agreement could only be finalised in March 1999, after four years and 24 successive rounds of negotiations (Lowe 2000: 39).

At the end of a 10-year transitional period, the EU will fully liberalise 95 percent of the current value of South African exports entering the EU. South Africa, on its part, will completely open up its market for 86 percent of the current value of total EU exports entering South Africa at the end of a 12-year period. Although the agreement stipulates asymmetry in favour of South Africa with regard to the timetable and final volume of trade in industrial products covered by the agreement, South Africa is likely to carry the greater burden (Eurostep 2000b: 7–8). It will have to remove a higher level of tariffs on a greater volume of mutual trade than the EU (Goodison 1999: 33). Besides, the EU accounts for a far greater volume of total South African imports (40 percent) than South Africa does for the EU's total imports, excluding intra-EU trade (1.4 percent).

Table 6.1 Percentage of zero duty imports from other party, in current trade 2000 and by end of transitional period

	Duty-free at entry into force			By end of transitional period		
	Agr.	Industry	Total	Agr.	Industry	Total
South Africa	34	62	60	81	86	86
European Union	21	86	75	62	100	95

Source: Eurostep (2000a), Eurostep (2000b), Lee (2002).

By the end of the 10-year transitional period, the EU will have gradually increased duty-free access for South African industrial goods from 86 percent to 100 percent (apart from six aluminium products). In general the tariff level is low on industrial products entering the EU market, in particular for those developing countries that have been granted GSP. In terms of the WTO charter South Africa was not really entitled to GSP but was granted GSP status for industrial products by special arrangement with the EU in 1994 (Volz 2001: 80). The lion's share of South Africa's non-agricultural exports was already entering the EU market duty-free as early as 1994, and the GSP preferences currently enjoyed will be locked in and extended by the FTA agreement. No fewer than 90–100 percent of the product lines of important industries such as iron and steel basic industries, machinery, electrical machinery, chemicals and motor vehicles and motor vehicles parts were granted GSP (IDC 1998). By the end of South Africa's 12-year liberalisation period, duty-free access for European industrial products will have increased gradually from the current 62 percent to 86 percent. Three percent will receive partial liberalisation (clothing and textiles) and products representing 11 percent of total imports from the EU are on the 'reserve list', i.e. have been kept outside the ambit of the free trade agreement but the products will periodically be reviewed (Partner in Progress 2003: 9).

The outcome of the negotiations in the agricultural sector was constrained by the EU's Common Agricultural Policy (Links 2000: 34, Lowe 2000: 42). The EU will increase duty-free access from the current 21 percent in value of total South African exports of agricultural products entering the EU to 62 percent. On South Africa's part, the agreement provided for a faster and higher level of duty-free access for European agricultural products, rising from a current value of 34 percent of total exports entering South Africa duty-free to 81 percent by the end of the 12-year period. Nineteen percent will remain on the 'reserve list', and many of these products, currently excluded but subject to review, are regionally sensitive for exporters in Southern African Development Community (SADC) countries (such as beef, sugar and cereal products).

Trade Policy Reforms in South Africa

After transition to democracy, trade policy reforms were introduced with the principal aim of improving the growth performance of the manufacturing sector, making the sector internationally competitive and generating a process of export diversification (Bell 1997: 80, Joffe et al., McCarthy 1998: 83). The signing of the WTO Agreement in April 1994 was the start of a major shift in trade and industrial policy with commitment to a drastic simplification of the tariff structure, reduction in tariff protection and the phasing out of the selected system of export incentives (McCarthy 1998: 70). The new macroeconomic strategy of 1996, the Growth, Employment and Redistribution Strategy (GEAR), another important step in the evolving new trade and industrial policy, rested heavily upon the assumption that manufacturing exports and private investments would accelerate growth and boost employment (Department of Finance 1996).

Trade liberalisation accelerated and became a sustained process when the country bound its reform program to the WTO. Most current imports are tariff-free, with the most extensive tariff liberalisation occurring in the manufacturing sector (Draper 2003: 15–16). South Africa has also made significant moves towards strengthening bilateral ties with its main trading partners. The government has negotiated two free trade areas to date, the one with the EU and another with 10 of the 14 members of the SADC. Besides, a number of 'strategic partnerships' are being considered with the aim of gaining improved market access opportunities and, as in the case of the US, to lock in preference levels currently being enjoyed (ibid.: 29–30).

EXPORT DIVERSIFICATION AND DEVELOPMENT

A recurrent issue of trade and development is that a high concentration of exports of primary products and resource-based commodities may have negative effects on a country's growth prospects (Bonaglia and Fukasaku 2003: 8–11). On the demand side, the argument is based on the notions of low growth in world demand for primary products, and that volatile prices of these products result in instability of export revenue. This makes economic planning difficult and reduces investment by risk-adverse producers. Besides, a boom in the primary sector may cause real exchange rate overvaluation, thereby worsening the international competitiveness of manufacturing production. On the supply side, low opportunities for skill and technical improvements in production and difficulties in establishing linkages with the rest of the economy may hamper growth. Other arguments are that the concentration of exports in a few resource-based activities increases unproductive rent-seeking activities. This may have negative effects on human capital developments and contribute to wage inequality.

A process of export diversification is often related to different phases in a country's trade policy and economic development (Bruton 1989: 1604–16, Imbs and Wacziarg 2003: 63). In a first stage of import substitution, economic activity is spread more equally across sectors, where production patterns respond to domestic demand. The argument rests on the assumption that a period of protection is needed for an 'infant economy' to develop the capacity to transform resources into a wide range of products. In the next phase, characterised by trade liberalisation, diversification of production may eventually lead to new export sectors. Finally, in a U-shaped development, economic activity may start to concentrate again in those sectors that benefit from comparative advantage.

In traditional trade theory, where trade structure is determined by cross-country differences in factor endowments and technology, export diversification is based on more efficient use of available endowments, by shifting production to commodities with a positive price trend and adding value to commodities through additional processing. Modern theories emphasise increasing returns to scale that may be either external to the firm or internal. In trade and geography theory, comparative advantages become endogenous, and export diversification into new export sectors may generate positive externalities for the rest of the economy, gained from dynamic learning-by-doing and learning-by-exporting, and fostered by competition in world markets. These externalities are usually limited in sector and geographical scope, which eventually may create a new phase of sector specialisation. Because strong externalities are largely confined to the manufacturing sector, this is used as an argument for diversification out of primary into manufacturing exports.

In the final stage of diversification, specialisation may also take place within sectors, leading to productivity gains through the exploitation of internal economies of scale, and to exports and imports of similar goods: intra-industry trade (IIT). Access to a larger market permits firms to increase plant size and/or engage in more plant specialisation, resulting in longer production runs and reduced unit costs. In a process of structural rationalisation at industry level, this leads to intra-industry specialisation, generating export diversity.

TRADE STRUCTURE AND SPECIALISATION

We use two data sets, classified according to the Standard International Trade Classification (SITC) in the analyses of South Africa's trade with the EU. Customs and Excise South Africa (SARS 2004) collected the first one with yearly data from 1990 to 2003. This is complemented by statistics from the OECD International Trade by Commodity Database, from which we borrow 'mirror' data for South Africa's exports of 'Non-monetary gold' to the EU countries for the period 1990–1995, and unit prices of exports and imports not reported in the South African database. Estimates of trade development are based on two- or three-year averages in order to limit the distortion arising from volatile trade flows.

In the analysis of South Africa's comparative advantages we apply a reclassification of trade data from the SITC two-digit level to a set of 10 industrial clusters proposed by Leamer, as shown in the appendix (1984: chapter 3). The clusters consist of two primary product aggregates (petroleum and primary products); four crops (forest products, tropical agricultural products, animal products and cereals); and four manufactured aggregates (labour intensive, capital intensive, machinery and chemicals). A distinguishing feature of each commodity group is that the clusters based on the correlation of net exports of manufactures conform well to clusters based on capital intensities and skill ratios. The extreme groups are the labour-intensive products, which use mainly unskilled labour and 'Chemicals' with high capital intensities and high skill requirements, while capital-intensive products and machinery have moderate levels of capital intensities and skill requirements. In addition to these 10 commodity groups, we add 'Non-monetary gold' as a separate commodity in the analyses.

For a decade after 1992, trade openness increased continuously with merchandise exports increasing from 20 to around 33 percent of GDP in 2002 (SARB 1997: S-78, S-100, SARB 2005: S-87, S-112). In addition to trade liberalisation, this growth was driven by surplus production capacity in the early 1990s combined with the ending of sanctions and depreciating exchange rate (Edwards and Schoer 2002, IMF 2005: 539). Thereafter, exports stagnated and declined in relative terms to around 23 percent of GDP in 2003 and 2004, largely explained by the significant appreciation of the rand by about 60 percent (IMF 2005: 539).

The EU is by far the biggest trading partner, and South Africa is the EU's largest trading partner in Sub-Saharan Africa. Since the early 1990s, three-year moving averages of the EU in South Africa's total world exports have been stable in the range 37–39 percent. Import shares of the EU in total imports have ranged from 41 to 45 percent. A few countries dominate EU trade with South Africa. In 2002/03, the United Kingdom, Germany, Italy and the Netherlands accounted for around 70 percent of the exports and imports.

Trade Structure and Comparative Advantages

Table 6.2 shows the distribution of South Africa's net exports to the world and to the EU across the 10 commodity groups proposed by Leamer, and non-monetary gold as the share of each commodity group in total inter-industry trade, $(X_i - M_i)/\sum_i |X_i - M_i|$, where X_i and M_i are the values of the exports and imports of commodity groups. The shares are interpreted as measures of comparative advantages according to factor intensities (De Ferranti et al. 2001: 20–23).

Since 1992/93, South Africa has been a net exporter of raw materials, crops and non-monetary gold in world trade and in trade with the EU. From 1992/93 to 2002/03 net export shares of these products in total inter-industry trade declined from about 47 to 39 percent in world trade and from 60 percent to around 33 percent in trade with the EU. The aggregates of labour- and capital-intensive products show net export values in world trade and shift from net imports to net exports in the trade with the EU. The main net import sectors are the clusters of machinery, chemicals and petroleum products.

Table 6.2 Distribution of South Africa's inter-industry trade in trade with the world and the EU (percent of total inter-industry trade)

Product groups[a]	World			EU		
	92/93	95/96	02/03	92/93	95/96	02/03
1. Petroleum products	-0.1	-6.5	-8.7	0.0	-0.6	-0.6
2. Raw materials	14.6	15.3	16.4	11.8	11.2	17.9
3. Forest products	1.2	1.6	2.1	-0.1	-0.1	0.3
4. Tropical agriculture	3.2	3.4	5.2	4.5	3.8	5.9
5. Animal products	0.9	0.3	1.3	1.2	0.9	2.2
6. Cereals etc	-2.3	-1.3	-1.3	-0.1	-0.2	0.0
7. Labour-intensive	7.1	5.3	3.1	-0.4	9.1	6.6
8. Capital-intensive	4.8	4.8	8.1	-1.3	-0.7	3.4
9. Machinery	-29.5	-36.7	-33.9	-28.0	-43.1	-44.3
10. Chemicals	-4.6	-3.9	-4.0	-9.6	-10.1	-11.6
11. Gold, non-monetary	29.9	20.6	15.7	42.9	20.2	7.2
12. Not classified	1.8	0.1	0.0	0.0	-0.1	0.0

Note: a The components of Leamer's 10 commodity clusters are found in the appendix.

Source: Compiled from statistics of SARS (2004) and Source OECD (2005).

The net export indicator reveals that South Africa has a comparative advantage in land and resource-based products, and that the country has maintained or developed a comparative advantage in labour and capital-intensive products over the decade. The country's strong disadvantage in sectors with high capital-intensity and moderate/high skill requirements ('Chemicals' and 'Machinery') prevails. The most striking change in South Africa's structure and destination of exports in the 1990s is the declining importance of non-monetary gold in world net exports, in particular in trade with the EU.

Export Diversification

In order to examine the recent trends in export revenue concentration we apply the Herfindahl index to South Africa's export flows to the EU between 1990 and 2003. Let E_{it} represent exports by South African industry i, and $s_{it} = E_{it} \Big/ \sum_i E_{it}$ the share of industry i's exports in total exports in year t. The static measure of specialisation, SPEC, is calculated as follows:

$$SPEC_t = \sum_i \left(s_{it}\right)^2 \tag{6.1}$$

A value of the index approaching one implies a high degree of export concentration while a value approaching 0 implies a high degree of export diversification. Figure 6.1 shows the behaviour of four calculated South African specialisation indices from 1990 to 2003, namely specialisation of South Africa's total exports to the EU and non-EU countries and exports to the EU divided up into the two aggregates of 'Manufacturing' (138 industries) and 'Primary, crops and gold' (96 industries).

In total trade to the EU and in the aggregate of 'Primary products, crops and gold', a high and increasing share of non-monetary gold in exports to the EU explains the increasing degree of specialisation prior to 1994. Then, in 1994, South Africa's gold exports to the EU were almost halved, resulting in a drastic fall in the specialisation indices of 'Primary products, crops and gold' and in total exports to the EU. Since then, the proportion of gold in total exports to the EU has continued to decline, contributing to declining concentration of export revenue, while exports of 'primary and crops' have been relatively stable.

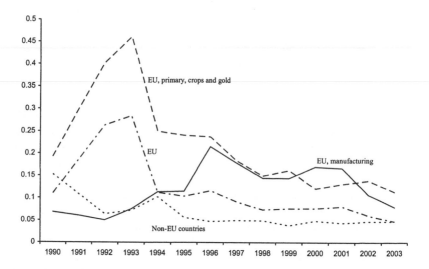

Source: See Table 6.2.

Figure 6.1 Specialisation indices of South Africa's exports 1990–2003

The index for South Africa's manufacturing exports to the EU shows a significant increased specialisation between 1992 and 1996. Trade liberalisation and the removal of sanctions resulted in a very uneven export development across industries, some experiencing a very high export growth while exports in other industries stagnated. In revenue terms, export expansion from 1992 to 1996 was dominated by the labour-intensive commodity group of 'Pearls, precious and semi-precious stones' increasing its share in total trade to the EU from 2.4 to 19.8 percent, and the export share of the EU in South Africa's world exports of these products increased from 13 percent to 74 percent. This is the main explanation for the large difference in the development of export concentration between the EU and Non-EU countries between 1992 and 1996. Thereafter, we find a weak trend of declining export concentration. Total exports to the EU show a higher degree of concentration than exports to the aggregate of non-EU countries, but since 1996 the two indices have gradually converged. Specialisation indices for South Africa's exports to individual EU countries are relatively stable with a high degree of export diversification, except for Italy and the UK. Since 1991, these two countries have been the destination for more than 90 percent of South Africa's gold export to the EU (Source OECD 2005).

Traditional and Non-Traditional Exports

The analysis of diversification and structural change in exports is based on commodity-specific cumulative export experience functions in constant US$ for the period 1990–2003 (de Piñeres and Ferrantino 1997: 379, IMF 2005: 602, UN 2004). The functions are defined as:

$$C_{it} = \sum_{t_0}^{t} E_{it} \left/ \sum_{t_0}^{t_1} E_{it} \right. \tag{6.2}$$

where t_0, t and t_1 represent the initial, current and terminal periods of the sample respectively. The variable C_{it} takes a value at or near 0 at the beginning of the sample period and rises to 1 in the terminal period. If the numerical values of C_{it} are plotted for two or more commodities together, the distribution functions differ according to whether exports are concentrated earlier or later in the period, or are roughly constant over the period.

Figure 6.2 illustrates cumulative distribution functions for four important South African export industries in trade with the EU. 'Iron and steel' shows a relatively moderate and stable increase in exports over the period compared to 'Road vehicles' and 'General industrial machinery' which show high export growth concentrated in the later years. Therefore the latter two commodity groups, which will be labelled as 'accelerating export' commodities, show cumulative export experience functions significantly to the right of the linear. Gold, finally, is a traditional export commodity of high export growth in the early 1990s, followed by three years of stagnating and declining exports to the EU after 1995.

In order to rank all industries according to accelerating performance, we construct an export performance index (AEP$_i$) as the mean of the cumulative export experience index for each industry for the entire sample period as:

$$AEP_i = \sum_{t_0}^{t_1} c_{it} \bigg/ (t_1 - t_0 + 1) \qquad (6.3)$$

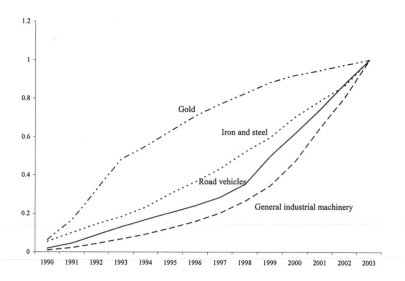

Source: See Table 6.2.

Figure 6.2: Cumulative exports: General industrial machinery, gold, iron and steel and road vehicles

The value of the AEP index differs between industries according to whether exports are concentrated earlier or later in the period. The weaker the export-accelerating performance of an industry, the higher the value of the AEP index. A higher value of the commodity-specific AEP index is usually assumed to reflect a more traditional export commodity (De Piñeres and Ferrantino 1997: 380, UN 2004: 38). However, traditional as well as non-traditional commodity groups may experience a period of high and accelerating export growth. Therefore, all industries will be classified as traditional (T) or non-traditional (NT) industries based on whether an industry shows net export surplus or deficit in the early 1990s, as measured by the net/gross ratio of revealed comparative advantage (RCA = (X-M)/(X+M)). The ratio ranges from -1 to 1 and negative indices are interpreted as comparative disadvantages and positive indices as revealed comparative advantages. In the analysis of export diversification, the focus is on accelerating export (AE) industries, which means a low rank and score for the AEP_i index. A benchmark will be used to separate industries with accelerating export performance (T-AE and NT-AE) from those with relatively stagnating or declining export performance, labelled non-accelerating export industries (Non-AE).

Sector Specialisation

In order to analyse 'sector' specialisation, commodity groups at the SITC two-digit level accounting for more than 1 percent of total exports to the EU in 2002/03 are shown in Table 6.3. The table includes revealed comparative advantages (RCA) 1990/91, the rank and score of export-accelerating performance (AEP) in South Africa's exports to the EU, average annual growth rates in constant US$ and percent of total exports to EU 1990/91 and 2002/03.

Table 6.3 Temporal sequencing of South Africa's major export products to the EU 1990–2003, RCA 1990/91 and annual average growth rates 1990/91– 2002/03 and share in total exports to the EU 1990/91 and 2002/03

AEP rank	Sector, SITC 2-digit (Leamer's classification)	RCA 90/91	AEP export to EU	Growth rates	Percent in total exports to EU	
					90/91	02/03
3	74 General ind. mach. (9)	-0.87	0.304	23.6	0.7	8.2
5	11 Beverages (4)	-0.67	0.322	25.2	0.2	2.7
11	78 Road vehicles (9)	-0.70	0.377	14.1	2.1	8.4
13	82 Furniture (7)	0.37	0.391	19.5	0.5	3.6
14	71 Power gener. mach. (9)	-0.80	0.401	12.3	0.4	1.4
16	66 Non-metallic manuf. (7)	0.12	0.409	13.4	3.4	12.4
19	77 Electrical machinery (9)	-0.84	0.438	9.9	0.6	1.5
24	67 Iron and steel (8)	0.39	0.450	6.0	5.2	7.9
28	03 Fish (5)	0.79	0.461	8.0	1.0	1.8
32	28 Metalliferous ores (2)	0.95	0.475	2.9	5.4	5.5
36	32 Coal and coke (2)	0.99	0.482	4.3	10.0	12.2
37	64 Paper (3)	-0.35	0.484	3.6	1.2	1.3
45	68 Non-ferrous metal (2)	0.70	0.497	-1.1	4.2	2.6
50	25 Pulp and waste paper (3)	0.97	0.526	1.1	1.4	1.1
54	05 Vegetables (4)	0.97	0.540	0.2	6.9	5.0
58	52 Inorganic chemicals (10)	0.09	0.559	1.3	1.5	1.3
61	26 Textile fibres (6)	0.50	0.602	-5.0	3.0	1.1
62	27 Crude fertilisers (2)	0.75	0.634	-6.1	3.3	1.0
63	97 Gold, non-monetary (11)	1.00	0.660	-8.3	35.8	8.2

Source: See Table 6.2.

Nineteen industries dominate exports, representing around 87 percent of South Africa's exports to the EU in 1990/91 as well as in 2002/03. The top seven, according to accelerating export performance, increased their share in total trade from 7.9 percent to 38.2 percent. According to the RCA criteria, five of these sectors are classified as non-traditional export sectors, and, according to Leamer's classification of factor intensity, four are characterised as moderate capital- and skill-intensive and one is classified as tropical agriculture. Production of the two traditional export sectors of the top seven are labour-intensive. Of the other 12 sectors with relatively low or declining growth, all but 'Paper' are traditional export sectors. Ten sectors are classified as raw materials or crops, while 'Iron and steel' is capital-intensive and 'Inorganic chemicals' is capital- and skill-intensive.

The conclusion is that although the period is characterised by a substantial change in export structure out of primary and crops into non-traditional manufacturing exports, a relatively few sectors continue to dominate exports.

INTRA-INDUSTRY TRADE AND EXPORT DIVERSIFICATION

Intra-industry trade is the value of total trade ($X_i + M_i$) remaining after subtracting the inter-industry trade of the sector, $|X_i - M_i|$. Because intra-industry trade refers to two-way trade within industries, the measure can be written $2\min(X_i, M_i)$ (Petersson 2002: 242). To facilitate comparisons of intra-industry trade for different industries and countries, it is useful to express intra-industry trade as a percentage of each industry's combined exports and imports. For an aggregate of industries, IIT can be measured as the weighted average of intra-industry trade across industries and calculated as:

$$IIT = 2 \cdot \min\left(X_i, M_i\right) \Big/ \sum_i \left(X_i + M_i\right) \qquad (6.4)$$

This index takes values between 0, for complete inter-industry trade, and 1, for complete intra-industry trade.

Increased export diversification may be the result of increased exports of import-competing product groups characterised by import surpluses, or reduced exports of product groups characterised by large export surpluses, thereby reducing export concentration. Finally, if exports and imports increase simultaneously, IIT increases regardless of whether a commodity group shows net export surplus or deficit. In these three cases export diversification leads to increased intra-industry trade. A comparison of IIT indices for different time periods therefore gives a broad indication of structural changes in the direction of export concentration or diversity.

In this section the analyses are restricted to the 224 industries with high and accelerating export performance, separated from the total number of 772 industries at the SITC four-digit level by a benchmark of AEP indices less than 0.41. The performances of South Africa's exports to the EU and IIT of these traditional and non-traditional accelerating export industries are found in Figure

6.3. The aggregate of 205 industries, classified as NT-AE industries by the revealed comparative advantage criteria, shows a steady increase in its share of total South African exports from less than 2 percent in 1990/91 to around 26 percent 2002/03. Until 2002, IIT also shows a stable increase, but declines in 2003, due to a substantial increase in imports. The similarity in performances of export share and level of IIT is explained by high growth rates of exports in industries, initially characterised by large import surpluses. As a result, trade has become increasingly 'balanced' at the industry level and the proportion of intra-industry trade in total trade (IIT) has increased.

The 19 industries in the aggregate of T-AE industries are all net export sectors vis-à-vis the EU. The share of total exports increased in the 1990s, in particular the period from 1993 to 1996 and in the year 2000. Thereafter the export share declined. Individual products and the aggregate showed relatively large fluctuations in export performance and in IIT. The aggregate is dominated by one industry – 'Diamonds, unworked, cut or otherwise worked, but not mounted or set' – in most years accounting for around 80 percent of total traditional accelerating export products. In this aggregate, periods of declining export share are characterised by increasing intra-industry trade.

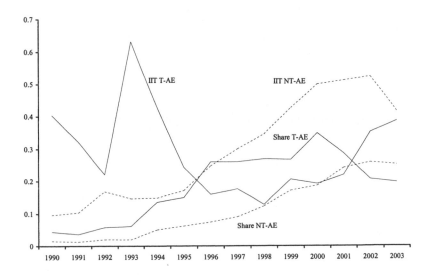

Source: See Table 6.2.

Figure 6.3: Share in total exports and intra-industry trade (IIT) of traditional and non-traditional accelerating export industries in South Africa's trade with the EU, 1990–2003

In summary, we found a significant relationship between accelerating export performance and change in the level of intra-industry trade. The aggregate of NT-AE commodity groups, comprising import-competing industries in the early 1990s, showed a stable pattern of growth until the early 2000s, with an accompanying stable increase in intra-industry trade. In contrast, traditional exports showed large fluctuations in performance and intra-industry trade.

Marginal Intra-Industry Trade

In order to ascertain the importance of changes in trade flows that generate increased intra-industry trade, the static measure of IIT is complemented by measures of marginal intra-industry trade. The following two indices of marginal intra-industry trade are used (Brülhart 1999: 46–8):

$$B = (\Delta X - \Delta M)/(|\Delta X| + |\Delta M|) \tag{6.5}$$

$$MIT = 1 - |B| \tag{6.6}$$

The MIIT index varies between 0 and 1, where 0 indicates that marginal trade in the particular industry is completely of the inter-industry type, and 1 that it is entirely of the intra-industry type (Brülhart 1999: 46). The B index can take values ranging from -1 to 1. The closer B is to 0, the higher is marginal intra-industry trade, whereas at both -1 and 1 it is entirely of the inter-industry type. Thus, -1 means that the whole change in trade flows concerns net imports, and 1 concerns entirely net exports. Accordingly, the B measure contains information about both the proportion of marginal IIT and the distribution of trade-induced gains and losses among industries, indicating changes in revealed comparative advantages. A drawback of the measure is that it cannot be meaningfully aggregated across industries, unless ($\Delta X - \Delta M$) have the same sign in all of the industries in the aggregate. Thus, in order to get some indication of changes in the pattern of specialisation, we aggregate and analyse industries with positive Bs (net exports in marginal trade) and the industries with negative Bs (net imports in marginal trade) separately.

Table 6.4 shows static and dynamic measures of the structure of marginal trade flows 1990/92–2001/03. The NT-AE and Non-AE industries are divided into two groups according to whether they show net exports or net imports in their marginal trade during the period. The table includes industries classified according to the clusters suggested by Leamer (1984) at the SITC four-digit level.

The two aggregates of non-traditional accelerating export products are dominated by the four manufactured aggregates of Leamer's 10 industrial clusters, but include several resource-based industries. The B index is positive for 140 NT-AE industries, which means that the increase in export values exceeded the increase in import values. In 83 of these industries imports declined (B = 1), suggesting improved performance on both world and domestic markets. As a result, the share of this sub-group of NT-AE industries in total exports to the EU increased substantially, while the share of imports declined. The B indices for most of the industries are very high and in the aggregate the index shows 63.0 percent, indicating that South Africa has increasingly specialised in these industries since 1992/93. Accordingly 37.0 percent of the marginal trade is the simultaneous increase in exports and imports (MIIT). The large increases of exports in these import-competing industries in 1990/92 imply a substantial increase of IIT.

The Herfindahl index applied to these 140 NT-AE industries indicates increased export concentration in the period 1990–95 followed by stagnation of the indices in the range 0.15 to 0.18. Three commodity groups account for almost two-thirds of NT-AE exports at the end of the studied period; the two moderate capital- and skill-intensive 'Filtering & purifying machinery for liquids & gases' and 'Passenger motor cars' with 7.3 and 5.0 percent, respectively, and 'Chairs and other seats and parts' (labour-intensive) with 2.7 percent. Finally, the total trade of the group of 65 NT-AE industries with negative B indices is relatively small and no industry dominates.

Table 6.4 Export and import shares, intra-industry and marginal intra-industry trade for export accelerating and non-accelerating export industries and components of Leamer's commodity clusters

	NT-AE ΔX>ΔM	NT-AE ΔX<ΔM	T-AE ΔX>ΔM	Non-AE ΔX>ΔM	Non-AE ΔX<ΔM
Number of industries	140	65	19	219	329
1. Petroleum	2	0	0	0	4
2. Raw material	11	3	3	14	32
3. Forest products	8	3	2	7	19
4. Tropical agriculture	6	2	3	7	28
5. Animal products	11	4	3	17	17
6. Cereals etc.	12	8	0	26	37
7. Labour intensive	20	6	2	27	42
8. Capital intensive	27	12	4	39	33
9. Machinery	32	16	0	55	75
10. Chemicals	13	11	0	27	42
Export share 1990/92	1.4	0.2	4.7	25.4	68.2
Export share 2001/03	23.4	1.7	23.0	32.4	19.6
Import share 1990/92	20.7	5.0	0.9	29.9	43.4
Import share 2001/03	16.0	6.6	4.0	12.9	60.6
IIT 1990/92	13.8	10.3	30.0	16.3	14.5
IIT 2001/03	50.9	39.0	31.1	17.6	15.5
B 90/92–01/03	63.0	-41.4	68.4	90.7	-92.8
MIIT 90/92–01/03	37.0	58.6	31.6	9.3	7.2

Source: See Table 6.2.

The aggregate of T-AE industries is characterised by high trade growth rates and increasing shares of both exports and imports in the trade flows with the EU, which result in a relatively high share of IIT and MIIT. In value terms, exports substantially exceed imports in marginal trade. The aggregate of T-AE industries is dominated by a labour-intensive industry – 'Diamonds' – which in 2002/03 accounted for 15 percent of total exports. Then follows 'Wine of fresh grapes' (tropical agriculture) with 2.3 percent and two raw material industries, 'Ores & concentrates of precious metals' (1.9 percent) and 'Platinum & other metals of the platinum group' (1.0 percent). The aggregate shows a relatively high and fluctuating export concentration with the Herfindahl indices in the range 0.35 to 0.80.

The two aggregates of non-accelerating export industries are dominated by inter-industry trade. Exports of the 219 Non-AE industries, which are characterised by exports exceeding imports in marginal trade, are dominated by a few traditional export industries in raw materials or resource-based products. For the 329 Non-AE industries, where the value of imports exceeds the value of exports in the marginal trade, the aggregated export share declines dramatically, largely explained by the decline of gold exports. In the period 2001/03 the exports of most of the industries are very small except for 'Non-monetary gold' with 8.0 percent and 'Other parts and accessories of motor vehicles' with 2.3 percent of total exports to the EU.

In summary, trade for non-traditional industries with accelerating export performance for the period 1990–2003 is characterised by a significant increase in intra-industry trade and trade expansion by a relatively large share of marginal intra-industry trade, compared to those with low and non-accelerating export performance. This suggests that the granted GSP status and trade liberalisation on the basis of reciprocity on the large EU market generated export specialisation within differentiated, import-competing product groups. The resulting export diversification also included several resource-based industries, which otherwise dominated the aggregate of traditional export accelerating export industries.

Intra-Industry Trade and Export Growth

The relation between accelerating export performance (AEP) and intra-industry trade is analysed with Pearson correlation coefficients in Table 6.5. The measures of intra-industry trade are IIT 1990/92 and 2001/03, the difference between IIT 2001/03 and 1990/92 (CIIT) and marginal intra-industry trade (MIIT) 1990/92–2001/03. The analysis includes 735 product groups of reported trade in South Africa's total trade and in all her main markets, the EU, the Southern African Development Community (SADC), US and rest of the world (ROW). Because the value of the AEP indices increases the weaker the cumulative export performance, negative coefficients indicate that accelerating export performance is positively related to the level of IIT.

Correlation analyses (of coefficients significant at the 0.01 level) show that accelerating export performance in trade with the EU is positively related to all measures of intra-industry trade, except for IIT 1990/92, indicating a positive relation to the level of inter-industry trade. There are relatively strong correlations between IIT 2001/03 on the one hand and IIT 1990/92, CIIT and MIIT on the other. The correlation between IIT 1990/92 and CIIT is, however, negative because significant increases in intra-industry are largely found in industries of low IIT (high level of inter-industry trade) in the early 1990s, and industries of high IIT 1990/92 often show stagnating or in some cases slightly declining IIT.

The interpretation of the testing taking into account the analyses of previous sections, is that accelerating export performance is largely found in import-competing product groups, where expanding exports result in increased intra-industry specialisation and trade, thereby contributing to increased export diversification.

Table 6.5 Correlation between acceleration export performance (AEP) and intra-industry trade (IIT and MIIT) indices for 1990/92 and 2001/03

	AEP in exports to		Measures of intra-industry trade			
	The EU	World	IIT 90/92	IIT 01/03	CIIT	MIIT
AEP EU	1.00	0.69[*]	0.12[*]	-0.19[*]	-0.29[*]	-0.14[*]
AEP world		1.00	0.06	-0.14[*]	-0.19[*]	-0.12[*]
IIT 90/92			1.00	0.41[*]	-0.49[*]	0.27[*]
IIT 01/03				1.00	0.59[*]	0.37[*]
CIIT 90/92–01/03					1.00	0.11[*]
MIIT 90/92–01/03						1.00

Note: * Correlation is significant at the 0.01 level (two-tailed).

Source: See Table 6.2.

The accelerating export performance of EU trade shows a strong correlation with the corresponding indices of South Africa's world trade (0.69), which is also found in her trade with other main markets (Petersson 2005: 793–94). Furthermore, Petersson (2005) found significant similarities of structural change in the development of South Africa's total trade and in trade with different trading partners: increases in IIT (CIIT) and in the proportion of IIT in marginal trade (MIIT) between 1990/92 and 2001/03 were positively related to accelerating export performance in total trade and with all trading partners, SADC excluded (significant at the 0.01 level) (ibid.: 795–96).

Export Diversification and Quality Differentiation

In this section we examine the quality of exports relative to the quality of imports within intra-industry trade. An important potential gain for the lower-income country from integration with more industrialised countries is increased quality of production, due to imports of cheaper or better quality intermediate and capital goods and learning spillovers.

A distinction is made between horizontal and vertical IIT. Horizontal IIT (HIIT) involves the simultaneous exports and imports of similar quality products of the same industry, and vertical IIT (VIIT) two-way trade of products in the same industry, where exports are of lower (VIIT inferior) or higher (VIIT superior) quality than imports. In the theoretical VIIT literature, product quality is usually linked to capital and/or human capital intensity. In the context of comparative advantage theory, this means that countries which are relatively capital-abundant will tend to export higher-quality varieties and labour-abundant countries lower-quality varieties. On the demand side, higher-income consumers will demand higher-quality varieties, while unequally distributed income within countries guarantees that there is a demand for every variety produced (Gullstrand 2002).

In order to separate a horizontal component and two vertical components in total IIT, we use the ratio between the unit value of exports, UV(X), and the unit value of imports, UV(M). The ratio is calculated at the SITC 4-digit level, using OECD data on EU external trade with South Africa. Subsequently, the IITs of these industries and each of the three groups of NT-AE, T-AE and Non-AE are assigned to one of three sub-groups. If the unit value of exports over the unit value of imports lies below 0.75, South Africa exports goods of lower quality than those imported, denoted inferior vertical IIT. Between 0.75 and 1.25, we have horizontal differentiation, since price differences are negligible, and above 1.25 we have superior IIT. In Table 6.6, we report IIT indices for the years 1995/96 and 2002/03 as well as the horizontal and vertical components of the matched flows.

The share of intra-industry trade of South Africa's total trade with the EU increases from 16.0 percent to 24.6 percent during the period. The most marked pattern seems to be the rising share of HIIT in the average of total intra-industry trade, increasing from 21.6 percent to 41.4 percent. In the aggregate of NT-AE products the combination of high export growth and significantly increase IIT in products of similar quality (HIIT) – compared to in particular products characterised by the inferior VIIT type of differentiation – explains the increasing share of HIIT in total intra-industry trade. Furthermore, in this aggregate of high and accelerating export growth, total exports are dominated by product groups in which intra-industry trade is of the horizontal or superior type of differentiation. The main structural change in the aggregate of Non-AE products is increased intra-industry trade in products characterised by HIIT. This aggregate of low growth in trade and non-accelerating export performance still dominates total trade in 2002/03, in particular in the aggregate of products classified by inferior VIIT type of differentiation.

Table 6.6 Average level of IIT and horizontal (HIIT) and vertical (VIIT) inferior (inf.) and superior (sup.) intra-industry trade and distribution of intra-industry trade by type of differentiation, 1995/96 and 2002/03

	IIT		Type of differentiation as % of IIT 1995/96			Type of differentiation as % of IIT 2002/03		
	95/96	02/03	HIIT	VIIT		HIIT	VIIT	
				Inf.	Sup.		Inf.	Sup.
NT-AE	22.7	45.7	39.0	40.2	20.8	53.4	293	17.3
T-AE	22.6	23.6	0.4	20.9	78.7	0.5	17.0	82.5
Non-AE	14.1	15.8	18.0	62.5	19.5	38.9	41.6	19.5
Total	16.0	24.6	21.6	53.9	24.5	41.4	32.7	25.8

Note: Industries where unit value is missing are excluded, accounting for 2.1 percent of exports and imports 1995/96 and 1.9 percent in 2002/03.

Source: Source OECD (2005).

Intra-industry trade of the two largest NT-AE industries, 'Filtering and purifying machinery for liquids and gases' and 'Passenger motor cars' is characterised by the superior VIIT and horizontal types of differentiation, respectively. Since the introduction of the Motor Industry Development Programme in 1995, substantial specific measures have been implemented in support of exports, and trade in motor vehicles and components has been liberalised. The reintegration of the industry into the global motor vehicle industry led to production-sharing arrangements and, in a few years, all domestic producers were at least partly controlled by multinational companies (Barnes 2000: 404–05). The benefits to the economy of the significant support to exporters have been questioned, due to distortions in the economy created by supply-side measures (Kaplan 2004). However, some studies argue that the export success is the result of the industry's competitiveness and efficiency (Barnes et al. 2004). This view finds some support in the rapidly rising trade in the industry dominated by horizontal differentiation, and the fact that the export/import unit price ratio has increased slightly.

The superior type of differentiation dominates the T-AE aggregate, largely due to the export/import unit value ratios of two important export industries slightly exceeding 1.25: 'Diamonds' and 'Ores and concentrates of precious metals', while 'Wine of fresh grapes' is an important exception characterised by the inferior type of differentiation.

With respect to quality, as measured by unit prices, the analysis suggests a slight improvement in the quality of South Africa's exports to the EU. The main changes are increasing shares of total exports and increasing IIT in import-competing product groups of the horizontal type of differentiation. This type of differentiation also characterises the major part of increased intra-industry trade in the aggregate of non-accelerating export performance. Products of low trade growth and non-accelerating export performance dominate total trade in the aggregate of products of inferior VIIT.

CONCLUSIONS

The purpose of this chapter is to analyse whether better terms of access to the EU market have promoted the diversification of South Africa's exports. The main instruments of trade promotion have been South Africa's ongoing trade liberalisation since majority rule in 1994 and the granted GSP status. These preferences have been locked in and mutual trade is being gradually liberalised due to the fact that the Trade, Development and Cooperation Agreement has been partially applied since 1 January 2000.

The ending of sanctions was followed by a few years of increased export concentration on traditional exports to the EU market. Thereafter, exports showed a trend of declining concentration, largely due to a significant decline of non-monetary gold exports. Relatively few sectors continued, however, to dominate, but there was a substantial change in export structure. Industries with expanding export shares in total exports included moderate capital- and skill-intensive non-traditional as well as labour-intensive traditional export industries, while stagnating or declining export shares were found in traditional resource-based industries.

In analyses based on cumulative export experience functions we find a large spread of emerging non-traditional export products across clusters of different factor intensities, together steadily increasing their proportion of total exports, while traditional exports showed large fluctuation in performance and intra-industry trade. The main explanation for structural change in the direction of export diversity was increased (marginal) intra-industry specialisation and trade in import-competing industries of high and accelerating export growth. Finally, with respect to quality, analyses based on relative unit prices of exports and imports suggest a slight relative improvement of exports, largely explained by accelerating export performance and increasing intra-industry trade positively related to quality.

Deepened integration with the EU and increased integration with other world markets are likely to further increase intra-industry specialisation and trade. This type of export growth driven by economies of scale and productivity gains is promoted by firm access to large competitive markets in a process which may eventually lead to a new phase of export concentration.

REFERENCES

Barnes, J. (2000), 'Changing Lanes: The Political Economy of the South African Automotive Value Chain', *Development Southern Africa*, **17** (3), 401–15.

Barnes, J., R. Kaplinsky and M. Morris (2004), 'Industrial Policy in Developing Economies: Developing Dynamic Comparative Advantage in the South African Automobile Sector', *Competition & Change*, **8** (2), 153–72.

Bell, T. (1997), 'Trade Policy', in J. Michie and V. Padayachee (eds), *The Political Economy of South Africa's Transition*, London: The Dryden Press.

Bonaglia, F. and K. Fukasaku (2003), 'Export Diversification in Low-Income Countries: An International Challenge after Doha', OECD Development Centre, Technical Papers No. 209, Paris: OECD.

Brülhart, M. (1999), 'Marginal Intra-Industry Trade and Trade-Induced Adjustment: A Survey', in M. Brülhart and R.C. Hine (eds) *Intra-Industry Trade and Adjustment. The European Experience*, London: Macmillan Press Ltd.

Bruton, H. (1989), 'Import Substitution' in H. Chenery and T.N. Srinivasan (eds) *Handbook of Development Economics*, Volume 2, Amsterdam: North-Holland.

Davis, R. (2000), 'Forging a New Relationship with the EU', in T. Bertelsmann-Scott, G. Mills, and E. Sidirpoulos (eds), *The EU-SA Agreement: South Africa, Southern Africa and the European Union*, Johannesburg: South African Institute of International Affairs (SAIIA).

De Ferranti, D., G.E. Perry, D. Lederman and W.F. Maloney (2001), *From Natural Resources to the Knowledge Economy: Trade and Job Quality*, Washington, DC: World Bank.

De Piñeres, S.A.G. and M. Ferrantino (1997), 'Export Diversification and Structural Dynamics in the Growth Process: The Case of Chile', *Journal of Development Economics*, **52** (2), 375–91.

Department of Finance (1996), *Growth, Employment and Redistribution:* A Macro-Economic Strategy, Pretoria.

Draper, P. (2003), 'To Liberalise or Not to Liberalise? A Review of the South African Government's Trade Policy', SAIIA Trade Policy Report No. 1, Johannesburg: South African Institute of International Affairs (SAIIA).

Edwards, L. and V. Schoer (2002), 'Measures of Competitiveness: A Dynamic Approach to South Africa's Trade Performance in the 1990s', *The South African Journal of Economics*, **70** (6), 1008–46.

Eurostep (2000a), 'The EU-South Africa Trade, Development and Co-operation Agreement: Analysis of the Negotiation Process, the Agreement and the Economic Impact', March 2000, Eurostep Briefing Paper.

Eurostep (2000b), 'The EU-South Africa Trade, Development and Co-operation Agreement: An Analysis of its Implications in Southern Africa', June 2000, Eurostep Briefing Paper.

Goodison, P. (1999), 'Marginalisation or Integration? Implications for South Africa's Customs Union Partners of the South Africa-European Union trade deal', European Research Organisation, IGD Occasional Paper No. 22, Braamfontein. South Africa: The Institute for Global Dialogue.

Gullstrand, J. (2002), 'Demand Patterns and Vertical Intra-Industry Trade with Special Reference to North-South Trade', *Journal of International Trade & Economic Development*, **11** (4), 429–55.

Imbs, J. and R. Wacziarg (2003), 'Stages of Diversification', *American Economic Review*, **93** (1), 63–86.

IDC (Industrial Development Corporation of South Africa) (1998), *Sectoral Prospects: Growth Guidelines for 80 South African Industries, 1997-2001*, Pretoria: IDC and Department of Trade and Industry.

IMF (International Monetary Fund) (2005), *International Financial Statistics Yearbook*, Washington, DC: International Monetary Fund.

Joffe, A., D. Kaplan, R. Kaplinsky and D. Lewis (1995), *Improving Manufacturing Performance in South Africa*, Cape Town: UCT Press (Pty) Ltd.

Kaplan, R. (2004), 'Manufacturing in South Africa over the Last Decade: A Review of Industrial Performance and Policy', *Development Southern Africa*, **21** (4), 623–43.

Leamer, E.E. (1984), *Sources of International Comparative Advantage: Theory and Evidence*, London: The MIT Press.

Lee, M.C. (2002), 'The European Union – South Africa Free Trade Agreement: In Whose Interest?', *Journal of Contemporary African Studies*, **20** (1), 81–106.

Links, E. (2000), 'Negotiating a Long-Term Relationship', in T. Bertelsmann-Scott, G. Mills and E. Sidirpoulos (eds), *The EU-SA Agreement: South Africa, Southern Africa and the European Union*, Johannesburg: South African Institute of International Affairs (SAIIA).

Lowe, P. (2000), 'Main Parameters of the EU-SA Partnership', in T. Bertelsmann-Scott, G. Mills and E. Sidirpoulos (eds), *The EU-SA Agreement: South Africa, Southern Africa and the European Union*, Johannesburg: South African Institute of International Affairs (SAIIA).

McCarthy, C. (1998), 'South African Trade and Industrial Policy in a Regional Context', in L. Petersson (ed.), *Post-Apartheid Southern Africa: Economic Challenges and Policies for the Future*, London: Routledge.

Partner in Progress (2003), 'The EU/South Africa Trade, Development and Cooperation Agreement for the 21st Century', European Commission, Directorate-General for Development.

Petersson, L. (2002), 'Integration and Intra-industry Trade Adjustment in South Africa', *Development Southern Africa*, **19** (2), 239–59.

Petersson, L. (2005), 'Export Diversification and Intra-industry Trade in South Africa, *South African Journal of Economics*, **73** (4), 785-802.

SARB (South African Reserve Bank) (1997), *Quarterly Bulletin*, **206**.

SARB (South African Reserve Bank) (2005), *Quarterly Bulletin*, **237**.

SARS (South African Revenue Service) (2004), 'Customs and Excise', Pretoria: Department of Finance.

Source OECD (Organisation for Economic Co-operation and Development) (2005), *International Trade by Commodity Statistics*, online, www.sourceoecd.org

UN (United Nations) (2004), 'Export Diversification and Economic Growth: The Experience of Selected Least Developed Countries', Economic and Social Commission for Asia and the Pacific, Development Papers No. 24, New York: UN.

Volz, E. (2001), 'The Trade, Development and Cooperation Agreement between the Republic of South Africa and the European Union: An Analysis with special regard to the Negotiating Process, the Contents of the Agreement, the Applicability of WTO Law and Port and Sherry Agreement', Thesis presented in fulfilment of the requirements for the degree of Master of Law, Stellenbosch University.

ANNEX 6

This appendix gives an account of the components of Leamer's 10 commodity clusters with SITC two-digit division code. Number of product groups of clusters at SITC four-digit level in parentheses.

1. Petroleum (7): 33 Petroleum and derivatives.
2. Raw materials (60): 27 Crude fertilizers and minerals; 28 Metal-ferrous ores; 32 Cole and coke; 34 Gas, natural and manufactured; 35 Electrical current; and 68 Non-ferrous metal.
3. Forest products (38): 24 Lumber, wood, and cork; 25 Pulp and waste paper; 63 Cork and wood manufacturers; and 64 Paper.
4. Tropical agriculture (46): 05 Vegetables; 06 Sugar; 07 Coffee; 11 Beverages; and 23 Crude Rubber.
5. Animal products (52): 00 Live animals; 01 Meat; 02 Dairy products; 03 Fish; 21 Hides and skins; 29 Crude animals and vegetables; 43 Processed animal and vegetables oils; and 94 Animal products n.e.c.
6. Cereals, etc. (80): 04 Cereals; 08 Feeds; 09 Miscellaneous; 12 Tobacco; 22 Oil seeds; 26 Textile fibres; 41 Animal oil and fat; and 42 Fixed vegetables oil.
7. Labour intensive (98): 66 Non-metal minerals; 82 Furniture; 83 Travel goods and handbags; 84 Articles of apparel; 85 Footwear; 89 Miscellaneous manufactured articles; 91 Postal packaging, not classified; and 96 Coins (non-gold).
8. Capital intensive (119): 61 Leather; 62 Rubber; 65 Textile yarn and fabric; 67 Iron and steel; 69 Manufactured metal n.e.c.; and 81 Sanitary fixtures and fittings.
9. Machinery (177): 71 Power generating; 72 Specialised; 73 Metalworking; 74 General industrial; 75 Office and data processing; 76 Telecommunications and sound; 77 Electrical; 78 Road vehicles; 79 Other transportation vehicles; 87 Professional and scientific instruments; 88 Photographic apparatus; and 95 Firearms and ammunition.
10. Chemical (94): 51 Organic; 52 Inorganic; 53 Dyeing and tanning; 54 Medical and pharmaceutical products; 55 Essences and perfumes; 56 Fertilizers; 57 Explosives and pyrotechnics; 58 Artificial resins and plastics and; 59 Chemical materials n.e.c.

7. The EU and Regional Integration in West Africa: Assessing the Effects of Deepening and Enlargement

Yves Bourdet and Joakim Gullstrand

INTRODUCTION

Regional integration, among developed as well as developing countries, has experienced a worldwide revival since the middle of the mid-1990s. The countries of West Africa, with their deepening and enlargement of existing integration schemes, are no exception to this pattern. The EU has played a decisive role in this revival of regional integration in West Africa, for two reasons. First, the EU considers regional integration *per se* as an engine for economic growth and development and, second, the setting up of partnership agreements, between the EU and regional groupings among developing countries, has been chosen by the EU to maintain preferential access for ACP countries in a form compatible with the rules of the WTO.

This renewed interest in regional integration raises of course the question of its impact on the economies of the countries concerned. The attempts at regional integration during the first wave of regional integration in the 1960s and 1970s, produced results that were at best mitigated and most often disappointing in terms of trade creation and acceleration of economic growth.[1] This is especially true of the experiments in regional integration among developing countries, in particular in sub-Saharan Africa.[2] The current situation is different with regard to the economic structure and the level of development of the countries engaged in regional integration schemes, as well as with regard to the kind of development strategy, less biased towards the domestic market, that is being implemented in the majority of these countries. The situation also differs as regards the trade policy environment, with an average level of tariffs and other trade barriers in the countries concerned as well as in the world in general clearly lower than it was 30 years ago. An implication of this is that there is less risk today that regional integration will result in a contraction of international trade and a slowdown of growth. In view of the differences between the past and present contexts, it is critical to evaluate the current experiments in regional integration in order to assess their relevance as an instrument of economic development.

The main purpose of this chapter is to assess the impact of the deepening and widening of regional integration in West Africa and, more specifically, to estimate the trade-creating effects of the customs union established in the mid-1990s and the distribution of these trade effects among the member countries. To the best of our knowledge, no study has so far attempted to estimate the trade effect of this customs union. The chapter also aims to estimate the potential for trade creation that the widening of regional integration in West Africa is likely to give rise to.

The chapter is structured as followed. The second section describes the various measures that have been introduced to deepen and then widen integration in West Africa. Emphasis is placed on the not always complementary roles of UEMOA (Union Économique et Monétaire Ouest Africaine) and ECOWAS (Economic Community of West African States). The third section assesses the quantitative impact of the deepening and widening of regional integration on the volume of trade within West Africa. Our study makes use of new developments in the empirics of gravity models, which improve the reliability of the estimates of the trade effects of regional integration. The final section summarises the main results and draws some conclusions on the pertinence of regional integration as an instrument of economic development in West Africa.

REGIONAL INTEGRATION IN WEST AFRICA

Two regional arrangements structure the process of regional integration in West Africa: in chronological order, ECOWAS and UEMOA. The creation of ECOWAS dates back to 1975 with the signing of the Treaty of Lagos by 15 countries from West Africa. UEMOA is more recent, its creation dating back to January 1994, the month of the huge devaluation (50 percent) of the CFA franc.[3] Several rather unsuccessful attempts at regional integration in West Africa preceded the formation of these two regional groupings. ECOWAS and UEMOA differ in terms of geographic coverage, characteristics of their Member States and the contents of the integration schemes. Nonetheless, the two regional groupings have strong ties with each other insofar as all the Member States of UEMOA (Benin, Burkina Faso, Ivory Coast, Guinea-Bissau, Mali, Niger, Senegal and Togo) also belong to ECOWAS, which contains, in addition, seven other countries from West Africa (Cape Verde, Gambia, Ghana, Guinea, Liberia, Nigeria and Sierra Leone). There are also strong disparities between the Member States of the two regional groupings in terms of size, average income per capita, structure of foreign trade, volume of development assistance and extent of poverty (see Annex 7). Moreover, certain countries are landlocked, like the countries of the Sahel, whereas others are coastal and have access to relatively well-developed harbour infrastructure. Finally, there are disparities of a linguistic and cultural nature, with a certain homogeneity within UEMOA, which is made up of French-speaking countries (except for Guinea-Bissau), and a great heterogeneity within ECOWAS, which brings together English-, French- and Portuguese-speaking countries.

The substance of the integration schemes differs in an important way between UEMOA and ECOWAS. Table 7.1 gives an overall picture of the measures taken, or planned, in the areas covered by the integration process (trade policy, factor mobility, monetary union, etc.). It suggests that the process of integration within UEMOA has gone farther than that within ECOWAS (i.e. between UEMOA and the other countries of ECOWAS). Economic integration within UEMOA rests on three pillars. The first is a customs union, which came into force in 2000 after a five-year transition period and *formally* guarantees the free movement of goods between the member countries. The second pillar consists of a set of positive measures, such as the harmonisation of commercial legislation and the adoption of a common competition policy, that encourage competitive practices and facilitate the integration of markets. The third pillar is a common currency, the CFA franc, which minimises the costs of transaction and promotes intra-regional trade.[4] There is also coordination of economic policies, through the adoption of common budgetary and macroeconomic criteria and a monitoring of these by the UEMOA commission, in order to guarantee macroeconomic and monetary stability in the currency union.

Table 7.1 Integration in West Africa, implemented (x) and planned (p) measures

	UEMOA	ECOWAS
Removal of intra-regional tariffs	x	p
Removal of non-tariff barriers		
Common external tariff	x	p
Other trade policy objectives	x	x
Free labor mobility	x	x
Free capital mobility	x	x
Harmonization of business laws	x	
Competition policy	x	
Monetary integration/common currency	x	p
Coordination of economic policies	x	p
Sector policies	x	p
Non-economic objectives [a]		x

Note: [a] Conflict prevention, peace and security, etc.

The strong level of policy integration between the Member States of the UEMOA, such as is illustrated in Table 7.1, should be mitigated because several measures are more formal than real; indeed, measures such as free trade for products from the primary sector and the free movement of workers or competition policy are only partly implemented. Although the process of integration within ECOWAS is less advanced, several commitments, undertaken in recent years, will permit integration within ECOWAS to move closer to the degree reached within UEMOA.

The customs union is a main component of the process of integration within UEMOA. Customs duties on intra-regional trade were eliminated gradually and a common external tariff (CET) was set up in 2000. UEMOA has adopted rules of origin, which determine the products exempted from customs duties and require at least 30 percent domestic value added in order to benefit from free regional trade. The creation of the customs union has led to a simplification and a lowering of customs duties on third countries' imports. The CET consists of four rates which range from 0 percent for a small number of basic commodities (like drugs) to 20 percent for the final consumer goods, with 5 or 10 percent for intermediate products and other inputs. In addition, there is an imposition of a statistical royalty of 1 percent on all imported products, and a tax of 1 percent, which is used to finance the institutions of UEMOA and some of its activities.

UEMOA also imposes two kinds of temporary taxes. A decreasing tax over time (TDP: *taxe dégressive de protection*) grants temporary protection to the sectors exposed to strong import competition from third countries following the introduction of the customs union. Currently the rates of this tax range between 2.5 and 5 percent of the value of import. This tax 'was extended until December 31, 2005 while waiting for the installation of a new protection system for industries'. There is also a kind of safeguard tax on imports (TCI: *taxe conjoncturelle à l'importation*), whose objective is to attenuate the impact of strong fluctuations on the world market upon products of the primary sector other than fishery products. The TCI can also be used 'to curb the unfair practices of some importers'. The TDP and TCI are national fees insofar as they apply only in those member countries that have made the appropriate request to the UEMOA commission. Unfortunately there does not exist, to date, a synthetic study on the share of the imports of each Member State that is subject to these two taxes. In view of these taxes, one cannot speak of a customs union in the strict sense of the term, since different levels of taxes are imposed on the same products imported from third countries. Rules of origin are necessary to determine whether these imported products are to be subject to a customs duty.

The customs union is planned to be extended to the whole of West Africa by 1 January 2008. Indeed, the Member States of ECOWAS have decided to align the external tariff of non-UEMOA countries with the common external tariff of UEMOA. It is also envisaged that the activities of ECOWAS will be financed by the customs duties on imports from third countries. There remain, however, some uncertainties about the date of introduction of the widened customs union and the participation of those ECOWAS countries that are not members of UEMOA. The negotiations carried out with the European Union, within the framework of the preparation of the Regional Economic Partnership Agreement, have contributed substantially to the revival of integration within ECOWAS and to the planned widening of the customs union to West Africa by 2008, which is the date of entry into force of the agreements of partnership between the European Union and the regional groupings among developing countries.[5]

TRADE EFFECTS OF REGIONAL INTEGRATION

The main economic objectives of regional integration are to promote trade between member countries and to further the specialisation of these countries according to their comparative advantages. The larger the volume of trade created, the larger the gains from trade and the impact on international specialisation will be. On the other hand, it is critical for the positive effects of integration that the trade created by integration is not at the expense of more competitive imports from non-member countries. The larger the volume of imports diverted from non-member countries, the more likely it is that regional integration will have negative economic effects for the member countries, in particular those countries that experience the largest volume of trade diversion.

The Empirics of the Gravity Model

In order to assess the trade impact of regional integration we make use of new developments in the empirics of the gravity model. The starting point of our empirical model is Anderson and Wincoop (2003), who derive a gravity equation from the assumptions that each country (or region) supplies a unique product and that consumers have identical and homothetic preferences (expressed by a CES utility function). This setting leads to the gravity equation:

$$x_{ij} = \frac{y_i y_j}{y^w} \left(\frac{t_{ij}}{\Pi_i P_j} \right),$$

$$\Pi_i = \left(\sum_j (t_{ij} / P_j)^{1-\sigma} \theta_j \right)^{1/(1-\sigma)}, P_j = \left(\sum_i (t_{ij} / \Pi_i)^{1-\sigma} \theta_i \right)^{1/(1-\sigma)},$$

(7.1)

where x_{ij} is region j's import demand for region i's goods, y is the nominal income (w stands for world), t_{ij} is the bilateral trade costs, P_i and P_j are consumer price indices (or 'indices of multilateral resistance'), σ the elasticity of substitution between all goods, and θ_i is the income share. An important implication of this equation is that the multilateral resistance variables 'depend on all bilateral resistance' (i.e. t_{ij}). Thus, a change in any bilateral trade cost between two trade partners affects all other trade patterns as well, and excluding these resistance variables may lead to omitted-variable problems. Furthermore, the bilateral trade cost is a function of several bilateral resistance variables and is assumed to take a log linear form:

$$t_{ij} = b_{ij} d_{ij}^\rho,$$

where b_{ij} is a bilateral trade-resistance variable (such as border effects), and d_{ij} is the bilateral distance.

One important drawback (as discussed in Anderson and Wincoop, 2003) of this model is that it predicts positive trade volumes between all trade partners since each country supplies a unique product demanded by all consumers in all countries. This is, however, not in line with empirical findings. Helpman et al. (2006) generalise the gravity equation of Anderson and Wincoop (2003) by introducing productivity heterogeneity across firms, transport costs and the sunk cost of exporting. This implies that each firm wishing to enter an additional market, other than the domestic, faces a fixed cost of exporting to this market. This cost may be asymmetric so that the fixed cost of exporting from i to j is not the same as from j to i. A fixed cost of exporting and heterogeneous firms imply that only a fraction (or none) of a country's firms serve a particular foreign market. That is, the model may predict two-way, one-way and zero bilateral trade. The implication of these results is that one has to consider that firms self-select (based on their productivity level) into export activities, which implies that the empirical specification has to control for biases due to the fact that only a fraction of firms export and that zero trade observations are excluded.

An alternative way to take zero-trade volumes into consideration is to assume a world with many homogenous products and that any given product is only supplied by a subset of the world's countries (as in the Heckscher-Ohlin or the factor specific model), as Haveman and Hummels (2004) suggest. In this setting (if we assume identical and homothetic preferences as above), bilateral trade patterns become indeterminate since consumers are indifferent to the origin of the product as long as the price is the same. If we introduce trade frictions that increase with distance, the indeterminacy in trade patterns disappears. Relative endowments determine the set of countries that produce a particular product, and the distance determines from which trade partner a particular country demands this product. Furthermore, the income of partners becomes important due to 'a set of adding-up constraints', which implies that the model predicts an on-average relationship between partner income and trade volumes that is in line with the gravity model.[6] That is, this perspective suggests that there is a self-selection of exporters due to country differences that leads to biased estimates in the gravity equation if zero-trade volumes are excluded.

In order to compare the different suggestions above, we use three specifications in our regressions. First, we use the Anderson and Wincoop specification (AW) without a selection process. Second, we use a selection process determined by country differences *à la* Haveman and Hummels (HH). Finally, we use the specification suggested by Helpman et al. (HMR).

The Selection Process

Although trade volumes are explained in a similar fashion in the three models mentioned above, two of them emphasise that there is a selection process behind bilateral trade patterns. Haveman and Hummels (2004) suggest that there may be a selection process determined by relative endowments and distance. Endowment differences fix the set of possible exporters to the importer i, while the distance between the potential exporters determines which of these actually export. Helpman et al. (2006) underline two sources of omitted-variable problems due to the fact that a firm selects into export activities. One stems from an exclusion of zero-trade observations and the other from the fact that only a fraction of all firms within a country export.

In order to control for this selection process, we use the two-step method of Heckman (1979), and the selection process is defined by the following probit:

$$\Pr(D_{ij} = 1 \mid observables) = \Phi\left(\sum_l \delta_l z_{lij} + \delta_i m_i + \delta_j n_j \right),$$

$$D_{ij} = 1 \mid x_{ij} > 0,$$

(7.2)

where z_{lij} is a set of explanatory variables, m_i is export-specific effects, and n_j is import-specific effects. The explanatory variables in the selection equation overlap with those used in the gravity equation below, Equation 7.3, except for GDP per capita differences. The latter variable is introduced on the basis of the suggestion of Haveman and Hummels (2004) that endowments differences may determine the set of potential exporters. As endowments differences are not included in the gravity equation, this variable provides the exclusion restriction for an identification in the second stage.

Empirical Specification of the Gravity Equation

All three models above suggest that trade volume increases with the income level of trading partners and that trade volumes are restricted by trade frictions between bilateral partners. In addition to these variables, Anderson and Wincoop (2003) underline that the gravity equation has to control for multilateral trade-resistance, which we control for with export and import country-specific effects.[7] Our benchmark specification of the gravity equation is as follows (excluding time dimension for simplicity):

$$x_{ij} = \alpha_0 + \beta_y y_i y_j + \beta_t t_{ij} + \lambda_i + \gamma_j + \beta_n n_{ij} + \beta_g g_{ij} + \varepsilon_{ij},$$

(7.3)

where y_i (y_j) is the exporter's (importer's) income, t_{ij} is the bilateral trade resistance, λ_i (γ_j) is the exporter's (importer's) fixed effect, n_{ij} controls for selection due to excluding zeros (Mills ratio in the HMR and the HH specification), and g_{ij} controls for the selection of firms in the export market (in the HMR specification). The two latter variables are excluded from the AW specification. The bilateral trade resistance is extended as in the following expression:

$$t_{ij} = dist_{ij} + landl_{ij} + island_{ij} + bord_{ij} + lang_{ij} + kol_{ij} +$$
$$+uemoa_i * \tau + uemoa_j * \tau + uemoa_{ij}, \tag{7.4}$$

where $dist_{ij}$ is the distance between the exporter's and the importer's capital, $landl_{ij}$ indicates if the exporter or the importer is landlocked, $island_{ij}$ is a dummy that takes the value one if the exporter or the importer is an island, $bord_{ij}$ indicates if the two trade partners share borders or not, $lang_{ij}$ indicates if they have the same language, and kol_{ij} is a dummy indicating if they have colonial ties. The rest of the variables are used to capture the effects of integration among the UEMOA countries. The two first variables, $uemoa_i$ and $uemoa_j$, are two dummies indicating whether the exporter or the importer, respectively, belongs to the integration area or not. Both these dummies are interacted with year dummies (τ), which implies that they indicate if this group of countries become more or less prone to export or import given their initial import (γ_j) and export resistance (λ_i) in Equation 7.3. The latter dummy, which takes the value 1 if both the exporter and the importer belong to UEMOA, captures the extra trade effect of belonging to the same integration area.

Data

We use the IMF Direction of Trade Statistics (DOTS) to define our bilateral trade flows between West African countries and all possible trade partners between 1992 and 2002. All trade flows are either exports from or imports of West African countries, which implies that all trade effects of UEMOA are compared to a norm based on a 'relatively homogeneous' set of countries.[8] The great circle distance is used to define distance between the capitals of trading partners, and longitudes and latitudes originate from CIA's *The World Factbook*. The same source is used to define whether countries are landlocked or islands, and whether trading partners share borders or have the same language and colonial ties. GDP and population statistics stem from the World Bank database, *World Development Indicators*.

Empirical Results

We begin with an investigation of the initial differences between UEMOA members and the other West African countries, and differences between the different empirical specifications. Specifications 1 and 5 are two selection procedures with the only difference being that the former only includes 12 broad exporter and importer dummies, while specification 5 includes country-level importer and exporter specific effects. The reason for these differences is that the non-linear specification of HMR turns out to be very sensitive to the inclusion of dummy variables. Table 7.2 shows that the specification of the selection process fits the sample rather well, especially if we incorporate importer and exporter fixed effects, and that (see specification 5) factor-endowment differences as well as distance seem to be important when West African countries select their trading partners.

Table 7.2 Comparing specifications

Variables	Selection equation (1) $D{=}1\lvert x_{ij}{>}0$	AW (2) x_{ij}	HH (3) x_{ij}	HMR (4) x_{ij}	Selection equation (5) $D{=}1\lvert x_{ij}{>}0$	HH (6) x_{ij}
$gdpcd_{ij}$	0.21 (.72)				0.58 (.00)	
$ln(gdp_i gdp_j)$	0.78 (.00)	0.86 (.00)	0.57 (.00)	0.97 (.00)	FE[a]	FE[a]
$ln(dist_{ij})$	-1.23(.00)	-0.78 (.00)	-0.35 (.00)	-0.80 (.00)	-1.26 (.00)	-0.69 (.00)
$landl_{ij}$	-0.41(.00)	-0.91 (.00)	-0.78 (.00)	-0.96 (.00)	-0.30 (.16)	0.01 (.96)
$island_{ij}$	-0.69(.08)	-1.45 (.00)	-1.07 (.17)	-0.97 (.17)	-0.65 (.27)	-1.70 (.17)
kol_{ij}	0.37 (.00)				0.13 (.26)	
$bord_{ij}$	0.39 (.02)	0.51 (.00)	0.39 (.01)	0.73 (.01)	0.29 (.20)	0.62 (.00)
$lang_{ij}$	0.22 (.00)				0.54 (.00)	
$uomea_{ij}$		0.64 (.00)	0.47 (.00)	0.61 (.00)		0.87 (.00)
n_{ij}			-0.71 (.00)	-0.93 (.00)		0.50 (.00)
g_{ij}				0.01 (.06)		
Sigma						
Exporter dummy	Yes[b]	No	No	No	Yes	Yes
Importer dummy	Yes[b]	No	No	No	Yes	Yes
Time dummy	n.a.	n.a.	n.a.	n.a.	n.a.	n.a.
R^2 (adj.)	0.42	0.38	0.39		0.68	0.63
Likelihood				-19,723		
No. obs	4,980	1,866	1,866	1,866	4,980	1,866

Notes: Figures within parentheses are p-values from a two-tailed t-test (H0: not different from zero), based on a heteroskedasticity-consistent covariance matrix. These results are based on data from 1992.
[a] Included in the fixed effect.
[b] Twelve broad regional dummies.

Turning to the gravity estimates in specifications 2–3, we can see that they have the same sign across specifications and they are all plausible compared to other studies.[9] We do not, however, comment on these findings until we use the whole time dimension of our dataset. The most important result in Table 7.2 is the evidence of a selection bias. And the most important selection bias, in this sample, is the matching process of importer and exporter (that is whether they trade or not), which we conclude from the significance of η in specifications 3 and 4. Biases due to a variation in the fraction of exporting firms seem to be less problematic in our sample.[10] We use the HH specification throughout the chapter to cope with the importance of selection bias trough importer-exporter and the lack of robustness of the non-linear specification of HMR.

Table 7.3 shows our base regression for the whole sample and compares ordinary least square estimates (AW) with those corrected for selection biases. The estimate of β_n suggests the presence of a selection bias, and therefore also a downward bias of the AW estimates of trade barriers due to the fact that trading partners with high trade barriers are likely to have small unobserved trade barriers. The results in Table 7.3 confirm this suggested bias.

Table 7.3 Results of the gravity equation, base regression

Variables	Selection equation (1) $D=1\|x_{ij}>0$	HH specification (2) x_{ij}	AW specification (3) x_{ij}
$gdpcd_{ij}$	0.34 (.00)		
$\ln(gdp_i\, gdp_j)$	0.55 (.00)	0.32 (.00)	0.18 (.07)
$\ln(dist_{ij})$	-1.29 (.00)	-1.09 (.00)	-0.72 (.00)
$landl_{ij}$	0.21 (.00)	0.14 (.00)	0.09 (.02)
$island_{ij}$	0.23 (.00)	-0.15 (.09)	-0.07 (.52)
$bord_{ij}$	0.40 (.00)	0.58 (.00)	0.52 (.00)
$lang_{ij}$	0.26 (.00)	0.19 (.00)	0.12 (.00)
kol_{ij}	0.22 (.00)	0.14 (.02)	0.05 (.04)
$uomea_{ij}$	0.62 (.00)	0.59 (.00)	0.47 (.00)
n_{ij}		0.87 (.00)	
Exporter dummy	Yes	Yes	Yes
Importer dummy	Yes	Yes	Yes
Time dummy	Yes	Yes	Yes
R^2 adjusted	0.56	0.64	0.63
No. of variables	352	332	331
No. of observations	54,780	24,237	24,237

Note: Figures within parentheses are p-values from a two-tailed t-test (H0: not different from zero).

The selection equation is in line with our expectations since the probability of countries trading with each other increases with differences in factor endowments. Column (1) indicates that, in most cases, the bilateral trade resistance has the expected effect on the propensity to trade between two trading countries. Distance reduces the likelihood of trading, while common borders and language as well as colonial ties increase it. Two results that are contrary to expectations concern the landlocked and island variables: column (1) actually indicates a positive impact on bilateral trade of being landlocked or an island.

The estimation of the gravity equation is the second step in the sample-selection model. All trade resistance variables, with the exception of the island variable, have a similar effect on bilateral trade volumes to the one they have on the probability of a positive trade volume. Contrary to expectations (see e.g. Carrère (2004)), the results in Table 7.3 indicate that landlocked countries trade on average 15 per cent more ((exp[0.14]-1)*100). All other variables have the expected signs although the island dummy seems to be insignificant in Equation (3). A main finding of Table 7.3 is that trade is higher (approximately 80 percent, (exp(0.59)-1)*100) among UEMOA countries, even after controlling for each country's propensity to trade with the help of importer and exporter specific dummies. This result is stable across specifications. The estimate pertains to the period 1992–2002 and captures, in addition to being natural trading partners as suggested in Table 7.2, the effects of trade policy as well as monetary integration in UEMOA. It can be compared with Carrère (2004), who found that UEMOA traded around 200 per cent more than the norm between 1962 and 1996.

The Deepening of Integration among UEMOA Countries

The estimates of Table 7.3 pertain to the period between 1992 and 2002. The question that now arises is whether the deepening of integration among

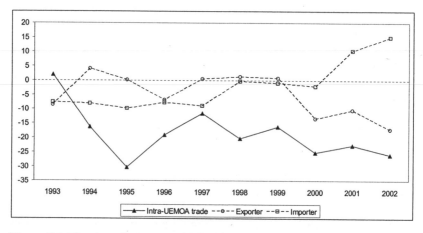

Figure 7.1 The time dimension of UEMOA, deviation from the average effect (%)

Note: Based on an extension of column (2) in Table 7.3.

UEMOA countries during the second half of the 1990s and the early 2000s has contributed to additional trade creation. The deepening of integration consisted in the creation of a customs union with lower tariffs on imports from third countries and a removal of tariffs on intra-UEMOA trade. In order to assess this impact, the extra intra-UEMOA trade dummy is interacted with time dummies and time-specific UEMOA import and export dummies are introduced. The result is illustrated in Figure 7.1, which shows the percentage deviation from the mean intra-UEMOA trade effect over the period 1992–2002. Figure 7.1 shows that both the propensity to export for the UEMOA members as a group and the extra trade effect when both trading partners belong to UEMOA seem to decrease over time. On the other hand, we can see that the UEMOA members seem to be more inclined to import over time.

The result in Table 7.4 (which divides the period between pre- and post-1995), extension (1), shows the same story. The UEMOA members, as a group, tend to be more willing to import and less prone to export, but the extra intra-UEMOA effect is unchanged over time. That is, the deepening of UEMOA integration during the 1990s had trade-creating effects with the rest of the world, but no effect among UEMOA countries. The increased inclination to import is included in a model with fixed bilateral effects that sweep away time-invariant variables (see extension (3) in Table 7.4). Extension (2) in Table 7.4

Table 7.4 Trade creation over time [a]

Extensions	(1) Extension of (2) in Table 7.3.[b]	(2) Extension of (2) in Table 7.2.[b]	(3) Bilateral fixed effects. [c]
$uemoa_{ij}\|t>95$	-0.04 (.51)	-0.13 (.07)	-0.12 [0.09]
$uemoa_i\|t>95$	-0.08 (.01)	-0.07 (.03)	-0.03 [0.03]
$uemoa_j\|t>95$	0.11 (.00)	0.14 (.00)	0.08 [0.03]
$uemoa_j \times ecowas_i$		-0.08 (.15)	
$uemoa_j \times eu15_i$		-0.08 (.17)	
$uemoa_j \times$ $ecowas_i\|t>95$		-0.01 (.94)	
$uemoa_j \times$ $eu15_i\|t>95$		-0.16 (.01)	

Notes: [a] See Table 7.2.
[b] We only include the new variables since all other coefficients are unchanged due to this extension.
[c] The estimates are based on fixed bilateral effects, which exclude all time-invariant bilateral variables over time in Equation 7.4. In this specification, following Wooldridge (1995), we use a Tobit selection process and incorporate the error term from the Tobit in our gravity equation. The results suggest the presence of a selection bias even with bilateral fixed effects. The figures within brackets are bootstrapped standard errors (using country blocs) based on 1000 replication.

investigates whether the external trade creation has benefited certain groups of countries (EU15, rest of ECOWAS or RoW). The results suggest that trade creation, on average (given distance, common language, colonial ties etc.), does not differ for these three groups of countries. We find, however, the confirmation of a structural change after 1995, with imports from non-EU members becoming all the more sizeable (since EU15 becomes less important) as the integration process among UEMOA members deepens.

Symmetric or Asymmetric Distribution of Gross Trade Creation

A recurrent issue when it comes to regional integration schemes among developing countries concerns the distribution of gains (and costs) among the member countries. The more different the member countries are in terms of economic development, economic structure or degree of openness, the more unequal the distribution of trade effects of integration is likely to be. Unequal distribution of gains (and costs) of integration is often considered an obstacle to integration, in particular in the absence of compensation schemes like regional policy.[11] The large differences that exist among the UEMOA countries (see Annex 7) make this issue very topical in the case of UEMOA integration. A critical difference here concerns the difference between the landlocked and coastal countries. The former countries are relatively poor countries with low income per capita (see Annex 7), while the latter are relatively rich and benefit from better developed transport and harbour infrastructures.

In order to investigate asymmetric trade effects of integration, the extra intra-UEMOA trade effect is interacted with dummies indicating whether the importer or the exporter is landlocked. Table 7.5 provides evidence of an asymmetric distribution of trade creation by showing that landlocked countries export less and import more than coastal countries. This supports the need for a compensation scheme in order to proceed with integration among UEMOA countries. Extension (1) in Table 7.5 suggests, however, that the deepening of integration since the mid-1990s has not aggravated this asymmetry.

Table 7.5 Symmetric or asymmetric trade creation [a]

HH-specification			
Extension			
Extension of (2) in Table 7.3.[b]	$Landl_i X$ $uemoa_{ij}$	$Landl_j X$ $uemoa_{ij}$	$Landl_i X uemoa_{ij}$ $X trend$	$Landl_j X uemoa_{ij}$ $X trend$
	-0.66 (.00)	0.86 (.00)	0.01 (.62)	-0.01 (.54)

Notes: [a] See Table 7.2.
[b] Only the new variables are included because all the other coefficients are unchanged as a result of this extension.

Potential Impact of ECOWAS

The customs union in force in UEMOA is planned to be extended to the whole of ECOWAS on 1 January 2008, with the alignment of the external tariffs of the ECOWAS countries that do not belong to UEMOA to the common external tariff. The question that then arises concerns the likely trade effects of this enlargement of the customs union. In order to estimate these effects, we use a gravity equation with only the UEMOA countries, and use the estimated coefficients to predict trade between non-UEMOA ECOWAS countries

(ECOWASRES) and UEMOA members, as well as among ECOWASRES countries. Then we compare the predicted trade volumes with the actual ones in order to calculate the trade potential if ECOWASRES trade as UEMOA countries. The estimates of trade potential take into account the potential impact of both trade policy and monetary integration in ECOWAS, which means that they will materialize only in case of completion of the proposed single currency for the whole of West Africa.

The potential trade indices in Table 7.6 are defined as the ratios of predicted trade to actual observed trade among the specified groups of countries. The results are unambiguous and rather stable over time, suggesting that there is much scope for increased trade between ECOWASRES and UEMOA countries. The trade potential is, however, not equally distributed across groups of countries. It is greatest for ECOWASRES, as our estimate suggests that trade within this group of countries will increase fourfold if integration within ECOWAS becomes as deep as in the UEMOA. Further, the trade potential is larger for import of ECOWASRES from UEMOA than the other way around.

Table 7.6 Trade potential of non-UEMOA ECOWAS countries

Year	Potential import volumes from UEMOA	Potential export volumes to UEMOA	Potential intra-ECOWAS (excl. UEMOA) trade
1996	2.20	2.01	4.55
1997	2.65	2.15	4.78
1998	2.18	2.22	3.92
1999	1.54	1.11	2.14
2000	1.28	0.89	2.04
2001	1.94	1.00	4.10
2002	2.34	1.22	4.80
Average 1996–2002	2.02	1.51	3.76

Note: Trade potential is defined as the ratio between the predicted and the actual trade volume between the countries in focus. Predicted trade volumes are derived from a two-step sample selection model with a sample consisting of intra-UEMOA trade volumes only. The right-hand side of the gravity equation consists of the following variables: constant, population (importer and exporter), GDP (importer and exporter), the share of primary production (importer and exporter), distance, landlocked dummy (importer and exporter), common border dummy, common language dummy, time dummies, and Mills ratio based on a probit (selection equation).

WHAT ARE THE LESSONS FOR EU POLICY TOWARDS REGIONAL INTEGRATION IN WEST AFRICA?

The creation of UEMOA has led to a deepening of regional integration in West Africa, but it is a deepening that has had no (or at best slight) trade-creating effects among the member countries. Poor transport infrastructure, strict rules of origin and numerous non-tariff barriers (administrative, technical, etc.) largely explain this outcome and the small gains achieved by regional integration in promoting international specialisation. Besides, the very specialisation of the member countries, often producers of primary products aimed at world markets and with an under-developed industry sector, limits the potential for intra-regional trade creation. On the other hand, the setting up of the customs union during the second half of the 1990s led to a simplification and lowering of import tariffs on imports from outside and an upsurge of imports from non-member countries. Increased import competition from outside, combined with the absence of trade creation within the integrated area, explains some of the difficulties faced by many manufacturing sectors in UEMOA during the past few years.

West Africa is now engaged in a process of widening regional integration. The adoption of the UEMOA common external tariff by the ECOWAS countries by 2008 is likely to facilitate trade among them. At the same time it is likely to boost import from countries outside the integration scheme. Estimates of trade potential within ECOWAS suggest that trade creation in the enlarged custom union is likely to be significant, but unequally distributed between groups of countries and dependent upon the introduction of a single currency for West Africa. The lowering and simplification of tariffs on third countries' imports are likely to increase external imports for the ECOWAS countries that are not members of UEMOA. This effect will be further strengthened by the establishment of the Regional Economic Partnership Agreement between the EU and ECOWAS, because a main component of it is the removal of tariffs on most imports from the EU in the longer run.

A main reason for the establishment of Economic Partnership Agreements between the EU and regional arrangements among developing countries is the maintenance of trade preferences for developing countries in a form that is compatible with the rules of the WTO. Another reason is the belief that regional integration *per se* can contribute to the economic development of the countries concerned. In the words of the European Commission 'EPAs will contribute to higher growth and greater opportunities through regional integration' (EPAs: Means and Objectives, European Commission). Our study suggests that regional integration in West Africa may fall short of expectations when it comes to its effects on trade and eventually growth. The deepening of integration among the UEMOA countries has not brought trade gains for the involved countries, but the enlargement to include the whole of ECOWAS is potentially beneficial to certain groups of member countries. There remain, however, serious difficulties in the process of enlargement, not least when it comes to monetary integration. These difficulties, some of them of a more political economy character, have to be overcome for the gains in trade and longer-term growth to materialise.

NOTES

1. See e.g. de la Torre and Kelly (1992), Schiff and Winters (2003), chapter 2, and World Bank (2005), chapter 3.
2. On the experience of regional integration in Sub-Saharan Africa, see Foroutan (1993), and Yang and Gupta (2005).
3. Prior to 1994, some of the UEMOA countries belonged to a regional integration arrangement called the Economic Community of West Africa (CEAO: Communauté Économique de l'Afrique de l'Ouest). Two francophone countries, Togo and Benin, chose not to adhere to the CEAO because of their strong trade ties with Nigeria. The CEAO was established in 1973 following the ratification of the Treaty of Abidjan by Burkina Faso (at that time Upper Volta), Côte d'Ivoire, Mali, Mauritania, Niger and Senegal. The CEAO consisted of a common external tariff (CET), free internal trade for products from the primary sector and preferential internal trade (lower tariff rates) for manufactured products that originate in member countries. The CET came into force in the mid-1980s. Preferential duties on manufactured imports varied across products and across member countries, implying that CEAO could not be considered a customs union *stricto sensu*. For a more detailed description of the CEAO integration arrangement, see Robson (1983), chapter 4.
4. Since its formation in 1975 ECOWAS has aspired to monetary integration but it was only in 2000 that a concrete project of monetary union was adopted by the ECOWAS countries that are not members of UEMOA, except for Cape Verde, which chose not to take part. The creation of an enlarged monetary union for all West Africa is envisaged in two stages. The first stage consists of the creation of a second monetary zone (WAMZ: West African Monetary Zone), bringing together the countries of ECOWAS that are not members of UEMOA (Gambia, Ghana, Guinea, Nigeria and Sierra Leone). Liberia has not taken part in WAMZ following the civil war. It is, however, expected that the country will join once peace returns and the political situation stabilises. The second stage will consist of the fusion of the two monetary zones, UEMOA and WAMZ, to arrive at the creation of an enlarged monetary union. The calendar initially envisaged, with the creation of WAMZ in 2003 and the fusion of the two zones in 2004, was modified and the expiry dates pushed back, following the non-observance of the conditions (criteria of convergence) for the creation of the second monetary zone. The launching of the second monetary zone was initially deferred until 1, July 2005. At the meeting in Banjul in May 2005, the Heads of State and the representatives of the five Member States made the decision to once again defer the creation of WAMZ, after reports on the non-observance of the criteria of convergence by the majority of the Member States. The launch is now fixed for 1 December 2009. No new date was decided for the fusion of the two monetary zones. For a thorough and recent analysis of the problems encountered by the projects of monetary integration in West Africa, see Masson and Patillo (2004), chapter 6.
5. It is interested to note that the European Commission, in a first stage, aimed at developing a partnership agreement solely with UEMOA (Maerten (1999)). There is a growing literature on the likely effects of economic partnership agreements. For analyses of some dimensions, effects and pitfalls of Economic Partnership Agreements between the European Union and West African countries, see e.g. Hinkle and Newfarmer (2005), Busse and Grossman (2004), and Oyejide et al. (2004).
6. See Haveman and Hummels (2004).
7. See Rose and Wincoop (2001).
8. Official statistics underestimate the volume of foreign trade because they ignore 'informal' unrecorded trade. It is generally admitted that unrecorded trade is important in West Africa. This should be kept in mind when analysing the trade impact of regional integration. By removing or lowering tariffs on intra-regional trade, regional integration is likely to decrease the share of unrecorded trade in total trade. Part of the increase in trade, following regional integration, is due in fact to 'informal' flows becoming 'formal'. This aspect is put forward in an econometric study of the trade-creating effects of African regional arrangements (Carrère (2004), p. 228). Meagher (1997) remains the best introduction to the 'informal' trade in West Africa and to the

networks which support it. Several studies, spanning the 1980s, consider unrecorded exports at 30-50 percent of total exports (ibid., p. 166). According to Meagher (pp. 182–83), unrecorded trade concerns primarily imported manufactured goods, often from third countries, and exports of the primary sector. The trade of the first kind of goods is often the product of price disparities occasioned by different trade policies on imports from third countries. The creation of a customs union with a common external tariff should decrease this kind of trade while tending to equalise prices between the member countries.

9. Note, for estimation purposes, that we exclude colonial links and language dummies in the gravity equation.
10. Helpman et al. (2006) found both these selection biases to be important but the latter (biases through a variation of exporting firms) was more serious.
11. Unequal distribution of gains/costs can also contribute to regional arrangements being a force for divergence rather than a force for convergence for member countries. On this issue, see Venables (1999).

REFERENCES

Anderson, J.E. and E. van Wincoop (2003), 'Gravity with Gravitas: A Solution to the Border Puzzle', *American Economic Review*, **93** (1), 170–92.

Busse, M. and H. Grossman (2004), 'Assessing the Impact of ACP/EU Economic Partnership Agreement on West African Countries', HWW Discussion Paper 294, Hamburg Institute of International Economics.

Carrère, C. (2004), 'African Regional Agreements: Impact on Trade with or without Currency Unions', *Journal of African Economies*, **13** (2), 199-239.

de la Torre, A. and M.R. Kelly (1992), 'Regional Trade Arrangements', IMF Occasional Paper 93, Washington, DC.

Foroutan, F. (1993), 'Regional Integration in Sub-Saharan Africa: Past Experience and Future Prospects', in Jaime de Melo and Arvind Panagariya (eds) *New Dimensions in Regional Integration*, Cambridge: Cambridge University Press, pp. 234–71.

Haveman, J. and D. Hummels (2004), 'Alternative Hypotheses and the Volume of Trade: The Gravity Equation and the Extent of Specialisation', *Canadian Journal of Economics*, **37** (1), 199–218.

Heckman, J.J. (1979), 'Sample Selection Bias as a Specification Error', *Econometric Society*, **47**, 153-62.

Helpman, E., M. Melitz and Y. Rubinstein (2006), 'Trading Partners and Trading Volumes', mimeo, Harvard University.

Hinkle, L.E. and R.S. Newfarmer (2005), 'Risks and Rewards of Regional Trading Arrangements in Africa: Economic Partnership Agreements (EPAs) Between the EU and SSA', mimeo, World Bank.

Maerten, C. (1999), 'Les accords de partenariat économique régionalisés entre les pays ACP et l'UE, in GEMDEV *L'Union européenne et les pays ACP - Un espace de coopération à construire*, Paris : Karthala, pp. 131–52.

Masson, P.R. and C. Patrillo (2005), *The Monetary Geography of Africa*, Washington, DC: Brookings Institution Press.

Meagher, K. (1997), 'Informal Integration or Economic Subversion? Parallel Trade in West Africa', in Réal Lavergne (ed.), *Regional Integration and Cooperation in West Africa*, International Development Research Centre: Africa World Press, Inc., Ottawa, pp. 165–87.

Oyejide, A., O. Ogunkola and A. Bankole (2004), 'Building Coherence of Objectives, Strategies and Modalities in the Negotiation of Bilateral, Regional and Multilateral

Trade Agreements Involving Sub-Saharan Africa', draft report, Trade Policy Research and Training Programme, University of Ibadan, Nigeria.

Robson, P. (1983), *Integration, Development and Equity – Economic Integration in West Africa*, London: George Allen & Unwin.

Rose, A.K. and E. van Wincoop (2001), 'National Money as a Barrier to International Trade: The Case for Currency Union', *American Economic Review*, **91** (2), 386-90.

Schiff, M. and A.L. Winters (2003), *Regional Integration and Development*, Washington, DC: The World Bank.

Venables, A.J. (1999), 'Regional Integration Agreements: A Force for Convergence or Divergence ? ', World Bank Policy Research Working Paper No. 2260.

Wooldridge, J.M. (1995), 'Selection Correction for Panel Data under Conditional Mean Independence Assumptions', *Journal of Econometrics*, **68**, 115-33.

World Bank (2005), *Global Economic Prospects – Trade, Regionalism and Development 2005*, Washington, DC: The World Bank.

Yang, Y. and S. Gupta (2005), 'Regional Trade Arrangements in Africa: Past Performance and the Way Forward', IMF Working Paper WP/05/36.

Internet Sources

CIA (2006), *The World Factbook*, http://www.cia.gov/cia/publications/factbook/

World Bank (2006), *World Development Indicators*, http://web.worldbank.org/WBSITE/ EXTERNAL/DATASTATISTICS/0,,menuPK:232599~pagePK:64133170~piPK:641 33498~theSitePK:239419,00.html

ANNEX 7 ECONOMIC INDICATORS

Table A7 Economic indicators

Country	Population in millions 2003	GDP per capita in $ 2002	Export concentration 2002 [a]	Taxes on foreign trade in % of total fiscal receipts (average 1995–2003)	Development assistance in % of GDP (average 1995–2003)	% of population under the poverty lines [b]
Benin	6.7	411	–	45	11	29
Burkina Faso	12.1	271	79	24	15	45
Côte d'Ivoire	16.8	708	34	37	6	37
Guinea-Bissau	1.5	141	79	31	41	49
Mali	11.7	294	84	46	16	64
Niger	11.8	190	–	48	14	63
Senegal	10.2	503	39	21	11	33
Togo	4.9	310	26	41	7	32
Cape Verde	0.5	1 345	–	40	20	–
The Gambia	1.4	266	13	42	11	58
Ghana	20.7	303	61	24	10	40
Guinea	7.9	414	78	17	9	40
Liberia	3.4	170	96	–	37	–
Nigeria	136.5	351	97	10	1	34
Sierra Leone	5.3	150	51	45	25	83

Notes: [a] The three most important export products in percent of total export.
[b] Most recent statistics.

Source: World Bank Africa Database 2005.

8. Effects of the EU Sugar Reform on Developing Countries

Marcel Adenäuer, Torbjörn Jansson and Helena Johansson

INTRODUCTION

The Common Agricultural Policy (CAP) in the European Union (EU) has gone through a sequence of reforms including the McSharry reform (1992), Agenda 2000 (1999) and most recently the 2003 reform. The purpose has been to increase the market orientation of the agricultural sector and level Community market prices of agricultural products with world market prices. In this process, support linked to production, like price support, has increasingly been replaced by decoupled direct payments to the farmers.

However, the EU Common Market Organisation (CMO) for sugar has long remained immune to such policy changes. Through a complex system of tariffs, export subsidies, guaranteed minimum price and national production quotas, the sugar price on the protected EU market has lingered at a level about two to three times as high as the world market price over the past 20 years. The main beneficiaries of the support system are the EU sugar industries and EU beet growers, but they are not the only producers benefiting from the high EU sugar price. Under the Sugar Protocol, which was renewed in the Cotonou Agreement of 2000, a number of former European colonies in Africa, the Caribbean and the Pacific (ACP), in addition to India, have preferential access to the EU market for their sugar exports. And new entrants are standing in line.

The least developed countries (LDCs) have been granted preferential access for sugar through the EU *Everything but Arms* (EBA) initiative of September 2001, which will be fully implemented in 2009. Hence, altogether 20 ACP countries, India and the 49 LDCs included in the EBA initiative (of which six are also in the ACP group) will benefit from preferential access to the Community market, at the latest with the full implementation of the EBA initiative in 2009. For the ACP countries and India, imports are currently limited by quotas, although the ongoing review of the preferential access agreement in the framework of the Economic Partnership Agreements (EPA) negotiations could lead to free access, while the LDCs will have free access and will be limited only by their own production capacity.

As the market price of sugar in the EU is high and protected by prohibitive MFN tariffs, in addition to the safety clause permitted under the 1994 WTO Agreement on Agriculture, the preferential agreements are of substantial value to their holders. Mounting external and internal pressures have, however, led the Commission to launch a sugar reform package, to come into force on 1 July 2006, where a main feature is a 36 percent reduction of the guaranteed price. A lower Community price means that the value of the preferential access will be eroded, and consequently, the reform has raised concern over its economic effects on the developing countries.

Using the CAPRI modelling system, the purpose of this chapter is to quantify changes in sugar prices, production, consumption and international trade for the LDCs, the ACP countries and the EU, and outline the complex mechanisms through which the developing countries benefit and lose from the existence of the EU sugar regime, and by changes in its structure. Special attention is given to the distribution of welfare within and between developing countries and the EU. In addition to computing the net welfare impact of the EBA initiative, the WTO panel decision and the reform for each country aggregate, it is also shown how producers, consumers, tax payers and the processing industries within the aggregates are affected.

The chapter begins with a short background to the reform followed by an outline of the CAPRI model and the simulation scenarios. Then comes an account of the simulation results and a sensitivity analysis of the model parameters. A discussion of the results concludes the chapter.

SUGAR IN THE EUROPEAN UNION

The European sugar policy dates back more than 300 years to the colonial era when sugar imports from the colonies were regulated to facilitate taxation of the lucrative sugar trade (Ballinger 1974). When introduced in 1968, the purpose of the CMO for sugar was to ensure a fair income to Community producers and keep the Community market self-sufficient in sugar (see details in Commission of the European Communities 2004). Following the accession of the United Kingdom in 1975, cane sugar exports from the signatories of the Sugar Protocol came under the auspices of the CMO, in practice receiving the same price as Community sugar producers for a fixed quantity of sugar.

For the EU member states, the Community price is reserved for sugar produced within a national quota, divided into two categories, A and B, with different levels of support. The quota sugar is partly consumed within the Community (A sugar) while the surplus is exported with export subsidies (B sugar). Sugar produced in excess of the quota (C sugar), can be stored and used by the refinery to fill its quota the following year. Otherwise, the C sugar must be exported without refund.

Although the CMO for sugar has long escaped the wave of reform sweeping through the CAP, pressure has been mounting up over time. First, as previously mentioned, the EBA initiative will allow unlimited preferential access of sugar from the LDCs from 2009 and onwards, with the implication that the supply of sugar from these countries to the EU market will increase. Second, a recent WTO dispute settlement panel, in response to a case filed by Australia, Brazil and Thailand, ruled against the EU sugar export subsidy regime. The panel decision, which was upheld by the Organisation's Appellate Body in 2005, classifies C sugar exports as subsidised, and requires them to be within the subsidised export limit of 1.273 million tonnes set in the 1994 Uruguay Round Agreement. In essence, although the export of C sugar does not receive any form of direct export subsidy, the panel ruled that the production of C sugar is cross-subsidised by the support to A and B sugar. In addition, the EU was not allowed to exclude the quantity imported from the ACP countries and India, amounting to 1.6 million tonnes of sugar, from its commitment schedule as spelled out in a footnote to the EU schedule of export subsidy commitments in the Uruguay Round Agreement. The footnote was found not to have the legal effect of modifying the EU commitments. Hence, the panel ruling all but prohibits C sugar exports, making it impossible for the EU to continue to dispose of large amounts of excess sugar on the world market in the future. Third, with the new farm premium scheme in place, the economic imbalance in the CAP in favour of sugar becomes increasingly apparent. Finally, several negative side effects of the sugar regime have been acknowledged, for instance that although the CMO for sugar stabilises sugar prices within the Community, it contributes to increasing price volatility on the world market (see the Commission of the European Community 2003).

In response, the Commission has launched a reform of which the core elements are a price cut of 36 percent to be phased in over four years, compensation to EU farmers averaging 64.2 percent of the price cut as part of the CAP single farm payment, a Restructuring Fund with the purpose of encouraging uncompetitive sugar producers to leave the industry, plus some assistance to the ACP countries who have benefited from the high Community price in the past. The reform agreement entails no quota cuts, but the Commission has proposed the reduction of sugar production to below quota during the first year of the reform, as a transitional measure to balance the market and avoid stocks of sugar piling up within the Community. According to the Commission, the reform will enhance the competitiveness and the market orientation of the EU sugar sector, as well as strengthening the EU negotiating position in the WTO Doha Round (see the Commission of the European Community 2005).

THE QUANTITATIVE ANALYSIS

The CAPRI Model

The analytical tool used in the chapter is the agricultural sector modelling system CAPRI (Common Agricultural Policy Regional Impact), which is designed for the assessment of CAP policy reform. CAPRI is a non-linear mathematical programming model for the EU25 agricultural sector, plus Bulgaria and Romania, composed of interlinked supply and market modules (see details in Britz 2005).[1] CAPRI is solved by iterating the supply and market modules, using data from EUROSTAT, FAOSTAT, OECD and the Farm Accounting Data Network (FADN, which is a farm-level database for a selection of farms in the EU).

The supply of agricultural crops and animal output in the EU is modelled by a quadratic programming model. This implies that supply depends approximately linearly on price, and the point elasticities of supply in the 2001 calibration point range from 0.2 to 2.5. A two-stage decision process is applied, where farmers first determine the optimal variable input coefficients per hectare, or head, for given yields, and then determine the profit-maximising bundle of crop and animal activities, at the same time as minimising feed and fertiliser costs. The aggregate profit function is subject to constraints regarding land, feeding and agricultural policy, and a non-linear cost term deals with all the factors not explicitly covered by restrictions. The non-linearity of the function makes it possible to calibrate the model to replicate observed behaviour in a base year, giving a smooth model response rooted in observed behaviour. For non-EU regions, supply is modelled slightly differently, using a normalised quadratic profit function and a simpler model structure based on elasticities borrowed from other sources. The basic behaviour of the function is, however, similar to the behaviour of the quadratic programming models in the EU.

The market module consists of a multi-commodity world market with bilateral trade flows, and attached prices, between 14 aggregates of major trade blocs, plus the EU. Three blocs of developing countries are included; the LDCs, ACP countries that are not LDCs, and India, enabling explicit modelling of preferential agreements with those aggregates. In addition to bilateral tariffs, the market module incorporates producer and consumer subsidy equivalent prices wedges, and for EU15, intervention stocks, tariff rate quota (TRQ) mechanisms and export commitment restrictions under the WTO are modelled.

Demand is modelled using a Generalised Leontief Expenditure system (Ryan and Wales 1996) combined with an Armington approach (Armington 1969), the latter meaning that consumption decisions are taken in several steps. First, the consumer decides how large a share of her income to spend on white sugar equivalents. Second, she decides how to allocate her sugar budget between imported and domestic sugar, where the domestic to imported sugar price ratio determines the relative shares in her consumption bundle. Finally, the budget share for imported sugar is allocated among imports from different origins. A central feature of this approach is that intra-industry trade can be taken into account by letting consumers view domestic and imported goods as less than perfect substitutes, and the Armington assumption is commonly used in Computable General Equilibrium Models (see for example Bowen et al. 1998).

In CAPRI, the demand for sugar at the upper level is determined as a function of price and income, while the demand function at the lower level is modelled as a CES utility function (Constant Elasticity of Substitution), where U is the utility in region r derived from consumption of sugar from different origins, M is the import quantity of sugar from origin r, and if $r = rl$ M, denotes domestic sales. The δ parameters are share parameters that are set when the model is calibrated to known import flows, while α is a shift parameter used to meet known quantities in the base year 2001 (the calibration point) giving,

$$U_{i,r} = \alpha_{i,r} \left[\sum_{rl} \delta_{i,r,rl} M_{i,r,rl}^{-\rho_{r,i}} \right]^{-\frac{1}{\rho_{r,i}}} \tag{8.1}$$

Deriving first order conditions for utility maximisation under the budget constraints and rearranging gives the relation between imported quantities,

$$\frac{M_{i,r,rl}}{M_{i,r,r2}} = \left[\frac{\delta_{i,r,rl}}{\delta_{i,r,r2}} \frac{P_{i,r,r2}}{P_{i,r,rl}} \right]^{\frac{1}{(1+\rho_{r,i})}} \tag{8.2}$$

where $1/(1+\rho)$ is the substitution elasticity. Hence, a lower price in region rl, or a higher price in $r2$ makes region rl more competitive and leads to an increase in import volumes from region rl.

Two issues arise regarding the applicability of the Armington assumption in the case of sugar. First, to what extent is sugar from different origins actually a differentiated good? Second, global national sugar trade is in fact dictated by policy rather than preferences, while consumer preferences are the underlying mechanism determining bilateral trade flows in the Armington approach.

To address the first issue, common sugar, or sucrose, extracted from sugar beet or sugar cane is *per se* chemically nearly identical irrespective of geographical source, but in the view of, for example, a retail chain, the product sugar is more than its chemical compounds. It is also the packaging, delivery conditions etc., so sugar from different sources can in fact be considered to be slightly different products.

Next, a drawback of the Armington approach is the inability to distinguish between consumer preferences and policy-induced restrictions. Prior to the EBA initiative, only some 50,000 tonnes of sugar is imported from the LDCs (some

ACP countries are also in the LDC group). In the model, this volume is interpreted as a manifestation of consumer preferences at the current price ratio when, in fact, the small import flow is due to quota restrictions in the Sugar Protocol and prohibitive tariffs under the CMO for sugar. When free access to the EU market is granted, EU sugar consumers will be able to buy LDC sugar at a much lower price and a surge in imports would be expected, but the CES function effectively limits the expansion. For instance, halving the EU/LDC price ratio would, with an elasticity of substitution of 10, which is very high, result in an increase in imports by a factor of 20, yielding 1 million tonnes. This might be too weak an expansion, since the initial import volumes did not reflect consumer preferences. Therefore, the substitution elasticity between domestic sales and imports is set at 10, while the substitution elasticity between import streams is set at 20 reflecting that consumers consider sugar and imported sugar to be imperfect substitutes, being less concerned with the origin of imported sugar.

Specific Features of the Sugar Module in CAPRI

Initially, the representation of the complex sugar regime in CAPRI was only rudimentary, but recent work by Adenäuer (2006) has significantly improved the model and has made impact analysis of changes in the CMO for sugar possible. Two important aspects that have been ameliorated are the treatment of beet prices and the EU supply behaviour. Although the CMO for sugar specifies how the minimum beet prices should be derived from the sugar intervention price, the total beet price is in fact set by the refineries, due to an array of additional costs and premiums, like premiums for different qualities, payments for pulps, transport costs etc. In addition, the sugar refineries act as monopsonists in dealing with the local growers because of the oligopolistic structure of the industry, a structure that is reinforced by the quota system (Blume et al. 2002). In order to capture the link between the sugar beet price and the market sugar price in Member State *MS*, a reduced form equation, linking the farm-gate price $\left(P_{MS,x}^{beet}\right)$ of sugar beets of type $x \in \{A, B, C\}$ to the relevant derived revenue from sugar and molasses $\left(R_{MS}^{molass}\right)$, is applied. Included are the applicable levy and the processing coefficient of sugar per tonne of beets $\phi_{MS,sugar}$ giving

$$P_{MS,x}^{beet} = \alpha_{MS}\left[\left(P_{MS,x}^{sugar} - levy_x\right)\phi_{MS,sugar} + R_{MS}^{molass}\right] \tag{8.3}$$

When calibrating CAPRI to reproduce the estimated differences between farm-gate beet prices and market sugar prices observed in the base period 2001, consistency with the observed beet price is achieved by the parameter α. The parameter is calculated using data from EUROSTAT Economic Agricultural

Accounts (EAA) and ranges from 0.41 to 0.66, showing how much of the sugar revenue a refinery passes on to the farmers.

The supply response in the EU depends crucially on the specification of the profit-maximisation assumption. Over time, EU producers have constantly supplied considerable quantities of sugar above the existing quota limit, so-called C sugar. One explanation is that farmers can lose part of their quota if they do not fill their quota during a bad year. Adenäuer and Heckelei (2005) show that a traditional profit-maximisation assumption is insufficient to take this behaviour into account, so therefore an assumption of expected profit maximisation under yield uncertainty is incorporated into the model instead.

Construction of the Scenarios

Three major changes exert pressure on the EU sugar market: the sugar reform, the EBA initiative and the WTO panel decision. In order to disentangle the mechanisms at work and analyse the expected impact of the reform in this context, three scenarios are constructed.

The first scenario, *Baseline*, presents a situation in which a non-reformed CMO is prolonged until 2012. The EBA initiative is not implemented, and nor is the result of the WTO sugar panel respected by the Community. All earlier reforms of the CAP are, however, taken into account and a full implementation of the 2003 reform is incorporated. Hence, the *Baseline* is to be interpreted as the most probable state of the EU agricultural sector in 2012 without any policy changes affecting the EU sugar market. As such it represents a *status quo* situation, serving as a starting point for the analysis.

In the second scenario, *EBA+WTO*, the EBA initiative is implemented as planned, giving all LDCs duty- and quota-free access to the EU sugar market from 2009. In addition, the level of EU sugar exports is restricted to 1.3 million tonnes per year according to the WTO sugar panel decision. Since the market module in CAPRI cannot accommodate limits to export volumes, a price wedge is introduced in the import price transmission function to make EU exports prohibitively expensive when the limit is reached. The price wedge simulates the dual value of the export restriction.

Finally, the third scenario, *Reform*, includes both the EBA initiative and the WTO sugar panel decision in addition to a full implementation of the EU sugar reform. In this scenario, the protected price is lowered by 36 percent. Further, by means of a sugar quota trade module, incorporated into the model for this purpose, a maximum of 1 million tonnes of quota is redistributed among the Member States. The quota is reduced in regions not filling their quota and increased in regions producing C sugar. In the simulations, it turns out that no additional quota reduction is necessary. The reduction in EU production and imports resulting from the price fall is sufficient to balance the market without overshooting the limit on subsidised exports. The scenarios are outlined in Table 8.1.

Table 8.1 Presentation of the simulation scenarios for 2012

Scenario Parameter	Baseline	EBA+WTO	Reform
Support price	unchanged	unchanged	-36 percent
Import	unchanged rules	unlimited and duty-free imports from LDCs	unlimited and duty-free imports from LDCs
Export	unchanged	a maximum of 1.3 million tonnes	a maximum of 1.3 million tonnes
Quotas	unchanged	reduced to keep the Community price up	redistribution within the Community

All results of the simulations refer to the year 2012 at constant 2001 prices, implying that all considered policy changes are fully implemented. When describing the simulation results, the word 'change' refers to changes relative to a reference scenario, most often the *Baseline*, and not to a situation before the reforms. That is, two different hypothetical outcomes in 2012 are compared to each other in the analysis, the difference between them being attributed to differences in earlier policy decisions. Note that the estimated changes are all yearly, meaning that for example an estimated gain in welfare is the gain accruing to the recipients every year.

RESULTS

Impact of the EBA Initiative and the WTO Sugar Panel

The first step of the analysis is to compare the outcome of *EBA+WTO* to *Baseline*, that is, to simulate what happens if the EU continues the implementation of the EBA initiative as planned and respects the outcome of the WTO sugar panel, but refrains from reforming the CMO for sugar. The simulation results are presented in Tables 8.2 to 8.6 below.

For the LDCs, the EBA initiative represents a considerable increase in the price paid for their sugar exports compared to Baseline. As free access to the EU market is gradually granted, the initiative will cause imports of sugar from the LDCs to escalate. At the same time, it is no longer possible for the EU to dispose of excess sugar on the world market by means of export subsidies as in Baseline, because of the WTO panel decision limiting EU sugar exports to a maximum of 1.3 million tonnes. This can be compared to the current export level which has amounted to approximately 5 million tonnes per year. Hence, the inflow of sugar to the EU market increases in *EBA+WTO*, while the possibility of disposing of sugar surpluses on the international market is substantially curtailed. Without a sugar reform, the price will be maintained at the politically decided high level, implying that the demand for sugar in the EU

Table 8.2 Market balances in EU25 2012 (million tonnes)

	Baseline	EBA+WTO	Impact
Production	19.55	12.52	-7.03
Consumption	15.66	16.54	0.88
Processing	0.45	0.48	0.03
Fodder	0.06	0.06	0.00
Imports	1.77	5.84	4.07
Exports	5.16	1.27	-3.89

Table 8.3 Market prices for sugar 2012 (euro/tonne)

	Baseline	EBA+WTO	Impact in percent
EU25	707	688	-2.7
LDC	367	496	35.1
ACP (not LDC)	386	403	4.4
Mediterranean countries	354	374	5.6

Note: The group of Mediterranean countries consists of Morocco, Tunisia, Algeria, Egypt, Turkey and Israel.

Table 8.4 Trade flows to and from EU25 2012 (million tonnes)

	Baseline	EBA+WTO	Impact
Imports LDC	0.06	4.16	4.17
Imports ACP (not LDC)	1.59	1.58	-0.01
European non-EU exports	1.39	0.67	-0.72
Mediterranean exports	2.56	0.40	-2.16
Exports LDC	0.13	0.02	-0.11
Exports ACP	0.58	0.07	-0.51

Table 8.5 Market balances in LDCs 2012 (million tonnes)

	Baseline	EBA+WTO	Impact
Production	3.50	4.60	1.14
Consumption	4.96	3.60	-1.40
Processing	0.16	0.10	-0.06
Imports	1.80	3.26	1.46
Exports	0.17	4.16	4.06

Source for the above tables: CAPRI simulations.

does not increase to absorb all the sugar supply. Thus, the only possibility of clearing the market is to reduce the level of production in the EU. In the non-reformed CMO, a declassification mechanism is in place that states that if a quota reduction is necessary in order to keep the internal price up, the quota reductions shall be made for each Member State in proportion to its B quota endowment. This mechanism is activated in *EBA+WTO* and the quotas are reduced until the EU market clears at the politically decided price level.

In Table 8.2 the market balances for sugar in the EU are displayed. As can be seen, *EBA+WTO* results in a substantial cutback of EU production by approximately 7 million tonnes compared to *Baseline*. Hence, more than a third of the entire EU sugar production is wiped out as a consequence of the EBA initiative and the WTO panel decision. Further, due to the substantial increase in imports by almost 4 million tonnes and the corresponding decline in exports, the EU will no longer be a net exporter of sugar. A theoretical possibility for relieving the pressure on EU producers would be to reduce the sugar quotas currently allocated to the ACP countries. However, this is not feasible, since the Sugar Protocol does not allow the EU to unilaterally cut the quotas of the beneficiaries of the scheme.

When trade flows to and from the EU are analysed in greater detail, as depicted in Table 8.4, it can be seen that sugar imports from the LDCs go from almost nothing in *Baseline* to more than 4 million tonnes in *EBA+WTO*. Underlying this estimate is the assumption that EU consumers regard sugar from different origins as close to perfect substitutes. The increase in the overall sugar supply slightly depresses the EU market price of sugar, as can be seen in Table 8.3. Turning to EU exports, the EU discards its sugar surplus mainly in the Mediterranean countries and in the non-EU European countries in *Baseline*. When the quantity of subsidised EU sugar exports is restricted, those countries experience a decline in imports from the EU, as do the ACP and the LDC countries to which the EU previously also exported sugar. Since export subsidies render sugar cheaper for the importing country, the price levels in the ACP and Mediterranean countries rise by 4.4 and 5.6 percent, respectively, when the volume of subsidised exports falls, as can be seen in Table 8.3.

The 35 percent price increase, shown in Table 8.3, triggers an overall expansion of sugar production in the LDCs of more than 30 percent, or 1.14 million tonnes, as shown in Table 8.5, drawing resources to the sugar sector from the rest of the economy in these countries. The volume of exports from the LDCs sky-rockets up to 4 million tonnes, which is a very large increase indeed compared to the initial 0.17 million tonnes in these countries in *Baseline*. The surge in production is not enough, though, to accommodate the large export increase. In addition, existing export flows are redirected to the EU market and a larger share of domestic production than before is exported. Without the EBA initiative, the local markets are largely served by domestic production. With the prosperous export opportunity in *EBA+WTO*, a high elasticity of substitution for sugar from different origins in the LDCs makes it possible for them to supply their own market with imports, directing almost their entire domestic production to the EU market. As a consequence, the volume of imports nearly doubles compared to *Baseline*.

The final aspect to consider is changes in total welfare for the LDCs, the ACP countries and the EU. To do so, the effects on consumer welfare, agricultural income, processing industry demand (pharmaceuticals, chemical industry etc.) and tariff revenues are computed. The change in consumer welfare is calculated as a *money metric*, computed straightforwardly with the Generalised Leontief Expenditure system in CAPRI. If the price rises, the money metric shows how much money the consumers would need in *EBA+WTO* to be as well off as in *Baseline*, the amount required being the loss in welfare. Agricultural income in the EU is calculated as the sum of revenues minus variable costs excluding capital and labour, which are not modelled. For non-EU regions, the change in agricultural income is computed using the normalised quadratic profit function governing their behaviour in the model. Profits from the industrial demand for sugar are also modelled using a normalised quadratic profit function, so the change in their profits can be computed in a way similar to that of the non-EU agricultural producers. Tariff revenues are computed using tariff rates and trade flows.

Table 8.6 Changes in welfare 2012 in WTO+EBA vs. Baseline (million euros)

	LDC	ACP (not LDC)	EU25
Money metric	-778	-181	716
Agricultural profits	1 195	191	-1 120
Profits of processing industries	-48	-8	75
Tariff revenues	586	-290	-53
Domestic support outlays	0	0	1 077
Remaining	-17	-1	-1
Total	938	-289	694

Source: CAPRI simulations.

In Table 8.6, changes in consumer welfare in *EBA+WTO* relative to *Baseline* are outlined. Starting with the EU, it can be seen that the producers lose more than 1 billion euros when the protected EU market is opened up to new entrants. However, their loss is more than compensated for by the reduction in domestic support outlays, mainly reduced outlays for export subsidies, plus the consumer gain, the net gain for the EU being 694 million euros. The consumer welfare gain is a consequence of the slightly lower price level in the EU, and a new composition of the Armington aggregate 'sugar', that is, a change in consumption patterns. Hence, the EU is a major net beneficiary when the EBA initiative and the WTO panel decision are considered.

Turning to the two groups of developing countries, it can be seen that consumers in both groups will experience a loss of welfare, since sugar will become more expensive for them. As shown in Table 8.3, the reduction in subsidised exports from the EU leads to an increase in the market prices of sugar in regions to which the EU used to export, and by trade interlinks to other regions of the world as well. The clear winners are the sugar producers, foremost in the LDCs, who benefit from the market access to the EU provided by the EBA initiative, but producers in the ACP countries also benefit to some extent. Although the latter group suffers from increased competition and the slight decline in the EU sugar price, they also have other export markets. Since the price of sugar rises in those markets, the net effect on ACP producer profit is positive.

An interesting and rather significant aspect in pecuniary terms is tariff revenues. Both the LDCs and the ACP countries extract import duties from the sugar trade. When the LDCs orient their sugar production towards the EU market and domestic demand is catered for by imports in *EBA+WTO*, the tariff revenues therefore rise. In the ACP countries, on the other hand, sugar imports fall when the price rises and, consequently, sugar tariff revenues fall as well. For the ACP countries, the loss of tariff revenue is the most important contributor to the net loss of welfare. This loss reveals one indirect mechanism through which the ACP countries benefit from the Sugar Protocol and the CMO for sugar in *Baseline*. A circular flow is present where the EU imports sugar from the ACP countries, thereafter discarding sugar surpluses on the world market with export subsidies, and where the ACP countries then import sugar at depressed prices and collect import duties. Whether it is actually the same ACP countries that export to and import from the EU cannot be retrieved from the CAPRI model, since the model does not single out separate countries in the LDC and ACP aggregates.[2]

Summarising the components of the welfare analysis, the overall result for the LDCs is a net gain of 938 million euro, while the ACP countries experience a net loss equal to 298 million euro. Hence, for the LDCs the EBA initiative brings about a yearly net transfer of nearly 1 billion euros from the EU, while the former beneficiaries of the system lose out. Also the EU is a net winner.

Additional Impact of the EU Sugar Reform

The second step of the analysis is to incorporate the EU sugar reform into the framework. In this section, the simulation results of *Reform* are compared to those of *Baseline*. In addition, some comments are made about how the impact outlined above of the EBA initiative and the WTO panel is modified when the sugar reform is taken into account. The simulation results are presented in Tables 8.7 to 8.11 below.

A first observation is that sugar demand, both human consumption and processing demand, is relatively inelastic, meaning that changes in the price level lead to small changes in consumption. Therefore, the reform can be expected to mostly affect the supply side, which is confirmed by the model simulations.

In the EU, the market price for sugar falls by more than 40 percent after the reform, as can be seen in Table 8.8. Because of tacit collusion among the sugar producers, the Community market price in *Baseline* is higher than the intervention price. In *Reform*, the market price is equal to the intervention price, rendering the price fall larger than the cut in the intervention price. The reason is purely technical; tacit collusion is not modelled in CAPRI.

The lower price makes it less attractive for the LDCs and ACP countries to export sugar, while, for the EU consumers, EU sugar becomes relatively cheaper than imported sugar. Instead of the surge in imports experienced in *EBA+WTO*, a slight decline occurs in *Reform* compared to *Baseline*. This decrease reduces the pressure on the EU market from imported sugar, and, as a consequence, a smaller production reduction is necessary in *Reform* in order to comply with the WTO panel than in *EBA+WTO*. As can be seen in Table 8.7, the reduction in EU production is limited to less than 3 million tonnes, compared to the reduction of 7 million tonnes in the scenario without the reform. As the level of EU export is restricted by the WTO panel decision, a similar reduction to the one in *EBA+WTO* takes place.

A closer look at EU international trade flows in Table 8.9 reveals that the composition of trade changes compared to *Baseline*. For the ACP countries, the lower price on the EU market leads to a fall in exports from 1.59 million tonnes to just above 1 million tonnes. The situation for the LDCs is, however, rather the opposite. Despite the fall in the intervention price compared to *Baseline*, the price level in the Community market is still above the world market price after the reform, so free market access through the EBA initiative is valuable. As can be seen, EU imports from the LDCs more than triple after the implementation of the EBA initiative and the sugar reform, although this is by no means close to the 4 million tonne increase in exports without the reform.

Table 8.7 Market balances in EU25 2012 (million tonnes)

	Baseline	Reform	Impact
Production	19.55	16.66	-2.89
Consumption	15.66	15.89	0.23
Processing	0.45	0.53	0.08
Fodder	0.06	0.08	0.03
Imports	1.77	1.13	-0.64
Exports	5.16	1.29	-3.87

Table 8.8 Market prices for sugar 2012 (euro/tonne)

	Baseline	Reform	Impact in percent
EU25	707	403	-42.0
LDC	367	374	1.9
ACP (not LDC)	386	387	0.3
Mediterranean countries	354	368	4.0

Note: The group of Mediterranean countries consists of Morocco, Tunisia, Algeria, Egypt, Turkey and Israel.

Table 8.9 Trade flows to and from EU25 2012 (million tonnes)

	Baseline	Reform	Impact
Imports LDC	0.06	0.22	016
Imports ACP (not LDC)	1.59	1.09	-0.50
European non-EU exports	1.39	0.68	-0.71
Mediterranean exports	2.56	0.41	-2.15
Exports LDC	0.13	0.01	-0.12
Exports ACP	0.58	0.06	-0.52

Table 8.10 Market balances in LDCs 2012 (million tonnes)

	Baseline	Reform	Impact
Production	3.50	3.56	0.06
Consumption	4.96	4.82	-0.14
Processing	0.16	0.15	-0.01
Imports	1.80	1.76	-0.04
Exports	0.17	0.34	0.17

Source for the above tables: CAPRI simulations.

The market balances in the LDCs are outlined in Table 8.10, showing that the total export volume is doubled. At the same time, both consumption and imports fall slightly because of the higher sugar price. As in *EBA+WTO*, the price increase in the LDC markets is caused by the restriction imposed upon subsidised EU sugar exports by the WTO.

Finally, changes in welfare are depicted in Table 8.11. Both the LDCs and the ACP countries experience a net loss in welfare in *Reform* compared to *Baseline*, while the net gain for the EU amounts to more than 4 billion euros, and as emphasised above, this is a *yearly* net gain. Consumers in the EU are the winners, both the processing industry using sugar as an input and final consumers. The main losers are EU sugar producers whose profits fall by 1.7

billion euros and also, albeit to a much lesser extent, EU taxpayers. The latter group has to finance an increase in direct support outlays following upon the reform, because of the financial compensation to EU beet sugar growers included in the reform package. To a large extent, this increase in support is offset by the reduction in outlays for export subsidies, so the net increase in domestic support outlays amounts to 298 million euros.

Table 8.11 Changes in welfare 2012 in Reform vs. Baseline (million euros)

	LDC	ACP (not LDC)	EU25
Money metric	37	50	5 931
Agricultural profits	-44	-81	-1 746
Profits of processing industries	1	2	444
Tariff revenues	-43	-367	-251
Domestic support outlays	0	0	-298
Remaining	1	6	-39
Total	-48	-390	4 041

Source: CAPRI simulations.

The overall impact on the LDCs compared to *Baseline* is a small loss of welfare, 48 million euros, which is equally divided between a reduction in agricultural producer profits and a loss of tariff revenues. As can be seen in Table 8.11, consumers are net beneficiaries, albeit by a small amount, which may seem contra-intuitive as the price of imported sugar rises. The explanation is that the sugar reform will lead to lower prices for food exports other than sugar from the EU, especially for cereals which are a close substitute for sugar beet for farmers. In *Baseline*, the subsidised sugar production pushes land prices upwards in the EU, indirectly taxing the cultivation of other crops. In *Reform*, both the production and exports of alternative crops increase when beet production is reduced, and the prices of those other commodities fall to some extent in export markets, for example by 0.3 percent for cereals. Hence, consumers in the LDCs lose because of the higher price of imported sugar, but they are more than compensated by the lower prices of other food items, foremost imports of cereals and poultry, for the latter which cereals is fodder. Here, a negative indirect effect of the CMO on sugar for the developing countries is revealed. For importers of food, the CMO means that imported food becomes more expensive than it needs to be. The price reductions of other commodities also affect agricultural profits in the developing countries. As can be seen, the LDCs experience a small loss in agricultural profits, despite the higher price of sugar.

The ACP countries also experience a net loss when the combined effect of the reform, the EBA initiative and the WTO panel is considered, compared to *Baseline*. As in *EBA+WTO*, ACP producers gain from higher prices in other export markets and lose because of a lower EU price. Since the price fall in the EU market is so much larger in *Reform* than in *EBA+WTO* compared to *Baseline*, the net effect on producers is negative in this case. ACP consumers are winners because of the fall in the prices of other imported food items, while tariff revenues drop because of the reduction in ACP sugar imports, in addition to the fall in world market prices on other food items on which tariffs are collected.

To summarise, the LDCs stand to gain a lot from the EBA initiative, but this gain is erased when the EU sugar reform is implemented. Further, the ACP countries lose in both cases, but the loss is greater when the EU carries through the reform. In addition, as emphasised above, all the changes that occur are not attributable to the sugar reform. Most importantly, the EU must fit its supply of imported and domestic sugar into a much narrower suit than before in order to comply with the 1.3 million tonne WTO export restriction. Hence, irrespective of the reform, the reduction of subsidised EU exports raises the world market prices of sugar so that developing countries importing sugar experience a welfare loss through deteriorating terms of trade, because of higher prices for consumers and a reduction in tariff revenues when imports fall, while sugar exporting countries gain from the higher prices in non-preference markets. Thus, part of the loss accruing to developing countries stems from the fact that they are no longer able to import sugar at a depressed price.

SENSITIVITY ANALYSIS

The quantitative results presented above are influenced by several parameters in the CAPRI model. For some of these parameters there is uncertainty about their correct value due to lack of data. Those are (i) the elasticities of supply for sugar producers in the EU, (ii) the elasticities of substitution for imports of different origin, and (iii) the elasticities of supply for sugar producers in the LDCs. In the following, these sets of parameters are discussed, and the results of changes in the parameter sets are reported. To avoid having an excessively large number of scenarios in the sensitivity analyses, only one set of parameters is manipulated at a time.

All in all, the sensitivity analysis shows that the simulation results remain qualitatively (in direction and order of magnitude) the same under different parameter values, although the quantitative effects sometimes differ.

Elasticities of Supply for the EU

In *Reform*, EU sugar production needs to be reduced to approximately 16 million tonnes to make room for imports from the LDCs and ACP countries, in order to keep within the subsidised exports limit according to the WTO panel decision.

A question is whether, in reality, a price drop from approximately 700 euro to roughly 400 euro per tonne results in a domestic sugar supply of 16 million tonnes in EU. With the elasticities currently in place in the model, it does, after some of the quota has been redistributed to the more competitive regions. However, if the elasticities of supply in reality are higher, a smaller price reduction would be required to provoke the same supply reduction. Since the LDCs are unable to supply a major share of the EU market, the resulting market price in the EU would then be higher.

The elasticities for EU sugar production in place in the model are estimated from farm level data (not published) and they range from 0.9 to 2.0 over the different NUTS II level regions in EU. In the sensitivity analysis, the elasticities are increased by a factor of about 1.5 (the exact factor in each region depends on regional characteristics like marginal cost and original elasticity), and as a consequence the sugar price in EU drops only to about 510 EUR per tonne, and in EU10 it stays even higher. At those higher prices, more sugar is imported from the LDCs and ACP countries, where the resulting market price is higher. As a result, the welfare loss of the reform is smaller for the developing countries.

Reducing the elasticities would have the opposite effect, but that effect would be bounded because of the mechanism in the CMO for sugar that reduces quotas if the market price drops below the minimum price. Thus no sensitivity analysis has been carried out with lower elasticities of supply.

Elasticities of Substitution for Imports of Different Origin

The two-stage consumer budgeting process incorporates elasticities of substitution between imported and domestic goods. A high elasticity of substitution means that a small change in the price ratio leads to a large change in the composition of consumption. In the simulations above, the substitution elasticities for sugar are set at high values (10 for substitution between imported and domestic sugar, and 20 for substitution between imported sugar from different sources), to reflect that sugar is a homogeneous product. It must be underlined that the substitution elasticities have not been estimated, but selected based on economic theory and plausibility considerations.

Additional simulations have been carried out to compute the effect of setting the parameters at twice or half of the values they had in the above simulations. It turns out that doubling them is mathematically difficult due to the extreme curvature of the resulting functions. Theoretically, it would make sugar of different origins very close to perfect substitutes, so that imports from LDC would increase more in *EBA+WTO* and *Reform* than is the case in this chapter. However, one must remember that the exports capacity of the LDCs is limited by their production capacity, as re-export of non-LDC sugar from the LDCs is prohibited. In *EBA+WTO*, the LDCs are already close to that amount of exports.

Halving the elasticities, that is using values of 5 and 10, reduces imports from LDCs by about 50 percent (to about 2 million tonnes) in *EBA+WTO*. That changes the absolute numbers, though not the direction of the welfare effects. For instance, the welfare gain in the EU in *Reform* compared to *Baseline* is reduced from 4.04 to 3.76 billion euros, and the corresponding welfare loss for LDCs increases from 48 to 87 million euros. For the ACP countries, the effect of halving the substitution elasticities is infinitesimal.

Elasticities of Supply for Developing Countries

In *EBA+WTO*, the sugar price in the LDC markets rises substantially. An open question is how much the LDCs' sugar supply actually increases in response to the higher price. In CAPRI, the supply elasticities of sugar for the LDCs and ACP countries are initialised with unity, and made consistent with microeconomic theory by using an estimation procedure. The result is elasticities of 0.94 for the LDCs and 0.95 for the ACP countries. Additional runs have been performed to analyse the effect of initialising the elasticities of supply of sugar for the LDCs and ACP countries to 2 instead of 1. With greater elasticity of supply, the supply reaction of the LDCs to a given price shock is stronger, or alternatively, a smaller price increase is necessary to provoke the same production increase.

The supply response of the LDCs to opened export opportunities in the EU is also determined by the limited substitutability of sugar in the EU. Doubling the supply elasticities for sugar in the LDCs thus leads to less than a proportional increase in the supply reaction. However, if *both* the substitution elasticities for the EU and the supply elasticities for the LDCs are higher, imports into the EU would be considerably higher than in the above simulations, and, conversely, if both elasticities were lower than in the simulations. If the parameters were misspecified in *opposite directions*, say with a too high substitution elasticity for the EU and a too low supply elasticity for the LDCs or *vice versa*, the errors would tend to cancel each other out. No additional simulations have been performed to quantify the latter effects.

DISCUSSION AND CONCLUDING REMARKS

A main impact of the sugar reform for the developing countries is that the Community price cut reduces the future values of preferential agreements for the ACP and LDC producers. The ACP countries suffer from preference erosion while the LDCs lose the rent that the EBA initiative would have yielded in the absence of the reform. The LDCs, with support from the ACP countries and several NGOs, have therefore argued in favour of a less far-reaching reform, incorporating shallower price cuts, in order to maintain some of the (anticipated) preference margins (see for example LDCs 2004 and Oxfam International 2004). One argument was that a high guaranteed price helps the countries to (re)build their sugar industries by providing a more secure environment for investment. Hence, an unusual alliance was formed between EU sugar producers and developing countries, both of whom wanted to restrict a reform of one of the most distorting regimes left within the CAP. What then, if the EU chooses to use its sugar regime as a form of development aid, and renounces the reform altogether?

Several aspects are of concern from this perspective, not only the welfare loss accruing to the producers in the developing countries because of the reform. It is also of interest to consider the effects on the distribution of welfare within the developing countries and the impact of trade preferences on the long-term production structure in the receiving country. An important question is also whether an unreformed CMO for sugar, combined with preferential access, is an efficient way to transfer resources from the EU to the developing countries.

In discussions regarding preference erosion, the focus tends to be on the producers in the developing countries, since they receive the direct benefit of the preference scheme. Less obvious are the impacts on other actors in the developing countries. As can be seen in Table 8.12, in which the level of welfare in *Reform* is compared to *WTO+EBA*, not everyone is made worse off by the reform. Given that the WTO panel decision and the EBA initiative are implemented, both consumers and the processing industry in the LDCs and ACP countries are better off with the reform, the consumer gain being 815 and 231 million euros respectively. Note that in the ACP countries, the consumers' gain in welfare is almost of the same magnitude as the producer loss. Hence, a transfer to the sugar producers in the developing countries via the EU sugar

Table 8.12 Changes in welfare 2012 in Reform vs. EBA+WTO (million euros)

	LDC	ACP (not LDC)	EU25
Money metric	815	231	5 214
Agricultural profits	-1 240	-272	-626
Profits of processing industries	48	10	369
Tariff revenues	-630	-77	-198
Domestic support outlays	0	0	-1 375
Remaining	21	7	-37
Total	-986	-101	3 347

Source: CAPRI simulations.

regime is, to some extent, at the expense of the local consumers and not a pure benefit for the receiving country.

The producers stand to lose from the reform though, and for the ACP group of countries, the reduction of future export earnings is likely to trigger structural adjustment in high-cost countries that are no longer competitive at the lower price. This adjustment can be costly, especially for countries in which sugar is a major export product. The (non-LDC) ACP countries with the highest EU quotas are Mauritius, with a third of the total quota, and Fiji and Guyana, with a quarter of the total quota together. They are all high-cost producers, and Chaplin and Matthews (2005) point out that their high-cost structure is a direct consequence of having a long-standing stable export market in the EU through the preferential access under the ACP Sugar Protocol.

This effect is one of the potential drawbacks of trade preferences as development aid. Prices that are administratively set at a high level create an artificial comparative advantage, giving less competitive countries an incentive to direct human and financial resources into the sugar industry, away from other sectors in which the resources can be more efficiently used. Further, the inherent protection from international competition in the preference system easily renders the industry inefficient. If the countries do not manage to become competitive, they are bound to face preference erosion and structural adjustment at some time in the future, especially since there is a general tendency to move away from agricultural price support in developed countries, while the current WTO negotiations in the Doha Round are striving to reduce agricultural tariffs. Hence, from a development perspective, trade preferences can potentially have a long-term negative impact on the development of the receiving country (see for example Brenton and Ikezuki 2005 for a discussion of agricultural trade preferences).

For the LDCs, the net loss of 986 million euros in Table 8.12 is the loss of future preferences margins and tariff revenues accruing from the EBA initiative because of the reform, not the loss of any *actual* export earnings. The real net loss of the reform is much smaller, 48 million euros for the group of countries as a whole, as can be seen in Table 8.11. This is not to say that this loss is unimportant. For very poor countries even welfare losses of small magnitudes may have a very detrimental impact on those who are affected. However, the loss of the preference margin as such may not be wholly negative for the countries involved. Given the potential problems with trade preferences hinted at above, a positive effect of reducing the preference margin for the LDCs is that they will have more accurate price incentives to start with. Even after the reform, the protected price in the EU will be substantially higher than in other countries, as can be seen in Table 8.8 in which the sugar prices in the LDCs, the ACP countries and the Mediterranean countries with the reform are outlined. If countries cannot export at this high price, it is less likely that they will have the potential to become competitive in the future.

Focusing on the transfer of resources to the developing countries, a question is whether the CMO for sugar is an effective way to provide development aid to the developing countries. Altogether, the analysis shows that this is not the case. Instead, an unreformed CMO for sugar is a costly and inefficient way of transferring resources to the developing countries. As shown in Table 8.12, the total cost for the EU of keeping the unreformed CMO in order to transfer approximately 1 billion euro per year to beneficiaries of the Sugar Protocol and the EBA initiative, amounts to more than 3.3 billion euros. That is, since the EU will gain 3.3 billion euros when reforming the sector, this amount will simply equal the cost of not carrying through the reform. The net gain for the EU is several times larger than the loss of the ACP countries plus the LDCs. This means that the EU can afford to transfer 1 billion euros every year directly to the developing countries, without the detour through the sugar regime, and still have a substantial net gain.

Turning to the EU, the reform is altogether a slight move away from the non-transparent and heavily distorting price support, in which an artificially high price brings about a transfer from the consumers to the producers, to a more transparent and less distorting support in the form of a direct payment to producers financed by taxpayers. As such, the sugar reform follows the logic in the 2003 reform where support is shifted from production to the producer. The reform is, though, far from an overhaul of the old regime. The price support mechanism for sugar as such, as well as the border protection, are both still in place after the reform. It is just the level of the intervention price that has been reduced, implying that sugar still receives special treatment in the Community compared to many other agricultural commodities.

Even this partial reform of the CMO for sugar is, however, a clear net gain in welfare for the EU, compared to only implementing the EBA initiative and respecting the WTO panel decision, as can be seen in Table 8.12. The benefit to consumers from the lower prices is much larger than the loss in producer income, tariff revenues and the increase in domestic support following upon the reform. The sugar producers in the EU lose in both cases, but they lose the most in *Reform*, in which agricultural profits is 626 million euros lower than in *EBA+WTO*. That is, from their point of view, a sharp reduction in EU sugar production levels is preferable to a sharp decline in the protected price.

To conclude, the analysis in this chapter confirms that producers in the ACP countries will suffer from preference erosion when the sugar reform is implemented, and producers in the LDCs will lose a substantial part of the future value of their preferential access to the Community market. However, the analysis also clearly shows that the CMO for sugar is an inefficient way to transfer resources to the developing countries. If the Commission kept the CMO for sugar unreformed, as a development aid, the cost of transferring 1 billion euros to the LDCs and ACP countries would amount to 3 billion euros yearly. In addition, not everyone in the developing countries is a winner in such a case.

The consumers in both the LDCs and the ACP countries will be worse off without a reform.

NOTES

1. CAPRI was developed within the EU Fourth Framework project under the coordination of Bonn University; see http://www.agp.uni-bonn.de/agpo/rsrch/dynaspat/dynaspat_e.htm
2. Note that the tariff revenues come from all imports, not only sugar imports. The change in tariff revenues therefore also stems from changes in the world market prices of all the agricultural commodities for which the country groups collect tariffs.

REFERENCES

Adenäuer, M. (2006), 'Modelling the European Sugar Sector: Economics of Sugar Beet Production and Analysis of Relevant Policy Options', Bonn University, Bonn.

Adenäuer, M. and T. Heckelei (2005), 'Economic Incentives to Supply Sugar Beets in Europe', paper presented at the 89th European Seminar of the EAAE, 3–5 February, Parma.

Armington, P.S. (1969), 'A Theory of Demand for Products Distinguished by Place of Origin', IMF Staff Working Paper 16, International Monetary Fund, Washington, DC.

Ballingar, R.A. (1974), 'A History of Sugar Marketing', US Department of Agriculture, Agricultural Economic Report No. 382, Washington, DC.

Blume, C., N Strand and E. Färnstrand (2002), 'Sweet Fifteen: The Competition on the EU Sugar Markets,' Swedish Competition Authority Report 2002:2, Stockholm.

Bowen, H.P., A. Hollander and J.M. Viaene (1998), *Applied International Trade Analysis*, Ann Arbor: Michigan University Press.

Brenton, P. and T. Ikezuki (2005), 'The Impact of Agricultural Trade Preferences, with Particular Attention to the Least-Developed Countries', in M. Ataman Aksoy and J.C. Beghin (eds) *Global Agricultural Trade and Developing Countries*, Washington DC: The World Bank.

Britz, W. (ed.) (2005), CAPRI Modeling System Documentation, Institute for Agricultural Policy, Market Research and Economic Sociology, Bonn University, Bonn.

Chaplin, H. and A. Matthews (2005), 'Coping with the Fallout for Preference-Receiving Countries from EU Sugar Reform', IIIS Discussion Paper No. 100/November 2005, Institute for International Integration Studies, Trinity College, Dublin.

Commission of the European Communities (2003), 'Reforming the European Union's Sugar Policy – Summary of Impact Assessment Work', Commission staff working paper, Brussels.

Commission of the European Communities (2004), *A Description of the Common Organization of the Sugar Market*, Brussels.

Commission of the European Communities (2005), 'EU Radically Reforms its Sugar Sector to Give Producers Long-Term Competitive Producers', Press release, 24 November 2005, Brussels.

LDCs (2004), 'Proposal of the Least Developed Countries of the World to the European Union Regarding the Adaptation of the EBA Initiative in Relation to Sugar and the Role of the LDCs in the Future Orientation of the EU Sugar Regime'.

Oxfam International (2004), 'A Sweeter Future? The Potential for EU Sugar Reform to Contribute to Poverty Reduction in Southern Africa', Oxfam Briefing Paper 70, November 2004.

Ryan, D.L. and T.J. Wales (1996), 'Flexible and Semiflexible Consumer Demands with Quadratic Engel Curves', Discussion paper No. 96–30, Department of Economics, University of British Columbia, Vancouver, Canada.

9. Comparative Effects of EU and US Food Aid on Local Production and Commercial Trade

Carl-Johan Belfrage

INTRODUCTION

Food aid – country-to-country donations of cereals and other food items – accounts for a mere 3 percent of world trade in food but is nevertheless a matter of controversy, particularly between its main donors: the United States and the European Union. The major sources of controversy are food aid's purported threat to domestic agricultural production in recipient countries and to its role as an export subsidy harming the commercial food exports of third countries.[1]

The threat to recipient country food production has received considerable attention in economic literature, at least since an article by Schultz (1960),[2] and is high on the agenda among development-oriented NGOs (see e.g. Oxfam, 2005). Important reasons for this are that agriculture is the primary activity of many of the poor in developing countries and that agricultural expansion is widely believed to be a key to economic development (see e.g. Sen (1999).[3] The main concerns are the pressure on prices expected from the addition to local food supply, and possibly also shifts in preferences towards imported food types that may occur (see Maren 1997 for what is claimed to be an example of this in the case of Somalia).

The major bone of contention between the main donors, however, and (as noted by the *Financial Times* on 28 September, 2005) 'an unlikely sticking point in the Doha round trade talks', is the expected negative impact of food aid on the commercial food exports of third parties. Those fears are often particularly acute with respect to food aid from the US, not only because it is by far the largest but also because one of its official purposes is the expansion of export markets for American agricultural products. The safeguards against food market distortions introduced (including a Food Aid Convention and a Consultative Committee on Surplus Disposal charged with establishing so-called 'Usual Marketing Requirements', which define limits on allowed reductions in commercial imports), are not considered sufficient by the EU, which wants food aid to be subjected to the WTO disciplines on export subsidies. While the US wants a continuation of the exemption for food aid, European agricultural commissioner Franz Fischler (2004) has even gone as far as stating that the EU will not be willing to move on export subsidization if food aid is not treated in parallel.

The actual effects of food aid on local production and commercial trade are thus of potential importance to development as well as to the credibility of the opposing positions taken by key players in the world trade negotiations. The EU plays a special role as the second largest donor, major critic of the food aid practices of the largest donor, and perhaps the most stubborn proponent of further restrictions.

Against this background it is of interest to get an idea of the actual short-term and longer-term effects of food aid on recipients' own food production and commercial food imports. This chapter is devoted to tracking those effects, with a keen eye on EU and US donations and the types of food aid used.

After a brief background on food aid characteristics, a review of the food aid consequences implied by a simple supply and demand analysis is provided. Following a brief review of previous empirical research on the topic, the method, data and procedures involved in the present attempt to trace the short-term and long-term production and trade effects of food aid are declared. The results of those attempts are then presented and finally become the subjects of a somewhat more speculative discussion in the concluding section.

A BRIEF BACKGROUND ON FOOD AID

By food aid, one usually refers to international transfers of food for which recipients pay nothing or at least considerably less than world market prices. While about one quarter of all food aid involves food purchased in the recipient country (local purchases) or in other developing countries (triangular purchases), the most controversial part of it (and the focus of this study) involves shipments of food produced in the donor countries.

Food aid mainly consists of cereals, which account for about 80 percent of the total in terms of grain equivalent weight.[4] The dominant donor is the United States with 54 percent of total food aid donations over the past 10-year-period (1995–2004), followed by the European Union (14 percent from the European Commission and 11 percent from individual member countries).

More than 100 countries have received food aid during this period, but some have of course received more than others. About 34 percent has gone to sub-Saharan Africa where Ethiopia and Eritrea (when counted as one) are together the world's largest food aid recipient (at 11.4 percent of world food aid over the past 10 years). Other recipients of large quantities of food aid are Bangladesh (6.4 percent) and North Korea (9.6 percent). In some recipient countries, like Cape Verde, Rwanda and Jamaica, more than half of food consumption often comes from aid.

Food aid is usually divided into three types or categories: emergency aid, project aid and program aid. Emergency aid (46 percent of all food aid in 1995–2004 but 58 percent in 2004) is generally given in instances of climate shocks and conflicts, while project aid (25 percent of all food aid in 1995–2004 but 28 percent in 2004) has an explicit development orientation and typically involves the use of donated food in food-for-work projects designed to improve rural infrastructure. Unlike the targeted and in many cases UN-distributed aid in the emergency and project categories, program aid (29 percent of all food aid in 1995–2004 but only 14 percent in 2004) is normally donated directly from government to government and used as budget support after being sold in recipient markets.

EFFECTS OF FOOD AID IN THEORY

Food aid may have effects on local production and commercial imports in the short as well as in the long run. Those effects depend on the answers to a number of questions: what would the supply of food look like in the absence of food aid, how well integrated are the world food markets, do the particular food items included in food aid complement or substitute for items supplied from other food sources, where is the food procured, what do the government and consumers of the recipient country do with the resources freed by food aid, etc.

Bhagwati (1986) and Srinivasan (1989) have shown how the effects of food aid can be analyzed in a two-sector general equilibrium model. The following is an attempt to demonstrate how, in the simplest possible manner, one may think about the short-run effects of an inflow of food aid on local production and commercial imports of food. Thereafter, potential long-run effects are discussed.

Effects on the Market for Food in Recipient Countries in the Short Run

In Figure 9.1, local food output is represented by a vertical line denoted S, in order to reflect the almost non-existent possibilities for local agriculture to adapt its output to price changes in the short run. Domestic food demand is represented by a demand curve denoted D, which is downward-sloping, reflecting the assumption that the lower its price the more food is likely to be demanded. If the transport-cost-inclusive price of imported food is low enough for consumers to want more than the sum of local output and food aid, and if the recipient country is too small in economic terms to influence world market prices, then there will be a supply of commercial food imports, which can be illustrated by the horizontal line drawn at the price p^* in the figure. That will also be the price that local producers receive and the per-unit market value of any food aid received.

Regardless of whether the items included in food aid are sold in local markets (as in the case of program aid) or whether they are distributed for free to individual consumers there, they constitute an addition to the supply of food in the recipient country, which is denoted A in Figure 9.1. Receipts of food aid can thus, in the absence of commercial imports, be expected to cause a fall in food prices in the recipient country or, if commercial imports are present, have no impact on food prices but cause a reduction in commercial imports.

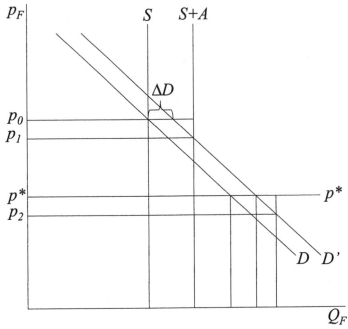

Figure 9.1 Short-run effects of food aid in the recipient country food market

The extent of those effects of food aid on food prices or commercial import quantities will however be determined by its effects on demand. If the food included in aid shipments is sold on the market by the recipient government, additional government revenue is created and an increase in the incomes of some local residents can be expected. To the extent that this additional income is devoted to food, the demand curve shifts to the right (as illustrated by the horizontal difference ΔD between the curves D' and D in Figure 9.1). The same kind of effect can be expected from food aid that is instead directly distributed to households in the recipient country (as is common in the cases of project and particularly emergency aid). Since the food that is received makes it possible to reduce market purchases, households can also under these circumstances be said to have received an addition to income that to some extent may be spent on food.

The increase in demand (at constant prices) that follows a food-aid-induced increase in food supply is sometimes referred to as *additionality*. It can be expressed as the ratio between the demand shift (ΔD) and the inflow of food aid (A), which is a little less than 50 percent in Figure 9.1. How close to full (100 percent) additionality is reached will primarily depend on who ends up with the extra income that food aid brings (targeting) and when that income arises (timing). Should the government for instance distribute the revenue from food aid sales (or directly distribute the food received as aid) to the very poorest at a time when their incomes are particularly low (so that they are on the brink of starvation), there will be very close to full additionality and very small effects on food prices or commercial import quantities.

To summarize, in Figure 9.1, the inflow of food aid A, giving rise to some but not full additionality, would cause a fall in the price of food from p_0 to p_1 if there are no commercial imports. If commercial imports are available at the transport-cost-inclusive price p^*, that price will prevail both with and without food aid, and the entire adjustment to food aid comes as a reduction in imports equal to the difference between food aid and the additional demand that it creates.

If, however, the recipient country government fulfills demands from donors to ensure that the inflow of food aid does not lead to a reduction in commercial imports (according to the 'usual marketing requirements' dictated by international agreements on food aid), there will be a negative effect of food aid on food prices (from p^* to p_2 in Figure 9.1).[5]

The simple analysis carried out so far thus implies that in the presence of commercial imports, food prices in the recipient country will be unaffected by food aid, unless the recipient country is forced to ensure that pre-aid import levels are maintained. An important implicit assumption is that the actual food items included in local production, commercial imports and food aid are identical or at least viewed as perfect substitutes by consumers in the recipient country. Food is, in other words, viewed as a homogeneous good. If, in practice, there are significant content differences, the effects of food aid will depend on (i) how close substitutes the items included in food aid are to the contents of local production and commercial imports, and (ii) how the additional income inherent in food aid affects the demand for locally produced and commercially imported food items. If, for instance, the contents of food aid are closer substitutes for local production than for commercial imports, and only a small part of any addition to income is devoted to locally produced food, then it is reasonable to expect a downward pressure on prices received by local producers also in the presence of commercial food imports.

Furthermore, the conclusions drawn do not take into account the fact that the cost of imported food may vary between regions in a recipient country. In practice, while some regions may have to rely completely on local production and food aid due to prohibitively high transport costs for imported goods, other regions (perhaps with better access to ports or road networks) may be able to engage in commercial imports at reasonable cost. In some countries, it may therefore be possible to observe a mix of the expected effects on food prices and commercial import quantities.

Effects on Net Incomes from Agricultural Production in the Short Run

If an inflow of food aid leads to lower food prices, a fall in agricultural sales revenue accruing to recipient country farmers can be expected. It is, however, far from self-evident that a fall in food prices caused by food aid will lead to a fall in their net income, even in the short run.

Through effects on costs as well as the use of freed resources, food aid might actually increase net farm incomes in the recipient country. The costs of agricultural production could in theory fall more than food prices, as shown by Mohapatra et al. (1999). If agricultural labor is paid with food (or if wages are indexed to food prices), labor costs will fall as much as food prices. If exchange rates are highly sensitive to changes in import quantities, for instance in the presence of balance of payments problems, then food aid which replaces commercial imports may carry the added benefit of significantly reducing the costs of importing inputs such as fertilizers and equipment.

Aside from the above-mentioned direct effects on labor and input costs, food aid may also affect the costs of agricultural production indirectly through reductions in the overall demand for intensively used resources. An even more indirect manner in which food aid could raise the net incomes of recipient country food producers, pointed out by Lahiri and Raimondos (1996), exists in the many cases where recipient countries have tariffs on industrial imports. Those tariffs make industrial production expand, which puts upward pressure on the costs of resources that are useful for both industrial and agricultural production. The industrial import tariffs thus do harm to food production by raising its costs, but they constitute a difficult to replace source of public revenue. By reducing the recipient government's need for tariff revenue, food aid can therefore indirectly support local agriculture by facilitating tariff removal.

Effects on the Market for Food in Recipient Countries in the Long Run

In those cases where receipts of food aid do end up causing lower net incomes from agricultural production in the short run, there may be effects on output in the longer run. If farmers have adaptive expectations, in the sense that low prices this year are seen as indications of low prices in coming years as well, land improvement and cultivation efforts may be reduced. Furthermore, credit market imperfections may make current agricultural investments sensitive to current farm incomes. If such links between short-run income declines and long-run output are important, a dependency on food aid could arise (at least if food aid does not contribute to sustained expansion of other economic activities).

A key factor is the utilization of the additional resources made available to the country through food aid. Prominent, at least among the official purposes of the non-emergency forms of food aid, is the promotion of food production in the recipient country. As already mentioned above, food aid provides an opportunity to finance trade policy reforms that would reduce the discrimination of agricultural production which often prevails in developing countries. One alternative use of the freed resources is to invest them in improvements of rural infrastructure such as roads, drainage and irrigation – common features of project food aid. Another is the development of and/or provision of information about more effective production methods. If well selected and implemented, such uses of the resources added or freed by food aid have the potential to raise future agricultural productivity in the recipient country. Under the right circumstances, one may hence expect positive long-run effects of food aid on local food production.

Receipts of food aid may also have long-run effects on food demand. If the food items of which the aid consists differ from locally produced foods and if the free sample of e.g. foreign cereal types leaves a taste for more, there may be a long-run shift in demand from locally produced toward imported food. If, on the other hand, successful targeting yields improved nutrition (and thus improved bodily strength, avoidance of disease and disabilities, as well as improved school attendance and learning), productivity improvements may follow and eventually local food demand will rise.

Reasons Why the Effects May Differ Between Donors

Since the empirical analysis below will in part be concerned with differences between the effects of EU and US food aid donations, let us now consider possible reasons for such differences to exist. One obvious reason would be the much greater propensity of the EU to purchase the food given as aid in the recipient countries or regions, but the analysis will only be concerned with donor-sourced aid. Another reason may be the distribution of aid between recipient countries given that food demand and supply patterns are likely to differ. There will be a role for that factor in the empirical analysis, but it will be limited by one of the requirements for sample inclusion, namely that a country has received food aid from both the EU and the US during most of the years.

Remaining reasons of potential importance are (i) the timing of donations, which is a key determinant of the extent of additionality; (ii) the commodity content of donations, determining substitutability for local and imported food items; (iii) the contents of programs and projects in which the aid is used, since that may be important for targeting (and hence the degree of additionality), as well as the impact on the future productivity of recipient agriculture, (iv) the share of donations that are monetized (sold in local markets upon delivery); and (v) any conditions attached to the aid, such as restrictions on recipient economic policies, food imports and re-exports.

EARLIER STUDIES OF FOOD AID CONSEQUENCES

The effects of food aid have been studied quite extensively since the 1970s. Due to space limitations, the following will simply be a guide to important reviews of this literature, together with a brief overview of the main methodological alternatives and the associated results.[6]

As far as methodological choices are concerned, earlier research was mainly confined to case studies of individual donors' aid to individual countries (see Shaw and Clay, 1993, for an overview). Those studies offered a great deal of detail but limited opportunities to identify causal relationships and little scope for making general conclusions. During the 1980s it became common to conduct regression analyses of food aid, using either cross-sections of recipient countries or time series for single countries (see Nathan Associates, 1990 for an overview). Since the 1990s, vector autoregression analysis has been introduced as a food aid research tool since it makes it possible to simultaneously trace both short-term and long-term effects of food aid. Lavy (1990), Barrett et al. (1999), and this study, are among the few studies in this genre so far.

Most studies of the effects of food aid on commercial imports and local production have dealt with the crowding out that is usually expected to take place in the short run. Nathan Associates (1990), Saran and Konandreas (1991), and others point to crowding out of commercial imports in the 40–70 percent range.[7] Assuming that no simultaneous crowding out of local production is possible, Barrett (2002) points out that those results imply a degree of additionality in the 30–60 percent range, which he claims is in line with the results of microeconometric studies of food consumption demand. The rather large study on the effects of food aid on commercial trade carried out by the OECD (2003) can be said to confirm those results, while adding detail about variations with regard to food aid categories and distribution channels. Those studies that focus on the effects of food aid on local agricultural production, yield conflicting results as noted by Barrett (2002).

Lavy's (1990) vector autoregression analysis is concerned with cereals food aid and recipient output of cereals in 33 countries in sub-Saharan Africa during the period 1970–1987.[8] He finds significant positive effects of cereal food aid on local cereal production, instead of the negative effects many would expect. In complementary analyses he finds that a contributing explanation is that food aid replaces commercial imports, since the total supply of cereals in the recipient countries seems unaffected by inflows of food aid.

Barrett et al. (1999) conduct an analysis similar to that of Lavy (1990) but are exclusively concerned with US program aid to those 18 countries that have received it most frequently during the period.[9] They find small but negative effects on local production in the short and in the long term, as well as some crowding out of commercial imports in the short term. They do, however, find positive long-term effects on commercial imports but that those effects mainly benefit third countries rather than the donor.

To summarize, the empirical literature, at least the part of it which allows some insight into both short- and long-term effects of the food aid that has been delivered in recent years, is quite scarce. A partial explanation is that it is difficult to come by relevant statistics further back in history than 1988. Possible differences in the effects of food aid according to donor have not been examined at all, despite claims of the use of food aid as a marketing tool. The empirical analysis described in the following pages is an initial attempt at filling those gaps in the literature.

EMPIRICAL ANALYSIS

Choice of Method

Considering the questions about local production and commercial import effects of EU and US food aid to be addressed, the key variables are clearly local production of food, receipts of donor-sourced food aid from the EU and the US, and commercial imports of food. Just as in earlier studies, the primary concern is with the per-capita quantities of these variables, since that (rather than country totals) can be expected to be the focus of food consumption and aid choices.

As noted in the review of possible theoretical relationships between those variables, they all may affect each other in the long as well as in the short run. The present choice of estimation method therefore follows Barrett's (2002) recommendation to use a kind of vector autoregression (VAR) analysis, which allows identification of temporal causality between variables, cross-sectional variations and takes into consideration the possibility of effects of food aid on trade and local markets over time.

More specifically, the key is to use a structural VAR on the form

$$\mathbf{B}x_t = \Gamma_0 + \Gamma_1 x_{t-1} + \Gamma_2 x_{t-2} + \dots + \Gamma_L x_{t-L} + \varepsilon_t \qquad (9.1)$$

where $x_t \equiv (P_t, U_t, E_t, M_t)'$ is the vector of per capita quantities of local food production, receipts of US food aid, receipts of EU food aid, and commercial food imports, respectively, all at year t, while $\mathbf{B}$ is a 4x4 matrix of contemporaneous correlation coefficients. Pre-multiplying by $\mathbf{B'}$ yields the reduced form VAR

$$\mathbf{x}_t = \mathbf{A}_0 + \mathbf{A}_1\mathbf{x}_{t-1} + \mathbf{A}_2\mathbf{x}_{t-2} + ... + \mathbf{A}_L\mathbf{x}_{t-L} + \mathbf{u}_t \tag{9.2}$$

where $\mathbf{A}_l = \mathbf{B'\Gamma}_l$, that is employed in the regression exercises. Restrictions on the $\mathbf{B}$ matrix will make it possible to estimate key short-term effects in addition to the longer-term ones. Since the estimation will involve panel data and a fixed effects analysis will be carried out, the vector of constants $\mathbf{\Gamma}_0$ (and hence also $\mathbf{A}_0$) will be allowed to take on different values for different recipient countries.

Data

As in most other studies of food aid, the present analysis is confined to cereals, which, according to available statistics from the WFP, constitute about 85 percent of world food aid by weight. Important reasons are data availability, that cereals are not as afflicted by output measurement problems as some other crops (Djurfeldt, 2001, pp. 26–28 provides a good discussion of those measurement issues), and that the different cereal varieties are more or less equivalent in terms of basic nutrient value per unit of weight, thus facilitating aggregation. In all the estimates below, the measure of choice is therefore kilograms per capita of the aggregate 'cereals' (where processed items such as wheat flour have been converted to their grain equivalent before aggregation). This aggregation does of course prevent discoveries of interesting effects across cereal types, but since a number of intertemporal relationships are to be estimated, the chosen method forces us to limit the number of variables to consider.

The quantities of cereal food aid – divided between donors and sources (the donor country, the recipient country, or a third country) – were obtained from the World Food Program during the fall of 2003. Data on cereal production, commercial cereal imports, and population in the recipient countries were collected at the same time from the FAO.[10] All references to the EU as a donor are concerned with aid administered by the European Commission and not at all with bilateral aid provided by individual EU member countries.

Some data adjustments have been necessary, particularly as the import quantities of some countries are reported for periods other than calendar years and often include food aid receipts.

Only the donor-sourced parts of cereal food aid have been included, since those are the primary concern in the debate on possible harmful effects of food aid and for positions taken in the global trade negotiations. In instances where it is possible that the estimates may be influenced by the omission of locally sourced food aid, this variable is added to the exogenous variables in the system.

The country sample selection takes into account the interest in comparisons of EU and US aid effects, as well as the need for a number of years of data coverage in order to obtain estimates of longer-term effects. The specific selection criteria for inclusion are that during the 14-year-period of common

Table 9.1 Data overview

Country	EU and US aggregate aid, project aid and emergency aid	EU and US aggregate aid to sub-Saharan Africa	EU and US program aid	Domestic production	Commercial imports	Aggregate aid	US aggregate aid	US program aid	US project aid	US emergency aid	EU aggregate aid	EU program aid	EU project aid	EU emergency aid
										Average quantity of cereals for the years 1988–2001 (kg per capita)				
Angola	Yes	Yes	Yes	36.18	20.93	10.35	5.73	0.86	0.08	4.79	2.85	1.56	0.01	1.28
Bangladesh	Yes		Yes	168.83	9.49	6.51	3.11	1.71	1.27	0.14	1.14	0.50	0.50	0.14
Bolivia	Yes		Yes	127.39	18.81	22.90	19.64	11.66	7.97	0.00	1.28	0.58	0.70	0.00
Burundi	Yes	Yes		44.37	1.72	1.47	1.03	0.00	0.11	0.93	0.13	0.00	0.08	0.05
Cape Verde	Yes	Yes	Yes	34.36	60.32	92.83	49.93	14.29	35.63	0.00	7.67	5.81	1.86	0.00
Congo-Kinshasa	Yes	Yes		33.24	7.02	0.99	0.78	0.66	0.01	0.11	0.11	0.10	0.00	0.01
Dominican Republic	Yes			51.34	119.80	3.76	3.47	2.50	0.84	0.12	0.11	0.07	0.04	0.00
Ecuador	Yes		Yes	117.62	43.52	2.81	1.67	1.43	0.25	0.00	0.05	0.02	0.03	0.00
Egypt	Yes		Yes	230.17	132.66	9.92	6.91	6.84	0.07	0.00	1.34	1.28	0.04	0.03
El Salvador	Yes		Yes	143.61	49.29	14.24	13.31	11.53	1.62	0.16	0.14	0.08	0.05	0.01
Ethiopia and Eritrea	Yes	Yes	Yes	122.62	15.56	15.29	8.76	2.44	1.44	4.88	2.09	0.36	1.10	0.63
Gambia, The	Yes	Yes		98.04	88.93	5.22	4.37	0.66	3.71	0.00	0.12	0.00	0.10	0.02
Haiti	Yes		Yes	52.05	37.99	13.16	10.20	3.04	5.95	1.22	0.85	0.02	0.74	0.09
Ivory Coast	Yes	Yes	Yes	87.90	58.42	2.29	2.09	1.79	0.28	0.02	0.11	0.11	0.00	0.00

172

Country													
Jordan		Yes	25.28	300.14	48.04	44.49	42.80	0.26	1.43	0.95	0.00	0.80	0.16
Kenya	Yes		110.95	19.53	4.34	3.02	0.67	0.53	1.82	0.78	0.14	0.26	0.38
Lesotho	Yes	Yes	97.82	88.41	8.34	4.31	0.00	3.80	0.51	3.70	3.04	0.31	0.35
Liberia	Yes		43.98	18.80	35.00	31.12	2.57	1.72	26.82	2.25	0.00	0.04	2.21
Madagascar	Yes		132.97	7.61	2.15	0.74	0.07	0.44	0.23	0.86	0.75	0.08	0.03
Malawi	Yes		167.17	8.80	7.97	5.47	0.22	0.18	5.06	1.19	0.23	0.13	0.84
Mauretania	Yes		64.95	119.76	14.82	5.35	1.75	1.74	1.87	4.00	1.81	1.49	0.70
Mozambique	Yes	Yes	62.28	10.95	17.76	10.70	5.24	1.85	3.61	2.97	2.21	0.04	0.71
Nicaragua	Yes	Yes	116.78	19.63	17.50	9.71	6.25	2.40	1.06	1.85	1.03	0.72	0.11
Peru	Yes	Yes	86.98	84.95	9.70	8.28	4.51	3.70	0.07	0.70	0.47	0.19	0.03
Rwanda	Yes		35.76	16.37	12.68	10.30	0.05	0.53	9.72	1.55	0.02	0.10	1.43
Sao Tome and Principe	Yes	Yes	24.30	33.28	35.30	10.56	0.00	10.56	0.00	6.30	6.20	0.10	0.00
Senegal	Yes		110.12	79.31	3.75	2.19	1.02	0.70	0.47	0.17	0.00	0.09	0.08
Sierra Leone	Yes		76.33	36.37	8.02	6.56	1.89	0.78	3.89	0.44	0.22	0.06	0.16
Somalia	Yes		46.43	12.11	8.60	4.19	0.00	0.16	4.03	2.42	0.27	0.02	2.13
Sudan	Yes		148.02	15.51	8.34	5.04	1.39	0.07	3.58	1.48	0.00	0.07	1.41
Tunisia	Yes		166.95	188.89	13.03	7.76	7.54	0.22	0.00	1.93	0.54	1.14	0.24
Uganda	Yes		90.92	2.06	1.32	0.86	0.00	0.24	0.62	0.25	0.00	0.15	0.10
Yemen	Yes	Yes	52.83	125.72	5.36	3.66	3.37	0.27	0.03	0.55	0.32	0.21	0.02

time series coverage (1988–2001), a country must have received cereal food aid from the EU for at least eight years and cereal food aid from the US for at least eight years as well. Those criteria yield a sample of 33 countries (with Ethiopia and Eritrea treated as a single recipient unit), of which most are situated in Africa (mainly south of the Sahara), but Bangladesh and some Latin American countries are also included (see the country data overview in Table 9.1).

Estimation Procedures and Issues

After ruling out the presence of unit roots and determining the appropriate lag length, the four individual panel regressions of the reduced form VAR (e.g. regressing recipient local production quantities on lags of local production, US aid, EU aid and commercial import quantities) are conducted with country fixed effects and cross-section weights.[11] The information thus obtained is sufficient for an evaluation of Granger causality between the different variables and for construction of the variance-covariance matrix.[12] In order to be able to estimate the same-year relationships between food aid, production and commercial imports, the following restrictions on the **B** matrix of contemporaneous correlations are introduced:

1. $b_{12} = b_{13} = b_{14} = 0$. Local production is unaffected by inflows of food aid and commercial imports during the same year, since the main activities affecting local production levels (like ploughing, sowing, etc.) have already been carried out before the effects of food aid and commercial imports on local market conditions are revealed.[13]
2. $b_{23} = 0$. On account of its dominant position as a food aid donor, the US does not take into account current EU food aid to a country when deciding on its own level of food aid to that country. It is not ruled out, however, that EU food aid takes into account concurrent US food aid flows.[14]
3. $b_{24} = b_{34} = 0$. Commercial imports are more flexible than food aid, which requires some planning and organizational efforts. Commercial imports may therefore be affected by food aid arriving in the same year, but any influence in the opposite direction can be ruled out.

The above-mentioned assumptions about contemporaneous correlations, together with the estimated error term variances and covariances, make it possible to calculate the non-zero contemporaneous correlation coefficients, and then carry out impulse-response analyses. The latter involves tracing out the consequences, for all current and future levels of the variables involved, of a hypothetical temporary increase in e.g. EU cereal aid by 1 kg per capita. The results of some of those exercises are exhibited in diagrams below, as well as in reports on cumulative effects of shocks presented in Table 9.2. Impulse-response analyses can also be used to obtain an indication of the relative importance of e.g. EU cereal aid for the future development of local production and commercial imports. This is done by calculating how an exogenous shock (amounting to one standard deviation) in e.g. current EU cereal aid would affect VAR-based forecasts of production, aid and import levels in future years, and relating those forecast error variances to the ones that would arise from similar exogenous shocks in the current values of the other variables. A large share of the overall forecast error variance is taken as a sign of substantial influence.

If the assumptions about no contemporaneous influence of commercial imports on local production or food aid are correct, then (no reverse causality issue arises and hence) it is also possible to consistently estimate a single (fixed effects panel OLS) regression of commercial imports on current as well as lagged food aid and local production. The resulting estimates are used to complement (and add indications about statistical significance to) the picture of influences on commercial imports.

Results

The key figures emanating from the estimation procedures detailed above are collected in Table 9.2. The main columns correspond to the results for different samples, periods and/or food aid categories. They are in turn divided into sub-columns with estimated effects of EU and US cereal food aid on local production (P) and commercial imports (M).[15]

Full Sample Estimates

The full sample estimates provide no support for the fears that food aid receipts threaten local food production. The share of EU aid in the 10-year forecast error variance for local food production is minuscule at 0.08 percent and the same can be said for US aid. Neither do the Granger causality tests allow conclusions to the effect that food aid receipts influence local production levels.[16]

Considering the absence of significant influences of EU (and US) aid on local production in the full sample estimate (with all aid types bunched together), one would expect to find effects on commercial imports. That is indeed the case for both EU and US food aid in these estimates, as can be seen from the p-values associated with the coefficients for contemporaneous influences in Table 9.2.[17] However, while the (in size terms dominant) US aid, as expected seems to cause recipient countries to cut back on imports, receipts of cereal food aid from the EU do instead seem to lead to an *increase* in commercial cereal imports according to the pattern shown in Figure 9.2.

Table 9.2 Summary of estimation results (1988-2001)

	Full sample		SSA		Full pre-1996		Full post-1996		Program aid		Project aid	
Recipient countries	33		22		33		33		16		33	
Lags	2		5		2		2		5		5	
	P	M	P	M	P	M	P	M	P	M	P	M
EU cereal food aid												
Influence on future levels of ...[a]	0.410	–	0.012	–	0.465	–	0.179	–	0.097	–	0.000	–
Share of 10-year forecast error variance in ... (%)	0.081	1.449	–	1.306	0.138	1.482	0.045	–	1.423	7.801	–	1.972
Cumulative effect of a shock after 10 years [b]	–	1.905	–	-0.106	–	1.610	–	–	-2.254	6.093	–	10.300
Contemporaneous influence [c]	–	0.622	–	-0.118	–	1.249	–	-0.273	–	2.543	–	-2.529
... associated p-value [d]	–	0.059	–	0.817	–	0.014	–	0.798	–	0.017	–	0.238
US cereal food aid												
Influence on future levels of ...[a]	0.470	–	0.039	–	0.034	–	0.587	–	0.085	–	0.000	–
Share of 10-year forecast error variance in ... (%)	0.070	3.986	0.692	1.821	0.816	5.401	0.038	13.040	0.701	18.741	–	1.372
Cumulative effect of a shock after 10 years [b]	–	-1.141	–	-0.518	–	-0.643	–	-0.500	0.233	-1.688	–	0.734
Contemporaneous influence [c]	–	-0.612	–	-0.403	–	-0.868	–	-0.890	–	-1.674	–	-0.616
... associated p-value [d]	–	0.000	–	0.033	–	0.000	–	0.003	–	0.000	–	0.109

Notes: a Granger causality test p-value.
b Cumulative effect of a 1 kg per capita shock after 10 years.
c Separate M-regression.
d Two tailed p-values.

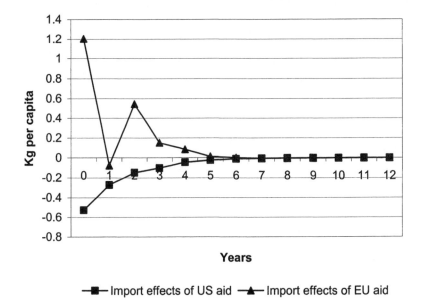

Figure 9.2 Commercial cereal imports by the average recipient country after a temporary increase of 1 kg per capita in cereal food aid from the EU and the US, in the year 0

Estimates for Sub-Saharan Africa Only

The full sample, as seen in Table 9.1, includes recipient countries with vast differences in potentially important characteristics. There is, however, one geographically defined sub-sample of sufficient size – sub-Saharan Africa. For this set of 22 countries, EU (as well as US) aid does seem to influence local production, as indicated by low p-values for Granger causality (particularly in the case of EU aid) and non-negligible shares of the forecast error variance. Figure 9.3 shows the result of impulse-response analyses where the estimated VAR system has been subjected to temporary food aid shocks. A temporary increase in EU aid of 1 kg per capita is estimated to make local production quantities in the average recipient country in sub-Saharan Africa initially (for two years) fall below what they would otherwise have been, but then come out higher in later years. A summation of those effects indicates a close to neutral long-term effect of EU aid (an estimated cumulative effect on local cereal production of -0.106 kg per capita over 10 years, as seen in the table). Judging from these, admittedly highly uncertain, estimates, a country in sub-Saharan Africa that is concerned with the long-term development of its own cereal production would be better off receiving cereal food aid from the US (for which a summation of local production effects during the first 10 years after the shock yields a positive value of about 0.692 kg per capita).

When the sample is confined to recipient countries in sub-Saharan Africa, the import-stimulating tendencies of EU aid do not seem to be present and the trade effects of US aid also seem less pronounced.

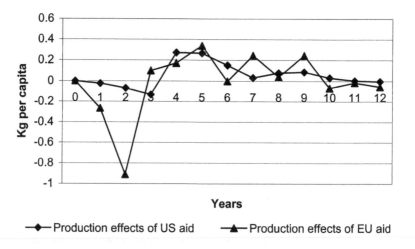

Figure 9.3   Local cereal production in the average recipient country in sub-Saharan Africa after a temporary increase of 1 kg per capita in cereal food aid from the EU and the US, in the year 0

Food Aid Before and After 1996

Next, the question of whether the new norms for EU food aid inscribed in Council Regulation No. 1292/96 have left any traces in terms of effects on local production, is dealt with by repeating the analysis for the periods 1988–1995 and 1996–2001 using the full sample of (33) recipient countries.[18] As seen in Table 9.2, the lack of significant production effects is as obvious in the individual sub-periods as in the full period estimate.

The effects of EU aid on commercial imports do seem to differ between the pre- and post-1996 periods, however. The significant positive short-term effect of EU aid on commercial imports in the early period is not seen in the post-1996 sample, whereas the effects of US aid look stable across periods.

Effects of Different Types of Food Aid

Since it may be argued that the different food aid types do not have the same objectives and therefore are likely to differ in terms of country distribution, timing and targeting, the consequences of each type have been subjected to separate estimations. The most controversial type, program aid, is concentrated on relatively few countries and in some instances for just a few years. Therefore, in order to make the necessary estimation procedures work and obtain meaningful results, the sample has been confined to the 16 countries that received program food aid (restricted to cereals as usual) from the EU or the US for at least eight of the 14 years for which data are available (1988–2001). For the other types of food aid which are delivered to a larger set of countries the regular sample of 33 countries has been used to obtain the estimates reported in Table 9.2. Direct comparisons between food aid types therefore require considerable caution.[19]

Emergency aid

The results for emergency food aid include no instances of Granger causality or significant contemporaneous effects on either local production or commercial imports, and have therefore been left out of the table for space reasons. Those results are only noteworthy in the sense that they do not contradict the position that emergency food aid (which is usually administered by the WFP), through well-targeted and timely deliveries, is associated with a high degree of additionality.

Program aid

While the 1.42 percent share in the forecast error variance attributed to EU program aid is not entirely negligible, the results of the Granger causality test point to a highly uncertain link between program aid receipts from the EU in past years and current local production. The impulse-response analysis points to a negative long-term effect of EU program aid on local production (a cumulative effect of –2.254 kg per capita over 10 years), while the heavily criticized US program aid, at least from the European end, seems to have a more limited impact on local production.

The most dramatic import effects of food aid are seen in the estimates focusing on program aid. Of the overall forecast error variance, 7.80 percent can be attributed to EU program aid (and more than twice that can be attributed to US program aid). While the direction of influence is the expected (negative) one for program aid from the US, the EU aid, curiously enough, appears to be import-promoting. With a coefficient of contemporaneous influence of EU program aid amounting to 2.7768, this effect is a magnified version of the one appearing in the estimate for the full sample of countries (pre-1996) with no discrimination between types of food aid.

Project aid

The estimates for project aid are quite different, pointing to significant positive long-term effects emanating from inflows of EU aid of this type. The impulse-response diagram in Figure 9.4 shows how a temporary additional inflow of EU project aid, according to the (of course quite inexact) estimates, would yield much higher local production levels in the recipient country in the years that follow (yielding a cumulative effect over 10 years of as much as 10.3 kg in additional local production per capita).[20]

No significant traces on commercial imports are left by either EU or US project food aid, as there are no significant contemporaneous influences to report.

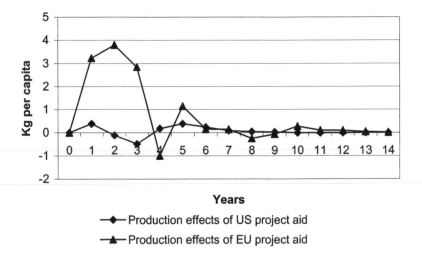

Years

—◆— Production effects of US project aid

—▲— Production effects of EU project aid

Figure 9.4 Local cereal production in the average recipient country after a temporary increase of 1 kg per capita in project cereal food aid from the EU and the US, in the year 0

CONCLUDING DISCUSSION

The above econometric analyses have yielded estimates of the net effects of a number of forces at different points in time, but little information of relevance for inferences about the underlying mechanisms. The simple theoretical framework drawn up above is of some help in efforts to explain the contemporaneous effects of aid receipts on commercial import quantities. As for effects of aid on local production quantities, however, the theoretical predictions are confined to effects on food prices in the year of aid arrival. The basis for the estimates is the assumption that (regardless of accompanying changes in food prices) local food production quantities are unaffected in the year when the aid arrives. Beyond that, the local production response depends on a mix of supply and demand factors pointing in different directions.

One cannot therefore go very far beyond mere speculation when trying to explain the results obtained above. Let us nevertheless conclude with a brief discussion based on comparisons between the results for different samples, and informed by some properties of those samples. Our focus will be on the presence of commercial imports which the food aid can replace and the relative importance of different types of food aid.

The full-sample, full-period estimates point to a rather curious effect of EU food aid on commercial food imports. Instead of some import replacement, as the simple theoretical framework would have us believe and as seen in the case of US food aid, EU food aid seems to be accompanied by increasing commercial food imports by its recipients. Effective targeting and timing of the EU aid, yielding a high degree of additionality in food demand, could explain an absence of import reductions, but not increases in imports, and what follows are some possible alternative reasons for the paradoxical result at hand:

- Despite the ban on re-exports that is normally included among the conditions attached to food aid, it is possible that the cereals contained in EU aid to some extent are exported in return for cereals of other kinds and qualities that better match domestic demand patterns.
- The effect would also arise if the EU were to request that recipient governments match their aid receipts with commercial imports – a kind of export subsidization that, if in existence, would violate the Food Aid Convention.
- One cannot rule out, however, that there are exogenous factors which make both EU aid and commercial imports rise simultaneously. A decline in world market prices of food may raise import quantities demanded, while making food aid a more attractive surplus disposal mechanism for the EU. Another possibility is that the EU often gives food aid in conjunction with other forms of aid, and that the latter, together with the additional food demand created by the food aid itself, add more to the demand for food than the food provided as aid.

For both major donors, the effects of their aid on commercial imports come out as more limited, and the effects on local production as somewhat more significant when the analysis is confined to recipient countries located in sub-Saharan Africa. One possible explanation is that at least some of those countries (or regions within them) have occasionally been without access to cereal imports at competitive cost. A weak indication in support of that hypothesis is that the average ratio between cereal imports and local cereal production among the observations in the sample of sub-Saharan African countries is 0.70, while it is 1.20 in the full country sample.

A complementary explanation is that the food items included in aid receipts have not been as close substitutes for the contents of commercial imports in sub-Saharan Africa as in the rest of the recipient countries. When the adaptation to an inflow of food aid is not entirely through reduced imports, at the same time as the targeting and timing are not good enough to ensure full additionality, farm incomes may fall (see the discussion on net income effects in the theory section) and, by way of effects on expectations and investment capacity, cause reductions in future local food production. That may just be the effect seen in the first couple of years of receipts of (primarily EU) food aid in Figure 9.3.

When looking separately at the effects of different aid types, the stimulus to local production that EU project aid seems to provide, and the rise in commercial imports accompanying EU program aid, both warrant some further discussion.

One cannot, of course, exclude the possibility that the inflows of EU project aid have coincided with other efforts to stimulate future local production which have not been captured by the variables included in the estimates. However, one such explanation that is close at hand – that locally purchased food aid has accompanied donor-sourced EU project aid – has been considered in the estimates by means of inclusion as an exogenous variable. An alternative, yet closely related, explanation is that technical and financial assistance, provided as part of the EU program for food security, has been part of the same larger aid package to recipient countries and has stimulated food production. Last but not least, a possibility is that EU project aid has indeed stimulated local production as intended. The resources freed by the aid may to some extent have been invested in ways conducive to local production, but it may also be the case that the agricultural production promotion elements of the projects themselves (including improvements in transport infrastructure and irrigation) have met with some success.

Reasons for the notable trade effects of EU program aid may (as noted above) be sought in re-exports, coinciding aid flows of other kinds that raise food demand, trade-related conditions attached to the aid, or possibly in a propensity to deliver this kind of aid at times when commercial import prices are low enough to attract additional imports. The re-export scenario is particularly relevant to program aid, since it is explicitly designed to be sold by the recipient government rather than distributed in kind. Imperfect substitutability between items included in the aid and commercial imports may leave the recipient government with an incentive to re-sell the aid abroad. The case for cyclicality (more aid when world market prices are low) is also particularly strong in the case of program aid, since it is not tied to emergency situations or long-term development projects.

In view of the significant, and somewhat odd, import-promoting effects that seem to arise most strongly with EU program aid, it is interesting to examine whether it is plausible that the relative importance of this type of food aid can account for the variation in estimated import effects of EU food aid across the different samples and time periods considered. While program aid amounts to 42 percent of total donor-sourced cereal aid from the EU in the full sample during the full period, it only amounts to 30 percent in the sample of countries in sub-Saharan Africa, which may help explain the lack of positive import effects in the latter sample. An even larger difference in the relative importance of program aid in EU donations can be seen in a comparison between the pre- and post-1996 periods. The most important change, at least in quantitative terms, that took place beginning in 1996, was the reduction in program aid. In the pre-1996 period, for which the estimates include a significant positive influence of aggregate EU cereal aid on commercial cereal imports by recipient countries, 51 percent of that EU aid was program aid. In the period beginning in 1996, for which no positive influence of EU cereal aid is detected, the program aid share was a mere 21 percent. Hence, the relative importance of program aid may be a key to the trade consequences of EU food aid.

Since no similar pattern arises with US program aid, a recommendation for further research is to look for unique characteristics and circumstances of EU program aid. Those may, as detailed above, include possibilities for re-export, trade-related aid conditions, and coincidence with other aid efforts that stimulate food demand.

NOTES

1. Another problem thought to arise with food aid is that it is pro-cyclical in character, i.e. that more is given when world food prices (and thus the opportunity costs of giving food away) are low, resulting in increased variability in the returns to agricultural production in recipient countries. When tied to food produced in donor countries, as is normally the case, food aid is also considered a highly inefficient form of aid. The question 'why not a check instead?' asked by Singer et al. (1987) is a relevant one, and a large study by the OECD (2005) makes the point that using the donor country as the source of the donated food typically adds one third to the cash amount needed for the recipient to obtain food of the same quantity and quality. However, as the inefficiency involved will hardly come as a surprise to donors, and since the option of writing a check instead has been available all along, it is reasonable to assume that much of the resources going into donor-sourced food aid do add to rather than substitute for other forms of aid.
2. Clay and Stokke (2000) and Barrett (2002) review this literature.
3. In a study of food aid to Ethiopia, however, Levinsohn and McMillan (2005) find that food aid there is pro-poor because the poor tend to be net buyers of food.
4. The most comprehensive statistics on food aid are kept by the World Food Program and the interested reader is recommended to visit www.wfp.org/interfais (which is also the source of the numbers in this brief overview) for more detailed information.
5. This does of course require that the recipient country government is indeed able to exercise control over the quantity of imports, either directly if there is a government monopoly on cross-

border food trade, or indirectly if it is possible to effectively administer instruments like tariffs and quotas (i.e. if smuggling can be prevented or at least be made more costly).

6. Substantial parts of this overview have been borrowed from Barrett (2002), who provides an excellent review of recent literature, with a focus on the trade effects of food aid but with substantial coverage also of studies dealing with the closely related effects on local agricultural production in recipient countries.

7. This summary is due to Barrett (2002).

8. The countries in Lavy's study were Angola, Burundi, Benin, Burkina Faso, Botswana, the Central African Republic, Chad, Cameroon, Djibouti, Ethiopia, the Gambia, Ghana, Kenya, Lesotho, Liberia, Madagascar, Mauritius, Mauritania, Mali, Malawi, Mozambique, Niger, Rwanda, Senegal, Sierra Leone, Somalia, Sudan, Tanzania, Togo, Uganda, Zaire, Zambia and Zimbabwe.

9. The countries included in the study of Barrett et al. (1999) were Bangladesh, Bolivia, the Dominican Republic, Egypt, Ghana, Guinea, Indonesia, Israel, Jamaica, South Korea, Morocco, Peru, Pakistan, Sri Lanka, Sierra Leone, Sudan, Tunisia and Zaire.

10. http://faostat.fao.org/collections.

11. The hypothesis of a presence of unit roots could in all cases be ruled out even at the 1 percent level of significance, when employing tests adapted to panel data recommended by Im et al. (2003). The appropriate lag length (with the restriction of an equal number of lags across equations) is selected among alternatives involving up to five lags with the help of variance-covariance matrix determinants using the Schwarz Bayesian criterion (SBC). The cross-section weights, derived from cross-section variance estimates obtained in a first-stage pooled regression, are designed to neutralize heteroskedasticity across recipient countries. The estimates have been obtained using EViews. All regressions include a time trend. Occasional comments on the statistical significance of coefficients in individual regressions are based on White's heteroskedasticity-consistent standard errors.

12. The evaluation of Granger causality involves a Wald test of the restriction that all coefficients of past values of a variable are equal to zero. The level of significance (p-value) associated with the F-statistics thus obtained are reported in tables below. A more detailed description of and motivation for the methods used can be found in e.g. Enders (1995, pp. 294–354).

13. The assumption that local production levels are insensitive to current receipts of food aid is supported by the results of Barrett et al. (1999).

14. This assumption was found to be of little consequence, however, as the estimates obtained using the reverse donor relationship were very similar.

15. The estimates of effects of local production and commercial imports on food aid flows, of which at least the former are significant in Granger causality terms, are not reported for space reasons but are of course available from the author upon request.

16. A general rule for the discussion of production effects is that they are considered insignificant when the p-value of the test for Granger causality exceeds 0.1 and the share in the forecast error variance is below 1 percent (those properties coincide in all cases except US program aid). In those cases, other impulse-response related kinds of output (impulse-response diagrams and cumulative effects of shocks) are not reported.

17. A general rule for the discussion of commercial import effects is that they are considered insignificant when the (two-tailed) p-value of the coefficient for contemporaneous effect of a food aid flow is above 10 percent. In those cases, other impulse-response related kinds of output (impulse-response diagrams and cumulative effects of shocks) are not reported.

18. Unfortunately, a shortage of degrees of freedom makes it impossible to repeat this exercise for the sub-Saharan African sample or the sample of frequent program aid recipients used below.

19. The use of lags and error term covariances in a relatively small sample with short time series in practice limits any structural VAR model estimations of this kind to at most four endogenous variables. That makes it necessary to consider one food aid type variable at a time as endogenous variables if both EU and US aid are to be included in the same system. In order to reduce estimation biases due to omitted influences from other types of aid on the system in question, lagged receipts of the other types of food aid have instead been included as exogenous variables in the individual regressions. In the separate import regressions, contemporaneous receipts of the other types of food aid have also been included as exogenous variables.

20. In order to control for influences from simultaneous receipts of food aid using locally purchased food, lagged values of total cereal food aid using local purchases have been included as exogenous variables in the individual regressions. Only minimal changes in the values or significance of the other coefficients are registered.

REFERENCES

Barrett, C.B. (1998), 'Food Aid: Is It Development Assistance, Trade Promotion, Both or Neither?', *American Journal of Agricultural Economics*, **80**, 566–71.

Barrett, C.B., S. Mohapatra, and D.L. Snyder (1999), 'The Dynamic Effects of U.S. Food Aid', *Economic Inquiry*, **37** (4), 647–56.

Bhagwati, J. (1986), 'Food Aid, Agricultural Production and Welfare', in S. Guhan and M.R. Shroff (eds), *Essays on Economic Progress and Welfare*, New Delhi: Oxford University Press.

Clay, E. and O. Stokke (2000), *Food Aid and Human Security*, London: Frank Cass.

Djurfeldt, G. (2001), *Mera Mat: Att brödföda en växande befolkning* [More Food: To Feed a Growing Population], Lund: Arkiv förlag.

Enders, W. (1995), *Applied Econometric Time Series*, Hoboken, NJ: John Wiley & Sons, Inc.

Financial Times (2005), 'The Folly of Food Aid', Editorial Comment, 28 September .

Gupta, S., B. Clemens, and E.R. Tiongson (2003), 'Foreign Aid and Consumption Smoothing: Evidence from Global Food Aid', IMF Working Paper 03/40, International Monetary Fund, Washington, DC.

Heckman, J.J., and B.S. Payner (1989), 'Determining the Impact of Federal Antidiscrimination Policy on the Economic Status of Blacks: A Study of South Carolina', *American Economic Review*, **79** (1), 138–77.

Im, K.S., M.H. Pesaran, and Y. Shin (2003), 'Testing for Unit Roots in Heterogeneous Panels', *Journal of Econometrics*, **115** (1), 53–74.

Lahiri, S. and P. Raimondos (1996), 'Food Aid and Food Production: A Theoretical Analysis', in V.N. Balasubramanyam and D. Greenaway (eds), *Trade and Development*, London: Macmillan.

Lavy, V. (1990), 'Does Food Aid Depress Food Production? The Disincentive Dilemma in the African Context', Working Paper No. 460, The World Bank, Washington, DC.

Levinsohn, J. and M. McMillan (2005), 'Does Food Aid Harm the Poor? Household Evidence from Ethiopia', Working Paper No. 11048, National Bureau of Economic Research, Cambridge, MA.

Maren, M. (1997), *The Road to Hell: The Ravaging Effects of Foreign Aid and International Charity*, New York: The Free Press.

Mohapatra, S., C.B. Barrett, D.L. Snyder, and B. Biswas (1999), 'Does Food Aid Really Discourage Food Production?', *Indian Journal of Agricultural Economics*, **54** (2), 212–219.

Nathan Associates (1990), *Food Aid Impacts on Commercial Trade. A Review of Evidence*, Washington, DC: Nathan Associates.

NR International (2000), 'Evaluation of EC Food Aid Security Policy, Food Aid Management and Programs in Support of Food Security, Regulation No. 1292/96 of 27 June 1996'.

OECD (2003), 'Export Competition Issues Related to Food Aid', *Working Paper for the Joint Working Party on Agriculture and Trade*, COM/AGR/TD/WP (2003)48, Paris: Organisation for Economic Cooperation and Development.

OECD (2005), *The Development Effectiveness of Food Aid: Does Tying Matter?*, Paris: Organization for Economic Cooperation and Development.

Oxfam (2005), 'Food Aid or Hidden Dumping', *Oxfam Briefing Paper*, March.

Saran, R. and P. Konandreas (1991), 'An Additional Resource? A Global Perspective on Food Aid Flows in Relation to Development Assistance', in E. Clay and O. Stokke (eds), *Food Aid Reconsidered: Assessing the Impact on Third World Countries*, London: Frank Cass.

Schultz, T.W. (1960), 'Value of US Farm Surpluses to Underdeveloped Countries', *Journal of Farm Economics*, **42** (5), 1019–30.

Sen, A. (1981), *Poverty and Famines: An Essay on Entitlement and Deprivation*, Oxford: Clarendon Press.

Sen, A. (1999), *Development as Freedom*, Oxford: Oxford University Press.

Shaw, J. and E. Clay (eds) (1993), *World Food Aid: Experiences of Recipients and Donors*, Portsmouth, NH: Heinemann.

Singer, H., J. Wood, and T. Jennings (1987), *Food Aid: The Challenge and the Opportunity*, Oxford: Oxford University Press.

SOU 2002:75 (2002), *Utrota svälten; Livsmedelssäkerhet, ett nationellt and globalt ansvar. Betänkande inför 'World Food Summit, five years later'* [Exterminate starvation; Food security, a national and global responsibility. Report to 'World Food Summit, five years later'], Stockholm: Fritzes.

Srinivasan, T.N. (1989), 'Food Aid: A Cause of Development Failure or an Instrument of Success?', *The World Bank Economic Review*, **3** (1), 39–65.

Tschirley, D., C. Donovan, and M.T. Weber (1996), 'Food Aid Markets: Lessons from Mozambique', *Food Policy*, **21**(2), 189–209.

Internet Sources

AgraEurope (2004), 'EU Tables WTO Offer to Scrap Agricultural Export Refunds', www.agra-net.com, accessed 14 May 2004.

Barrett, C.B. (2002), 'Food Aid and Commercial International Food Trade', aem.cornell.edu/faculty_sites/cbb2/Papers/BarrettOECDReportMar2002.pdf, accessed 17 June 2004.

Cairns Group (2004), 'Negotiating Proposal on Export Competition', www.cairnsgroup.org/proposals/export_competition_fc.html, accessed 25 April 2004.

European Commission (2000a), 'EU Food Aid and Food Security Program. Towards Recipient Country Ownership of Food Security, Biannual report', 1998–1999., europa.eu.int/comm/europeaid/projects/resal/Download/report/fact/9899fspeng1.pdf, accessed 17 June 2004.

European Commission (2000b), 'European Communities Proposal: Export Competition' (dated 15 September 2000), europa.eu.int/comm/agriculture/external/wto/document/prop4_en.pdf, accessed 17 June 2004.

European Union at United Nations (2004), 'WTO-DDA – EU Ready to Go Extra Mile in Three Key Areas of the Talks', europa-eu-un.org/article.asp? id=3490, accessed 10 May 2004.

FAO (1999), Food Aid Convention, www.fao.org/Legal/rtf/fac99-e.htm, accessed 21 April 2004.

FAO (2002), 'Declaration of the World Food Summit: Five Years Later', www.fao.org/DOCREP/MEETING/005/Y7106E/Y7106E09.htm, accessed 17 June 2004.

Fischler, F. (2004), speech to the European Parliament on 13 January 2004, europa-eu-un.org/article.asp?id=3150, accessed 26 April 2004.

International Grains Council (1999), 'New Food Aid Convention', www.igc.org.uk/press/pr990331.htm, accessed 17 June 2004.

USDA (2001), 'US Food Aid Programs Description: Public Law 480, Food for Progress and Section 416 (b)', fas.usda.gov/excredits/pl480/pl480ofst.html, accessed 21 April 2004.

WTO (1994), *Uruguay Round Agreement on Agriculture*, www.wto.org/english/docs_e/legal_e/14-ag.pdf, accessed 17 June 2004.

WTO (2003), 'Annexes to the draft Cancun Ministerial Text', www.wto.org/english/thewto_e/minist_e/min03_e/draft_decl_annex_e.htm, accessed 21 April 2004.

10. Does EU Aid Promote Growth?

Pontus Hansson

INTRODUCTION

For a number of decades, rich countries have given poorer countries assistance in the form of aid. Aid comes in many different shapes. It may be grants or subsidized loans, it may be strictly monetary or consist of goods or technical assistance. Regardless of shape, a common element is that aid should be intended to benefit economic development or economic welfare. These two targets are not necessarily mutually compatible. Aid that promotes long-run economic development may harm income distribution and welfare in the short run and vice versa. Therefore, it is not obvious that all aid has economic growth in the recipient country as the ultimate target. Nevertheless, growth is likely to be the prime target as long-run development is the best way to ensure that poverty is diminished or even eradicated in the longer term.

Most aid is given bilaterally from one country to another, but aid is also provided by multilateral bodies such as the European Union. In fact, the European Union is the largest multilateral donor of aid in the world. It is therefore of interest to examine whether aid from the European Union affects recipient countries any differently to aid from other sources.

Previous studies on aid and growth have come up with a diverse range of conclusions. Some find that aid is good for growth, others find the opposite and yet others find that aid is good for growth in certain circumstances or provided that certain conditions are fulfilled. Virtually all of those studies examine the effects of total aid flows. In this chapter, we seek to shed light on the issue of whether the particular aid flows that come from the European Union have been beneficial for growth. We concentrate on the multilateral aid flows from the European Union, i.e. aid that is granted by the central administration of the European Union. Thus, we exclude aid from individual member states of the European Union as well as aid from other organizations or countries of the world.

The empirical approach mimics those of most previous studies. We use cross-country panel data regressions with two stage least squares estimation and control for the standard variables that are generally believed to affect growth. Essentially, the result is that we cannot find a significant relation between aid flows from the European Union and growth in the recipient country.

AID AND GROWTH

The vast literature on economic growth identifies three basic sources of growth in per capita GDP: investment in physical capital, investment in human capital and technological progress.[1,2] By investing in physical capital, the capital stock per worker increases. By investing in human capital, the skill level of the workforce is improved. And by adopting more advanced technology and better organization, output is raised for a given level of inputs. In order for aid to improve growth in poor countries, these are the sources of growth that need to be targeted.

Aid, in its various forms, can affect all three sources of growth positively. After all, it is not unreasonable to believe that a poor country that is given funds to increase investment in key areas such as infrastructure, education and health care, should benefit in terms of higher growth rates and improved living standards. But despite the strong belief that aid contributes to productive investment in the recipient country, it is not obvious that poor countries receiving sizable sums of aid experience higher growth rates than countries receiving less aid.

Empirical studies on the link between the provision of aid and subsequent growth rates at best provide mixed evidence. Results range from the completely opposite outcomes of aid having the suggested positive impact, to aid not only being inconsequential but detrimental to a country's growth rate. Some studies fail to identify any impact of aid and some suggest that aid is good for growth only in countries with certain characteristics such as a good domestic economic policy. Whether aid actually benefits poor countries in terms of growth is therefore still an open issue.

To summarize the discussion of why aid is or is not likely to make a contribution to a country's growth rate, this section provides a brief overview of the link between aid and growth from a theoretical and an empirical perspective.

Theoretical Aspects

The theoretical grounds for believing that aid should improve growth are quite straightforward, but there are also theoretical reasons why aid might not render the desired outcome in terms of growth. Our discussion on the theoretical link between aid and growth starts with a focus on investment in physical capital, then turns to investment in human capital and ends by discussing how aid can improve technological standards.

Turning first to investment in physical capital, the inflow of aid into a country is likely to increase the level of investment. Often, aid is tied to specific projects such as roads, hospitals, schools, energy provision or factories, which by definition increases the capital stock of the recipient country. And even if aid is not directly linked to a particular investment purpose, it swells the budget of the recipient country and thereby allows it to finance a larger amount of investment. The latter argument is formally underpinned by Dalgaard, Hansen and Tarp (2004), who use a standard overlapping generations model and show that aid transfers improve steady state productivity through raising the capital stock per person.

However, the seemingly straightforward positive link between aid and investment is not without qualification. Whether grants that are not tied to a specific project but simply relax the budget restriction of the recipient country are actually used for investment purposes depends on the recipient country's marginal propensity to save, which tends to be low. If a poor country is given extra funds, there is likely to be a strong opinion in favour of expanding consumption rather than investment. If aid is used for consumption purposes, short-term utility increases and poverty may initially decrease if funds are directed towards the poor, but there will be no effects on long-term growth.

Furthermore, even if a grant is intrinsically linked to an investment project, the problem of fungibility may result in no actual increase in the overall level of investment. Fungibility in this context means that aid receipts that finance a project are not necessarily added to the domestic funds allocated to the same project. Instead, they may replace domestic funds, thereby making the previously allocated domestic funds available for consumption purposes elsewhere in the economy. For example if a grant is provided conditional on its use in assisting in building a road, the government of the recipient country may remove funds of equal size that were already allocated towards building the road, leaving total investment at the same level as before.

Moving on to human capital, there is a good chance that aid can improve the education level and educational standards of a poor country. If aid is used to build schools, finance school material and increase teachers' salaries, both the quantity and quality of investment in human capital are likely to improve. But the same caveat that regards investment is applicable here. If grants merely replace domestic spending on education, nothing is gained in terms of human capital formation.

Another channel through which aid can indirectly stimulate the formation of human capital is through the physical presence of foreign aid workers and their interaction with domestic workers. The transfer of skills and knowledge that takes place as a natural part of encounters between people may be an important source of improvements in human capital for key personnel at a more advanced level. In turn, such advanced skills may be crucial for the present and future adoption of new and more advanced technology by the recipient country.

A similar argument can be put forward for technological advances. Rich countries' involvement in aid-financed projects may constitute an important source of technology transfer, both through the transfer of know-how from aid workers to domestic workers and the physical transfer of machinery and equipment. Romer (1993) states that in order for poor countries to improve their technology, it is necessary to bridge both an idea gap – the absence of technological know-how and the absence of the required skill level of the workforce to handle more advanced technology – and an object gap – the absence of the actual machinery and equipment that embody the more advanced technology and the absence of facilities in terms of infrastructure to make the implementation of more advanced technology possible. The involvement of rich countries in investment projects in poor countries has the potential to contribute simultaneously to reducing both of those gaps. However, criticism has been directed at this argument on the grounds that many aid projects involve the transfer of technological know-how for the duration of the project only. If all machinery and equipment are withdrawn when a project is terminated, it is hard for the local community to bridge the object gap without further assistance.

The technology transfer argument also breaks down if aid solely comes in the form of a cheque without any accompanying personnel or equipment. In that case, the basic channel through which aid can affect technology is if the money is used for investment in areas that benefit the local industry. In an economic environment with an improved infrastructure, the potential gains from innovations are larger and more innovations in local businesses are likely to follow. Hence, if aid finances e.g. infrastructure and human capital, it is likely to spill over into improved overall technology as entrepreneurs identify new ways of making profits based on the new opportunities that arise.

Even though the above arguments in favour of aid exerting a positive influence on growth are compelling, there are also arguments pointing in the opposite direction. We have already discussed the problem of fungibility, but there are more potential problems that cloud the picture. Hudson and Mosley (2001) put forward the notion that aid affects relative prices and individual behaviour in the recipient country with unintended consequences. If aid comes in the form of goods, it may distort incentives by making domestic production less profitable. If a regular stream of funds is coming in from abroad, domestic saving may become less attractive. In other words, aid can be detrimental if its effect is to create a dependence on aid rather than complementing domestic efforts at increasing and improving production.

Rajan and Subramanian (2005) suggest additional problems. If government spending in the recipient country is financed to some extent by grants from other countries, the pressure to raise sufficient taxes domestically to pay for public outlays is reduced. Hence, the efficiency of the central administration with respect to taxes and spending becomes less important and the quality of fiscal institutions may decline over time, not least because the time and energy of the country's fiscal authorities to a large extent are devoted to administering aid instead of administering government spending and taxes.

In addition, Rajan and Subramanian argue that a large inflow of aid can lead to a real appreciation of domestic currency and reduce the country's competitiveness on the international market. The reasons for this effect are threefold. First, the inflow of money increases demand for the local currency, bidding up its value. Second, aid is funnelled towards capital-intensive industry to a larger extent than labour-intensive industry. But it is in the labour-intensive industry that most aid-receiving countries enjoy their comparative advantage. Hence, the sector that finds it harder to compete on the export market is strengthened at the expense of the sector with higher immediate export potential. Third, the inflow of aid stimulates demand and increases domestic prices. This will hit the sector producing traded goods harder than the sector producing non-traded goods, since the former sector faces international competition. All of those effects contribute to a worsening of the trade balance. Since Hausman, Pritchett and Rodrik (2005) identify increased exports as one of the main and most common factors associated with growth accelerations, this may be highly detrimental to growth prospects in an aid-receiving country.

A final interesting perspective on the relation between aid and growth comes from Clemens, Radelet and Bhavnani (2004). They quite rightly argue that aid is not a homogenous concept. It is given in different forms and is used in different ways. Some forms of aid, such as help in the wake of catastrophes or natural disasters, are not intended to promote growth. It is merely acute help in dire circumstances. And even aid that is intended to stimulate growth may do so on various time horizons. Investment in physical capital is likely to affect growth over a much shorter time horizon than investment in human capital. Therefore, they argue that aid should be disaggregated and not treated as a single concept when discussed in relation to its effect on growth.

As we have seen, there are theoretical arguments both in favour of and against aid having a positive influence on the growth rate of an aid-receiving country. To an extent, it is likely to depend on how aid is used, but even if aid is used in a supposedly wise and growth-enhancing manner, unintended side-effects working in the opposite direction can reverse any positive effect on growth. Therefore, we cannot rely on theory alone in determining if aid is good for growth or not. Instead, we must turn to empirical results and see if they shed any light on the issue.

Empirical Research

During the last decade, there has been an upsurge in the literature on the link between aid and growth. The starting point is Boone (1994), but arguably the most widely known and debated are the contributions of Burnside and Dollar (2000). They note that their forerunners in the area have reached widely different conclusions regarding the impact of aid on growth. In response to those ambiguous results, they suggest that the effect of aid may depend on the nature of the recipient country's economic policy. Their hypothesis is that aid given to a country with a sound domestic policy is put to better use and thereby increases growth more than aid given to a country with a less successful domestic policy. Using instrumental variable techniques (the standard approach in the aid and growth literature), they find support for their hypothesis in a regression analysis of 56 countries and the time period 1970–1993. It emerges that aid in itself is not a significant factor in generating economic growth unless it is accompanied by good domestic policy. Good policy in this sense means low inflation, low budget deficits and openness to international trade.

The results of Burnside and Dollar explain the failure of e.g. Boone (1994, 1996) to identify a positive correlation between aid and growth, despite the fact that he uses a similar approach. That aid does not generate growth unless it is accompanied by a good economic policy in the recipient country is confirmed by Collier and Dollar (2001, 2002). They also study the issue of whether aid is more beneficial for growth in countries with a high institutional quality. However, contrary to expectation, this notion is not given any support by the data.

In the context of the Burnside and Dollar findings, it is important to point out that they are important not only for their academic contribution, but for policy reasons as well. As their research constituted a part of a large-scale investigation by the World Bank into the effectiveness of aid, it has been highly influential in actual donor policy. While this particular research result has not been the only reason for the change in donor policy, e.g. Dollar (2001) concludes that, during the 1990s, more aid has been given to countries pursuing good economic policies than other countries.[3]

In a similar vein to Burnside and Dollar, Svensson (1999) finds that aid stimulates growth if the recipient country is democratic but not otherwise. He argues that a democracy uses the additional resources in a way that promotes the economic well-being of the country and its citizens, whereas dictatorial leaders tend to promote their own personal interests. Guillaumont and Chauvet (2001) extend the Burnside and Dollar investigation by adding the external environment as a factor determining whether aid is beneficial for growth or not. A bad external environment is defined in geographical terms as climatic factors and in economic terms as large variations in exports and a negative trend in the country's terms of trade. They find that aid raises the growth rate not only in countries pursuing good economic policies but also in countries with negative external factors hampering the development of the economy. Hence, their conclusion is that aid should be given to countries pursuing a good economic policy and countries with a large number of negative external factors.

Although the fundamental Burnside and Dollar finding on aid and domestic economic policy has unquestionably exerted a huge influence on actual donor policy, it has been challenged by several economists. A large amount of criticism has been directed towards it on methodological grounds. Dalgaard and Hansen (2001) point out a number of theoretical and econometric issues and, in particular, show that the Burnside and Dollar results are sensitive to the arbitrary choice of outliers removed from the analysis.[4] If another set of outliers were removed or if no outliers were removed, the main result that aid is not effective unless the recipient country pursues a good economic policy is altered. Furthermore, they argue that the Burnside and Dollar choice of outliers to be removed is not supported by standard econometric considerations. The results in Dalgaard and Hansen are that aid has a positive impact on growth on its own and that the finding that aid is more effective in countries with a good economic policy is not robust. An additional methodological question mark regarding the Burnside and Dollar finding emerges from a study by Easterly, Levine and Roodman (2004). By extending the time period to 1997, they find that there is no longer any evidence that aid is more efficient when combined with good domestic policies.

The idea that the influence of aid on the recipient country depends on the size of aid relative to the recipient country's GDP is given empirical support by Lensink and White (2001), who introduce the square of aid receipts as an explanatory variable in their growth regressions. They suggest that too much aid generates a dependency on external transfers rather than spurring growth-promoting forces within the recipient country. Hence, aid is initially good for growth, but if the amount of aid received exceeds a threshold level, it becomes negative instead. Hansen and Tarp (2001) and Hudson and Mosley (2001) incorporate this notion in studies of whether good economic policies increase the efficiency of aid in stimulating growth. Both of those studies find that (a) good policies are good for growth, (b) aid is on average good for growth, (c) aid becomes a hindrance to growth if a country receives too much aid and (d) there is no evidence that aid works better in combination with good domestic policies. Ovaska (2003) qualifies those results by noting that the result that aid is good for growth does not hold for all empirical specifications.

Furthermore, Dalgaard, Hansen and Tarp (2004) find that the introduction of a variable measuring whether or not a country is situated in the tropics supersedes the policy effect. A country whose land area is in the tropics does not benefit from aid in terms of improved growth to the same extent as a country that is not in the tropics.[5] Domestic economic policy is inconsequential for the effect of aid on growth as soon as the land area in the tropics is taken into account.

There are also attempts to examine the channel through which aid affects growth. Hansen and Tarp (2001) find that aid affects growth through its positive impact on the level of investment. Once the impact of aid on investment is controlled for, there is no additional effect of aid on growth. This outcome may explain the importance of the budget surplus in the variables constituting policy in the Burnside and Dollar specification. Mosley, Hudson and Horrell (1987) specifically relate the state of government finances to the share of aid used for investment purposes. They identify a positive correlation between countries running a budget surplus and countries using a large share of aid for investment. However, they also note that if a country is hit by a negative external shock, its tax base is likely to shrink, thereby forcing the government to allocate a larger share of aid transfers to consumption. Hence, the direction of causality is not clear.

In a study of particular relevance to our investigation into the effects of European Union aid, Ram (2003, 2004) divides aid into multilateral aid and bilateral aid in order to examine if there are any differences. This extension produces two interesting results. First, it is no longer possible to identify a link between good economic policies and the impact of aid on growth. Second, bilateral aid increases growth whereas multilateral aid decreases growth. This may be due to the fact that bilateral aid to a larger extent is given to countries with close cultural and linguistic ties to the donor, where institutional structures are similar and where donors develop a long-run relationship with the recipients in the specific development fields the aid resources are targeted at. If this finding has any bearing on the effectiveness of multilateral European Union aid, the implication is that its scope for promoting growth is limited. However, Ram (2003, 2004) and Berthélemy (2006) also note that bilateral aid is driven to a significant extent by the strategic motives and self-interest of the donors. Although this effect is not present in the empirical results of Ram, the connotation is that European Union aid is likely to be more beneficial for growth than bilateral aid.

Aid can be disaggregated in more ways than according to donor. In line with this reasoning, Clemens, Radelet and Bhavnani (2004) perform an empirical analysis with aid disaggregated according to what purpose the aid is assigned to in the recipient country. Their notion that different forms of aid should have different effects on growth and, in particular, affect growth over different time scales is borne out in their study. In a panel regression with growth over four-year periods as dependent variable, they find no significant effect on growth from emergency and humanitarian aid, nor from aid that affects growth only over a long time horizon such as aid financing education, health or political institutions. However, they find a significant positive effect on growth from aid going to physical investment, budget and balance of payments support and aid going directly to productive sectors.

Finally, Roodman (2004) notes that there is a large number of stories told and results produced concerning the link between aid and growth. The various results are all generated by empirical studies that resemble each other closely but are not identical. They differ with respect to time period, choice of data, country sample, estimation method and other econometric considerations. Roodman therefore lets a selection of the more influential analyses undergo a battery of rigorous econometric testing to see what conclusions are robust to alternative specifications. He finds that the result that aid works well in promoting growth outside the tropics but has no effect in the tropics survives virtually all alternative specifications. The result that a good domestic economic policy is a necessary condition for aid to enhance growth is the most vulnerable and is very dependent on a particular setting of econometric method, data and time period. In between come the notions of too much aid reducing its effect on growth and of aid stimulating growth in countries with a negative external environment in geographic and economic terms.

The contribution of Roodman is a good summary of the current state of the empirical literature on aid and growth. There is as of yet no consensus on the important question of whether aid promotes growth or not and under what circumstances aid produces better or worse results. In our study on European Union aid, we do not primarily attempt to add to the debate on what factors are important for aid to work. Instead, we incorporate a number of those factors identified as important in the literature and assess whether their interaction with European Union aid lends support to the other studies or works differently from the interaction with aid in general.

EUROPEAN UNION AID

Aid donors can be divided into two basic categories: bilateral and multilateral.[6] The European Union falls into the latter category (although aid given by individual member states of the European Union falls into the former category). Bilateral donors provide roughly three-fourths of total aid. During the time period 1975–2003, aid from the European Union constituted approximately 12 percent of total aid, which makes it the largest multilateral donor.

Table 10.1 Summary statistics on European Union aid

	Number of countries receiving aid	Aid, 1975–2003 (millions of 2003 dollar)	Share of aid, 1975–2003 (percent)
Africa	51	55,901	49.5
Asia	43	17,137	15.2
Central America	23	5,373	4.8
Europe	22	29,406	26.1
Oceania	7	1,486	1.3
South America	12	3,550	3.1
Total	158	112,853	100.0

Table 10.1 summarizes some characteristics of European Union aid. Aid has been given to a total of 158 countries. The main aid flows have been going to Africa, although aid to other European countries has increased dramatically after the break-up of the Soviet Union. Figure 10.1 shows the development of aid flows from the European Union to different parts of the world over time. Compared to other donors, the European Union gives relatively more to African countries and other European countries and relatively less to other areas, in particular to Asia and Oceania. Berthélemy (2006) notes that ACP countries (associated states from Africa, the Caribbean and the Pacific Ocean according to the Lomé and Cotonou agreements) receive relatively more aid from the European Union. (However, he also notes that this in part is compensated for by those countries receiving relatively less bilateral aid from the member countries of the European Union.) However, the correlation between European Union aid and total aid from other sources is as high as 0.58, suggesting that, in spite of the differences, there are also many similarities in aid policy across donors.

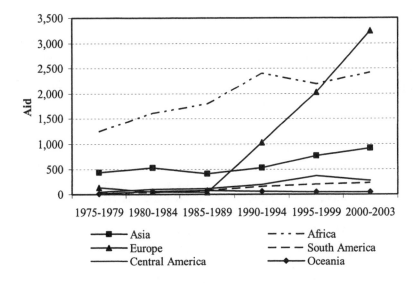

Figure 10.1 Average annual aid from the European Union (millions of 2003 dollar)

Regarding the size of European Union aid in relation to the size of the economy in the recipient country, it is hard to give a concise picture. One observation emerges, though, and that is the tendency for small countries to receive more aid in relation to their GDP. This tendency is the same for other donors. But apart from this observation, no clear pattern is visible. Aid in relation to GDP varies across countries and over time for a given country. The magnitudes range from a fraction of a percent of GDP to over 15 percent on rare occasions.

Berthélemy (2006) investigates empirically how various aid donors choose recipients. Is the choice of recipient based on the needs of the recipient, e.g. aid is channelled to poor countries or heavily indebted countries, on the merits of the recipient, e.g. aid is channelled to democratic countries or countries with no internal or external conflicts, or for reasons of self-interest, e.g. aid is channelled to countries with past colonial links or where the donor has commercial interests? His findings are that European Union aid is driven mainly by self-interest. In particular, countries that are linked to British export interests receive more aid. He finds no significance for any variable representing the needs of the recipient country and the only merit-related factor that appears to affect aid flows (negatively) is the presence of conflicts in the recipient country. This is in contrast to other multilateral donors and bilateral donors, where the needs and, for bilateral donors, the merits of the recipient are important.

EMPIRICAL MODEL

Most empirical studies on growth use the basic empirical set-up emanating from Barro (1991). In general, the literature on aid and growth follows this tradition and so does this analysis. This section is divided into two parts. First, we describe the empirical equation to be estimated and the estimation method and, second, we present the variables that are included in the analysis.

Empirical Set-up

The purpose of this analysis is to evaluate the impact of European Union aid on growth in the countries receiving aid. To this end, we estimate an empirical equation that corresponds to the basic structure used in the aid and growth literature. More specifically, it is a standard two stage least squares regression where the growth rate is regressed on aid and a number of economic, political, institutional and geographic control variables:

$$g_{i,t} = \alpha + a_{i,t}\beta_a + a^*_{i,t}\beta_{a^*} + z'_{i,t}\beta_z + w'_{i,t}\beta_w + d'_t\beta_d + \varepsilon_{i,t} \qquad (10.1)$$

where i is a country index, t is a time index, $g_{i,t}$ is the growth rate, α is a constant, $a_{i,t}$ is European Union aid relative to GDP in the recipient country, $a^*_{i,t}$ is aid from other sources relative to GDP, $z'_{i,t}$ is a vector of exogenous control variables, $w'_{i,t}$ is a vector of interaction terms, d'_t is a vector of dummy variables allowing for fixed time effects and $\varepsilon_{i,t}$ is a disturbance term with mean zero and variance σ^2.

The exogenous variables are included to capture any country-specific effects that affect growth. We also include some interaction terms that previous research has found to be important, in order to assess if aid stimulates growth more when combined with a good economic policy or a favourable geographic climate. The vector of dummy variables is included to take account of time-specific phenomena due to variations in worldwide business cycles.

The time period in our estimations is 1975–2003. Since it is unlikely that aid affects growth on a year-to-year-basis, the data are aggregated into five five-year periods and one three-year period to allow for a time lag between the provision of aid and its possible effect on growth.[7] The choice of five-year periods is standard in most of the growth literature. However, following Burnside and Dollar (2000), most of the literature that relates aid to growth use four-year periods. The lack of a theoretical underpinning for a specific time lag renders the choice arbitrary. Here, we follow the main growth literature and use five-year periods.

The sample is based solely on data availability. All countries that received aid from the European Union during the period 1975–2000 have been considered and are included if data on all variables are available. This results in an effective sample of 66 countries and 284 usable observations. The countries that are included are listed in Annex 10.2.

To estimate Equation 10.1, we use a two stage least squares approach rather than ordinary least squares. The reason for using the former method is the possibility of a two-way causal link between aid and growth. If the donation of aid influences the growth rate in the recipient country, and aid is given to countries based upon criteria involving the recipient country's historical growth record, the relationship between the two main variables is such that there may be an endogeneity problem if ordinary least squares is used. If aid were handed out based on future growth prospects (as opposed to the current growth rate), it would not constitute a problem as long as the regression analysis is carried out on a year-to-year basis. However, it may still occur when data are aggregated into time periods covering more than one year.

In the previous literature, two main approaches have been employed to come to terms with this potential problem. One is performing a two stage least squares regression using instrumental variables and the other involves using generalized method of moments estimation. Here, we follow e.g. Burnside and Dollar (2000), Hansen and Tarp (2001) and Guillaumont and Chauvet (2001) and use two stage least squares.[8]

Data and Variables

Apart from the main variables of interest, aid and growth, the empirical equation contains a set of exogenous control variables and a set of instruments that are drawn both from the overall growth literature and from the more specific aid and growth literature. In addition, the aid and growth literature has identified a number of interaction terms among some of the variables that may be significant determinants of the effect of aid on growth. We therefore include a set of interaction terms as well. In this section, we discuss the variables and how they are measured. In the section covering the empirical results, we discuss the correlation structure among the variables and its implications. All data sources are listed in Annex 10.1.

Aid and growth
The variables in focus in the analysis are aid (from the European Union) and the growth rate of GDP. We use GDP data from the World Bank and calculate growth as the average annual growth rate in per capita GDP for each five-year period. Data on aid is Official Development Assistance from the DAC database. By aid from the European Union, we mean the multilateral aid given by the European Union and not the bilateral aid given by individual member states. Although the aim is to examine the impact on GDP growth of aid from the European Union, we also include aid from other sources so as not to confuse any positive effects of European Union aid with effects of aid generally. The aid variables are measured as the total amount of aid donated to a country relative

to the recipient country's GDP. Since data are aggregated into five-year periods, we use the ratio of aid to GDP over the entire five-year periods. In line with the findings of, among others, Lensink and White (2001), we also use the square of the ratio of aid to GDP as a proxy for the notion that aid is good for growth at first but turns negative when aid donations become too large in relation to GDP.

Exogenous variables

Naturally, aid is not the only determinant of a country's growth rate. The exogenous control variables are included in the regression equation because they are expected to affect the growth rate for reasons other than aid. The growth literature identifies a large number of growth-enhancing or growth-retarding variables that may be considered for inclusion in this setting. Among those, we choose a set of variables based (a) on underlying endogenous growth theory and (b) on the robustness of the outcome in previous empirical research.

First, we have variables that empirical studies on growth have found to be among the most robustly correlated with growth. Conditional convergence suggests that poor countries have higher growth rates once other relevant factors such as physical and human capital are controlled for. We therefore include the logarithm of per capita GDP at the beginning of each five-year period among our exogenous variables. We also include gross capital formation per capita as a measure of the investment rate and the average years of education for the population aged 15 and above as a measure of the education level. In line with e.g. King and Levine (1993a and 1993b), we include a proxy for the state of the financial sector. Various proxies, such as the money stock relative to GDP, have been used as a measure of financial depth. Here, we use domestic credit to the private sector since access to credit markets is likely to be one of the main obstacles to growth in developing countries.

Second, to investigate the impact of domestic economic policy and its possible interaction with aid, we include the same variables as Burnside and Dollar and the aid and growth literature succeeding them. Those are (a) the natural logarithm of the inflation rate in percent, (b) the government budget surplus divided by GDP and (c) the Sachs–Warner index of a country's openness to international trade. Others, such as Guillaumont and Chauvet (2001) and Hudson and Mosley (2001), have suggested other policy-related variables, but we stick to the most widely used specification as a proxy for domestic economic policy. We combine the three policy variables into a composite policy index in the same manner as Burnside and Dollar (2000).

Third, there is a set of institutional and political variables that may affect both growth and aid. Standard variables in this literature are a measure of ethnic fractionalization in the population of the aid-receiving country and a measure of the average number of assassinations per million inhabitants. In addition, we include the polity variable from Marshall and Jaggers (2002) as a measure of the degree of democracy and a war variable that measures the extent of armed conflicts in a country. All of those variables are averaged over each five-year period.[9]

Fourth and finally, we have a couple of geographic variables that have been identified as significant in some previous studies. Following Dalgaard, Hansen and Tarp (2004), we include the share of the land area in a country that is situated in the tropics.[10] We also include a dummy variable for countries in East Asia.

Interaction terms

Some variables may affect growth in a different manner when their presence is combined with the presence of other factors. The key Burnside and Dollar (2000) result, which has been challenged, is that aid stimulates growth in an environment of good economic policy but not otherwise. Similarly, Dalgaard, Hansen and Tarp (2004) show that aid works well in promoting growth outside the tropics but not in the tropics. We capture effects such as those by including interaction terms consisting of two variables multiplied by each other.

Four interaction effects are considered. We use both European Union aid and aid from other sources multiplied by the policy and tropics variables, creating four possible interaction effects in the spirit of Burnside and Dollar and Dalgaard, Hansen and Tarp.[11]

Instruments

Finally, the two stage least squares approach requires a set of instrumental variables. In addition to the exogenous variables that are all used as instruments, we add a number of variables in line with the previous empirical literature on aid and growth. The variables included are the logarithm of the size of the population, the ratio of arms imports to GDP, the Freedom House indices for political rights and civil liberties, an interaction term between ethnic fractionalization and assassinations, an interaction term between the logarithm of population and the policy variable, and dummy variables for Egypt (an important ally and large recipient of aid from the United States), countries in Central America, countries in sub-Saharan Africa and countries belonging to the franc zones in Western and Central Africa.

EMPIRICAL RESULTS

This section contains the empirical analysis. The main question that is addressed is what effects European Union aid exerts on a country's growth rate. Along the lines of the empirical literature on aid and growth, we investigate if aid is more favourable for growth in certain circumstances, such as in countries pursuing good domestic economic policy or countries situated outside the tropics.

The section is divided into three parts. First, we examine the data using simple statistical tools. Second, we construct an index of domestic economic policy in order to investigate its impact on aid effectiveness. And third and finally, we carry out the main regression analysis to assess the effect of European Union aid on growth.

Preliminary Analysis

Before carrying out the formal regression analysis, it is instructive to look at simple correlation statistics among the variables. In Table 10.2a, we show the correlation among the variables involving aid and in Table 10.2b the correlation among the rest of the variables (including their correlation with variables involving aid).

Table 10.2a Simple correlation coefficients for variables involving aid

	EU aid /GDP	Other aid /GDP	(EU aid /GDP)^2	(Other aid/GDP)^2	EU aid · tropics	Other aid · tropics
EU aid/GDP	1.00					
Other aid/GDP	0.58	1.00				
(EU aid/GDP)^2	0.89	0.53	1.00			
(Other aid/GDP)^2	0.44	0.84	0.54	1.00		
EU aid* tropics	0.95	0.57	0.87	0.45	1.00	
Other aid* tropics	0.56	0.97	0.52	0.84	0.61	1.00

Note: The table lists the simple correlation coefficients among the aid variables and all interaction terms involving aid.

Two basic conclusions emerge from this analysis. First, there exists a fairly high degree of correlation among the variables involving aid. This is due to the fact that the correlation between European Union aid and aid from other sources is 0.58, which suggests that there are some similarities between the aid policy of the European Union and the aid policy of the rest of the world when it comes to recipients. It is therefore not surprising to find a high correlation among the interaction terms, since all interaction variables include either European Union aid or aid from other sources.

Second, both European Union aid and other aid are negatively correlated with initial GDP with correlation coefficients of –0.50 and –0.58, respectively. Thus, the data lend support to the very reasonable assumption that poor countries receive more aid than rich countries. Since there is a strong correlation between the initial level of GDP and the level of education, this means that there is a negative correlation between the education level and aid as well.

Table 10.2b Simple correlation coefficients

	Growth	Inflation	Budget surplus	Open-ness	Initial GDP	Investment/GDP	Financial lending
Growth	1.00						
Inflation	−0.22	1.00					
Budget surplus	0.26	−0.23	1.00				
Openness	0.36	−0.15	0.26	1.00			
Initial GDP	0.14	0.12	0.21	0.35	1.00		
Investment/GDP	0.17	−0.16	−0.09	0.14	0.19	1.00	
Financial lending	0.27	−0.25	0.12	0.34	0.54	0.29	1.00
Education	−0.24	0.11	0.14	0.44	0.72	0.18	0.48
War	−0.04	0.13	−0.05	−0.09	−0.06	−0.10	−0.10
Democracy	0.17	0.08	0.12	0.37	0.43	−0.05	0.21
Ethnic fractionalization	−0.07	−0.07	−0.08	−0.11	−0.38	−0.02	−0.13
Assassinations	−0.14	0.13	0.04	−0.01	0.06	−0.07	−0.10
East Asia	0.40	−0.26	0.20	0.28	0.11	0.29	0.46
Tropics	−0.23	−0.04	−0.04	0.01	−0.33	−0.10	−0.26
EU aid/GDP	−0.21	0.00	−0.24	−0.14	−0.17	−0.17	−0.28
Other aid/GDP	−0.16	−0.02	−0.27	−0.20	−0.08	−0.08	−0.35
(EU aid/GDP)^2	−0.15	0.02	−0.20	−0.09	−0.12	−0.12	−0.18
(Other aid/GDP)^2	−0.09	0.03	−0.23	−0.12	−0.01	−0.01	−0.23
EU aid*tropics	−0.23	0.00	−0.25	−0.16	−0.18	−0.18	−0.30
Other aid*tropics	−0.23	0.00	−0.23	−0.20	−0.10	−0.10	−0.37

	Education	War	Democracy	Ethnic fractionalization	Assassinations	East Asia	Tropics
Education	1.00						
War	0.01	1.00					
Democracy	0.40	0.04	1.00				
Ethnic fractionalization	−0.33	0.20	−0.12	1.00			
Assassinations	−0.01	0.45	0.09	−0.07	1.00		
East Asia	0.27	0.09	−0.08	0.07	−0.09	1.00	
Tropics	−0.35	−0.03	0.06	0.28	0.02	0.03	1.00
EU aid/GDP	−0.46	−0.14	−0.24	0.26	−0.15	−0.20	0.32
Other aid/GDP	−0.52	−0.14	−0.20	0.18	−0.12	−0.25	0.33
(EU aid/GDP)^2	−0.34	−0.07	−0.16	0.19	−0.10	−0.11	0.21
(Other aid/GDP)^2	−0.38	−0.12	−0.14	0.14	−0.09	−0.16	0.22
EU aid*tropics	−0.47	−0.12	−0.23	0.29	−0.14	−0.18	0.38
Other aid*tropics	−0.48	−0.12	−0.14	0.25	−0.08	−0.20	0.53

Note: The table lists the simple correlation coefficients among all variables not involving aid, including their correlation with the aid variables.

Apart from these insights about the variables involving aid, there is no correlation coefficient that particularly catches the attention. Correlation does not seem to be very strong among the rest of the variables.

Construction of Policy Index

If we believe that a prerequisite for the growth rate of an aid-receiving country to be increased by aid is that the country pursues good domestic economic policies, we need a measure of domestic economic policy. Following Burnside and Dollar (2000), we construct a composite index consisting of the inflation rate, the government budget surplus and the degree of openness to international trade. Thereby, we get a concise measure of policy and of the interaction between aid and policy.

There are a number of possible shortcomings of this approach. First, the three components in the index may interact with aid in different ways, invalidating the approach of a single policy index. However, it is likely that it is the overall policy environment that matters for the effectiveness of aid rather than single policies. To the extent that those three factors capture the overall policy environment, the approach of a policy index is likely to be valid.

Second, other aspects of economic policy apart from those included in the index may be relevant for the impact of aid. Nevertheless, we restrict ourselves to the main strand of defining policy in the aid and growth literature by using the method and variables applied by Burnside and Dollar to construct the policy index.

The third problem concerns the technical construction of the index and the relative weights given to the three components of the index. In line with Burnside and Dollar, the weights are assigned on the basis of what the data say. We regress growth on a constant, the three components of the index and all other exogenous and dummy variables from Equation 10.1. Variables involving aid (including all interaction terms) in (10.1) are left out. Then, we construct the policy index by weighting the components of the index by their estimated coefficients.

The result of the regression is found in Table 10.3. Both the budget surplus and openness are significant at the 5 percent level and the inflation rate is significant at the ten percent level, suggesting that all three variables are important for growth. The other exogenous variables have the expected sign apart from education, financial lending and war, but none of those three is significant. The estimations for the policy variables produce the following policy index:[12]

$$\text{policy} = -0.002 \text{ inflation} + 0.080 \text{ budget surplus} + 0.016 \text{ openness} \quad (10.2)$$

This policy index is used as an exogenous variable in the regressions on aid and growth in the next section.

Applying the policy index to the countries in the analysis, we get a diverse set of values, ranging from –0.034 to 0.023. Negative values occur if the inflation rate or the budget deficit is sufficiently large. The policy index exhibits a mean value of –0.003 and a standard deviation of 0.010.

Table 10.3 Constructing the policy index

	OLS
Inflation	−0.002*
	(0.083)
Budget surplus	0.080**
	(0.010)
Openness	0.016**
	(0.000)
Initial GDP	−0.005**
	(0.026)
Investment	0.018
	(0.421)
Financial lending	−0.000
	(0.716)
Education	−0.000
	(0.943)
War	0.000
	(0.792)
Democracy	0.001**
	(0.000)
Assassinations	−0.003**
	(0.009)
Ethnic fractionalization	−0.005
	(0.429)
East Asia	0.027**
	(0.000)
Tropics	−0.020**
	(0.000)
Observations	284
R^2	0.35

Note: The table contains the results of an ordinary least squares regression of Equation 10.1 with the aid variables $a_{i,t}$ and $a_{i,t}^*$ omitted and no interaction terms. The dependent variable is the growth rate of per capita GDP. For each variable, the table lists the estimated coefficient with p-value in parentheses. Two asterisks next to the coefficient indicate that a variable is significant at the 5 percent level and one asterisk indicates that the variable is significant at the 10 percent level. The purpose of the regression is to construct a policy index using the estimated coefficients for inflation, the budget surplus and openness.

The Effect of European Union Aid on Growth

In the previous section, we constructed the policy index by excluding variables involving aid from Equation 10.1. We now include the aid variables in order to assess the effect of European Union aid on growth in aid-receiving countries. This means estimating the full version of 10.1 using two stage least squares. The two stage least squares approach is necessary because of the potential endogeneity problem that may occur if aid is given to countries based on their growth record or growth prospects.

We estimate a set of regressions where different combinations of the aid variables and interaction terms involving aid are included. This is done to check the robustness of the results to various specifications. The results are found in Table 10.4. The coefficients are shown with p-values in parentheses. Because of the high correlation among the various aid-related variables, we complement the inspection of the t-statistics for each variable with standard F-tests to test for the joint exclusion of groups of the aid-related variables. The results of those tests are shown at the end of each column. Since we find evidence of serial correlation in the residuals of the estimated equation, inference is based on the Newey–West heteroskedasticity and autocorrelation consistent standard errors. The R^2 values are 0.35–0.36 for all regression specifications.

The first column of Table 10.2 merely replicates the regression from Table 10.1 by excluding all aid variables. In the second column, we add European Union aid and aid from other sources to get a first indication of the effects of European Union aid. Then, in column 3, we drop aid from other sources from the specification and include all variables involving European Union aid in the regression to assess the importance of including aid from other sources in the regression. In columns 4–6, we use European Union aid and aid from other sources as the base and include a pair of interaction or aid squared variables. Finally, in column 7, we include all aid-related variables.

With respect to the non-aid variables, the results are in general as expected. The policy variable is significant and its coefficient is close to 1 for all specifications, suggesting that good domestic macroeconomic policy has a positive effect on growth and that the presence of aid does not affect this result. Apart from policy, four variables are significant throughout. Polity as a measure of democracy and the dummy variable for East Asia are significantly positive, whereas assassinations and the share of land in the tropics are significantly negative. The latter three are in accordance with previous findings in the vast literature of empirical growth studies. The significance of the polity variable and its implication that democracy may be good for growth is noteworthy, since previous results on the link between democracy and growth are mixed.

Apart from those variables that are robustly significant, initial GDP is negative and significant at the 10 percent level in some specifications. This provides some evidence of conditional convergence, i.e. countries that are below the steady state level of per capita GDP grow faster, but the evidence is weaker than is normally found. Among the other variables, both the ratio of investment to GDP and financial lending are significant in most empirical growth studies but not here. Although education is widely believed to be a key aspect of the growth process, variables that act as a proxy for education are rarely significant in growth regressions. This is probably due both to the difficulty of capturing the relevant aspects of education and human capital in a quantitative measure and to the time lag between the actual education effort and its effect on a country's growth rate.

Table 10.4 Regression results on aid and growth

	(1)	(2)	(3)	(4)
Policy	1.000**	0.992**	1.159**	1.007**
	(0.000)	(0.000)	(0.000)	(0.000)
Initial GDP	−0.005	−0.006	−0.006*	−0.006*
	(0.104)	(0.120)	(0.090)	(0.093)
Investment	0.018	0.015	0.016	0.015
	(0.447)	(0.536)	(0.480)	(0.506)
Financial lending	−0.000	−0.000	−0.000	−0.000
	(0.771)	(0.813)	(0.795)	(0.823)
Education	−0.000	−0.000	−0.000	−0.000
	(0.953)	(0.928)	(0.751)	(0.888)
War	0.000	0.000	0.001	0.001
	(0.825)	(0.868)	(0.570)	(0.720)
Democracy	0.001**	0.001**	0.001**	0.001**
	(0.000)	(0.000)	(0.000)	(0.000)
Assassinations	−0.003**	−0.003**	−0.003**	−0.003**
	(0.009)	(0.005)	(0.004)	(0.006)
Ethnic fractionalization	−0.005	−0.004	−0.006	−0.005
	(0.514)	(0.579)	(0.406)	(0.474)
East Asia	0.027**	0.026**	0.026**	0.027**
	(0.000)	(0.000)	(0.000)	(0.000)
Tropics	−0.020**	−0.019**	−0.022**	−0.020**
	(0.000)	(0.000)	(0.000)	(0.000)
EU aid / GDP (a)		−0.254	0.101	0.556
		(0.496)	(0.945)	(0.358)
Other aid / GDP (b)		0.031		−0.109
		(0.754)		(0.576)
(EU aid / GDP)^2 (c)			−24.09*	−23.02
			(0.059)	(0.121)
(Other aid / GDP)^2 (d)				1.18
				(0.536)
EU aid policy (e)			−30.65	
			(0.122)	
Other aid*policy (f)				
EU aid*tropics (g)			0.283	
			(0.854)	
Other aid tropics (h)				
Observations	284	284	284	284
R^2	0.36	0.35	0.36	0.36
Exclusion test of		a, b	a, c, e, g	a, b, c, d
		$\chi^2 (2) = 0.469$	$\chi^2 (4) = 10.27$	$\chi^2 (4) = 2.8$
		(0.791)	(0.036)	(0.591)
			a, e, g	
			$\chi^2 (3) = 4.61$	
			(0.203)	
			a, c, g	
			$\chi^2 (3) = 5.91$	
			(0.116)	

Table 10.4 (continued): Regression results on aid and growth

	(5)	(6)	(7)
Policy	1.115**	0.984**	1.114**
	(0.000)	(0.000)	(0.000)
Initial GDP	−0.006	−0.006	−0.006*
	(0.121)	(0.133)	(0.086)
Investment	0.014	0.016	0.017
	(0.540)	(0.493)	(0.430)
Financial lending	−0.000	−0.000	−0.000
	(0.786)	(0.793)	(0.796)
Education	−0.000	0.000	0.000
	(0.822)	(0.928)	(0.983)
War	0.001	0.000	0.001
	(0.711)	(0.923)	(0.000)
Democracy	0.001**	0.001**	0.001**
	(0.000)	(0.000)	(0.000)
Assassinations	−0.003**	−0.003**	−0.003**
	(0.003)	(0.006)	(0.005)
Ethnic fractionalization	−0.004	−0.004	−0.006
	(0.529)	(0.596)	(0.413)
East Asia	0.025**	0.026**	0.026**
	(0.001)	(0.001)	(0.001)
Tropics	−0.020**	−0.016**	−0.017**
	(0.000)	(0.003)	(0.002)
EU aid / GDP (a)	−0.520	−1.10	−0.695
	(0.175)	(0.403)	(0.565)
Other aid / GDP (b)	0.053	0.223	0.073
	(0.648)	(0.113)	(0.696)
(EU aid / GDP)^2 (c)		0.976	−31.04**
		(0.498)	(0.042)
(Other aid / GDP)^2 (d)		−0.245	2.24
		(0.136)	(0.241)
EU aid policy (e)	−34.34		−27.98
	(0.143)		(0.247)
Other aid policy (f)	1.56		1.16
	(0.843)		(0.875)
EU aid tropics (g)			1.50
			(0.311)
Other aid tropics (h)			−0.348**
			(0.045)
Observations	284	284	284
R^2	0.35	0.35	0.36
Exclusion test of	a, b, e, f	a, c, g, h	a, b, c, d, e, f, g, h
	$\chi^2 (4) = 4.09$	$\chi^2 (4) = 4.77$	$\chi^2 (8) = 15.25$
	(0.394)	(0.312)	(0.054)
			a, b, d, e, f, g
			$\chi^2 (6) = 9.32 \ (0.156)$

Note: The table contains the results of a two stage least squares regression of Equation 10.1. The policy variable is constructed from inflation, the budget surplus and openness using the results of the regression presented in Table 10.3. The dependent variable is the growth rate of per capita GDP.

Each column represents a regression including a different set of aid-related variables. For each variable, the table lists the estimated coefficient with p-value in parentheses. Two asterisks next to the coefficient indicate that a variable is significant at the 5 percent level and one asterisk indicates that the variable is significant at the 10 percent level. At the bottom of each column, the table presents joint exclusion tests of groups of the aid-related variables. For notational purposes, the variables are labelled with the letters a–h in the presentation of the exclusion tests. The letters a–h appear in the left-hand column of the table, indicating what variable they represent.

Turning now to the main issue of aid and growth, the results are fairly discouraging. It is impossible to discern any significant effect of the basic European Union aid variable on growth. Regardless of specification and whether the significance test is carried out for the single variable or for a group of variables, the coefficient on the ratio of European Union aid to GDP is not significantly different from zero. The same result applies to aid from other sources. Hence, based on this study, it appears that aid is inconsequential for growth in aid-receiving countries.

However, the result that aid does not matter for growth is not the full story emanating from the regressions. The end result becomes even more disheartening. For European Union aid, not only is the ratio of aid to GDP insignificant, but the squared ratio of aid to GDP is negative and significant in two out of three specifications in which it appears. This suggests that European Union aid does not have any impact on growth as long as the aid volume is small compared to the recipient country's economy, but for sizable aid volumes, European Union aid becomes harmful for growth.

A similar story applies to aid from other sources. In line with Dalgaard, Hansen and Tarp (2004), we cannot reject, in our full regression with all aid variables included, the significance of the interaction variable between aid and the share of land situated in the tropics. Since the variable is negative, it suggests that aid is harmful for growth when given to countries in the tropics and that aid has no effect on growth otherwise. The remaining aid variables are insignificant in all specifications.

To summarize the main results from our regressions, the conclusions on aid and growth are the following: (a) we find no evidence that aid, from the European Union or from other donors, has any effect on growth on average, (b) if aid from the European Union becomes large in relation to the GDP of the recipient country, it starts having a negative effect on growth, (c) aid from other sources than the European Union is negative for growth in the tropics and (d) we find no evidence that aid is more positive for growth in countries pursuing good domestic policies.

CONCLUSIONS

This chapter sets out to investigate the effects of European Union aid on growth in per capita GDP in the countries receiving aid. To this end, we estimate a panel regression including aid and a set of control variables. The conclusions regarding aid are meagre. We cannot discern any significant effect of European Union aid on growth and therefore must conclude that, based on this evidence, aid does not seem to improve growth. Furthermore, we find that aid from the European Union starts to have a negative effect on growth as it becomes large in relation to GDP in the recipient country.

In the analysis, we also include aid from sources other than the European Union as a control variable. We cannot identify any significant effect of such aid either, but do find support for previous findings that aid is less beneficial for growth (in our case, harmful for growth) in the tropics than outside the tropics.

For the control variables, we find expected significant coefficients for a number of variables: countries in East Asia and democratic countries have experienced higher growth on average, whereas countries with a large number of assassinations and countries in the tropics have experienced lower growth on average. In addition, we find some support for conditional convergence, i.e. a higher growth rate in countries with low initial income relative to their potential when other factors have been taken into account.

But returning to the failure to identify a positive effect on growth of European Union aid, we may ask why we fail to find such a relationship. There are a number of possible explanations. One obvious explanation is that perhaps there is no such relationship. It may be the case that aid is not a useful tool for stimulating growth on the macroeconomic level. Another possible explanation is that aid has been given for other reasons. The more cynical view is that the choice of countries receiving aid is based on the self-interest of the donor rather than the need of the recipient. But it is also possible that aid has been given with the best interest of the recipient at heart, but has been targeted at relieving poverty in the short term rather than improving growth in the long run. A third explanation is that aggregate aid is not the proper variable to investigate. Different forms of aid may have different effects and may affect the economy with different time lags, which means that the positive growth effects that exist do not show up when all forms of aid are restricted to having the same effect and being visible only within the confines of a five-year period.

Hence, even though the results of this chapter indicate that there is no effect of European Union aid on growth, it would be unwise to take it as conclusive evidence that no such effect could possibly exist. A more modest conclusion is that aggregate European Union aid does not appear to affect economic growth in recipient countries in a positive (or negative) manner during the course of five years after the aid is provided.

NOTES

The author thanks Carl-Johan Belfrage, Yves Bourdet, Pernilla Johansson and Jaya Reddy for valuable comments and helpful suggestions and discussions.

1. Good overviews of current growth theory are provided by Barro and Sala-i-Martin (2003) and Aghion and Howitt (1999).
2. Within the scope of technological progress in this sense lies everything from major innovations to small organizational improvements.
3. The Burnside and Dollar article was already available as a working paper in 1997 and has therefore exerted its influence on donor policy before its appearance in the American Economic Review in 2000.
4. Burnside and Dollar (2000) remove five big outliers that are crucial for the results.
5. In a sense, this result is not so much a result as a new question: why does aid not promote growth in the tropics?
6. Berthélemy (2006) further subdivides the multilateral category into multilateral donors with a regional constituency (such as the European Union), multilateral donors with a regional client (such as regional development banks) and truly multilateral donors.
7. It is the final period that is three years only. For simplicity, we will refer to five-year-periods throughout in the text.
8. In previous studies on aid and growth where OLS regressions are performed alongside two stage least squares regressions, the difference in the estimated coefficients and in inference is small, suggesting that the endogeneity problem may be of a small magnitude as well.
9. The Freedom House indices of political rights and civil liberties were also among the variables tested. However, these variables turned out to be highly correlated with the other institutional and political variables and were insignificant in the growth regressions. They were therefore left out of the results included in this chapter.
10. Many growth regressions use a dummy variable for countries in sub-Saharan Africa. Such a dummy variable would have been insignificant in the regressions of this chapter, presumably because of its high correlation with the tropics variable.
11 In addition, we tested including European Union aid multiplied by aid from other sources. A positive sign of this variable would indicate that aid from the European Union works better when added on to aid from other sources. A negative sign would indicate that aid from the European Union is most beneficial for growth when given to countries lacking other major donors. However, this variable was not significant.
12. Burnside and Dollar include the constant from the regression in the policy index. We choose to omit the constant from the index because the constant represents the average growth rate rather than policy. This is of no consequence for the ensuing analysis.

REFERENCES

Aghion, P. and P. Howitt (1999), *Endogenous Growth Theory*, Cambridge, MA and London, England: MIT Press.

Barro, R. (1991), 'Economic Growth in a Cross Section of Countries', *Quarterly Journal of Economics*, **104**, 407–44.

Barro, R. and J. Lee (2000), 'International Comparisons of Educational Attainment: Updates and Implications', CID Working Paper no. 42, April, Cambridge, MA: Harvard University.

Barro, R. and X. Sala-i-Martin (2003), *Economic Growth*, Cambridge, MA and London, England: MIT Press.

Berthélemy, J.-C. (2006), 'Aid Allocation: Comparing Donors' Behaviours', forthcoming, *Swedish Economic Policy Review*.

Boone, P. (1994), 'The Impact of Foreign Aid on Savings and Growth', Centre for Economic Performance Working Paper No. 677, London School of Economics.

Boone, P. (1996), 'Politics and the Effectiveness of Foreign Aid', *European Economic Review*, **40** (2), 289–329.

Burnside, C. and D. Dollar (2000), 'Aid, Policies, and Growth', *American Economic Review*, **90** (4), 847–68.

Clemens, M., S. Radelet and R. Bhavnani (2004), 'Counting Chickens when they Hatch: The Short Term Effect of Aid on Growth', Working Paper 44, Center for Global Development, Washington, DC.

Collier, P. and D. Dollar (2001), 'Can the World Cut Poverty in Half? How Policy Reform and Effective Aid Can Meet International Development Goals', **29** (11), 1787–802.

Collier, P. and D. Dollar (2002), 'Aid Allocation and Poverty Reduction', *European Economic Review*, **45** (1), 1–26.

Dalgaard, C.-J. and H. Hansen (2001), 'On Aid, Growth and Good Policies', *Journal of Development Studies*, **37** (6), 17–41.

Dalgaard, C.-J., H. Hansen and F. Tarp (2004), 'On the Empirics of Foreign Aid and Growth', *Economic Journal*, **114** (496), 191–216.

Dollar, D. (2001), 'Some Thoughts on the Effectiveness of Aid, Non-Aid Development Finance and Technical Assistance', *Journal of International Development*, *13* (7), 1039–55.

Easterly, W., R. Levine and D. Roodman (2004), 'New Data, New Doubts: A Comment on Burnside and Dollar's "Aid, policies, and growth"', *American Economic Review*, **94** (2), 774–80.

Guillaumont, P. and L. Chauvet (2001), 'Aid and Performance: A Reassessment', *Journal of Development Studies*, **37** (6), 66–92.

Hansen, H. and F. Tarp (2001), 'Aid and Growth Regressions', *Journal of Development Economics*, **64** (2), 547–70.

Hausman, R., L. Pritchett and D. Rodrik (2005), 'Growth Accelerations', *Journal of Economic Growth*, **10** (4), 303–29.

Hudson, J. and P. Mosley (2001), 'Aid Policies and Growth: In Search of the Holy Grail', *Journal of International Development*, *13* (7), 1023–38.

King, R.G. and R. Levine (1993a), 'Finance, Entrepreneurship and Growth. Theory and Evidence', *Journal of Monetary Economics*, **32**, 513–42.

King, R.G. and R. Levine (1993b), 'Finance and Growth: Schumpeter Might be Right', *Quarterly Journal of Economics*, **108**, 717–38.

Lensink, R. and H. White (2001), 'Are There Negative Returns to Aid', *Journal of Development Studies*, **37** (6), 42–65.

Levine, R.N., Loyaza and T. Beck (2000), 'Financial Intermediation and Growth: Causality and Causes', *Journal of Monetary Economics*, **46** (1), 31–77.

Marshall, M. and K. Jaggers (2002), 'Polity IV Project, Political Regime Characteristics and Transitions', Center for International Development and Conflict Management, University of Maryland.

Mosley, P., J. Hudson and S. Horrell (1987), 'Aid, the Public Sector and the Market in Less Developed Countries', *Economic Journal*, **97** (387), 616–41.

Newey, W. and K. West (1987), 'A Simple Positive Semi-definite, Heteroscedasticity and Autocorrelation Consistent Covariance Matrix', *Econometrica*, **55**, 703–8.

Ovaska, T. (2003), 'The Failure of Development Aid', *Cato Journal*, **23** (2), 175–88

Rajan, R. and A. Subramanian (2005), 'What Undermines Aid's Impact on Growth?', NBER Working Paper 11657.

Ram, R. (2003), 'Roles of Bilateral and Multilateral Aid in Economic Growth of Developing Countries', *Kyklos*, **56** (1), 95–110.

Ram, R. (2004), 'Recipient Country's Policies and the Effect of Foreign Aid on Economic Growth in Developing Countries: Additional Evidence', *Journal of International Development*, **16** (2), 201–11.

Romer, P. (1993), 'Idea Gaps and Object Gaps in Economic Development', *Journal of Monetary Economics*, **32**, 543–73.

Roodman, D. (2004), 'The Anarchy of Numbers: Aid Development, and Cross-country Empirics', Working Paper 32, Center for Global Development, Washington, DC.

Svensson, J. (1999), 'Aid, Growth and Democracy', *Economics and Politics*, **11** (3), 275–97.

ANNEX 10.1 DATA SOURCES

Aid: Development Assistance Committee, Official Development Assistance and Official Aid

Population: World Development Indicators

GDP: World Development Indicators

Investment: World Development Indicators

Financial lending: World Bank

Inflation: World Development Indicators

Budget surplus: World Development Indicators

Openness: Sachs–Warner index updated by Roodman (2004)

Education: Barro and Lee (2000)

Democracy: Marshall and Jaggers (2002)

War: PRIO dataset, International Peace Research Institute, Oslo

Political rights: Freedom House

Civil liberties: Freedom House

Ethnic fractionalization: Levine, Loyaza and Beck (2000)

Assassinations: Levine, Loyaza and Beck (2000)

Arms imports: Levine, Loyaza and Beck (2000)

Share of land in tropics: Levine, Loyaza and Beck (2000)

ANNEX 10.2 COUNTRIES IN THE EMPIRICAL ANALYSIS

Algeria	Haiti	Paraguay
Argentina	Honduras	Peru
Benin	Hungary	The Philippines
Bolivia	India	Poland
Botswana	Indonesia	Rwanda
Brazil	Iran	Senegal
Burundi	Israel	Sierra Leone
Central African Republic	Jamaica	Singapore
Chile	Jordan	South Africa
China	Kenya	Sri Lanka
Colombia	Republic of Korea	Syria
The Comoros	Malawi	Thailand

Costa Rica	Malaysia	Togo
Cyprus	Mali	Trinidad and Tobago
Dominican Republic	Mauritania	Tunisia
Ecuador	Mauritius	Turkey
Egypt	Mexico	Uganda
El Salvador	Nepal	Uruguay
Gambia	Nicaragua	Venezuela
Ghana	Niger	Yemen
Guatemala	Pakistan	Zambia
Guyana	Papua New Guinea	Zimbabwe

Index